Celtic Texts of the Coelbook

The Last Five Books of The Kolbrin Bible

Celtic Texts of the Coelbook

The Last Five Books of The Kolbrin Bible

Janice Manning, Editor

Marshall Masters, Contributor

Your Own World Books
yowbooks.com
kolbrin.com

COPYRIGHT

No part of this book may be reproduced or transmitted in any form or by any means, graphic, electronic, or mechanical, including photocopying, recording, taping, or by any information storage retrieval system, without the written permission of the publisher.

The Kolbrin Bible: 21st Century Master Edition

Anonymous Original Authors: 2nd Century B.C.E to 1st Century C.E.

Public Domain Manuscript — Final Compilation: 19th Century C.E., UK

Kolbrin Citation System: Marshall Masters, 2005-2006 USA

First Edition Copyright ©2005 Your Own World, Inc.
USA Copyright Registration Number: TXu-1-262-967

Second Edition Copyright ©2006 Your Own World, Inc.
For Additional Front Matter, Editing and Index

*Celtic Texts of the Coelbook: The Last
Five Books of The Kolbrin Bible*

First Edition Copyright ©2006 Your Own World, Inc.

All rights reserved.

Your Own World Books
First Edition – May 2006
DOI: 10.1572/kolbrin.coelbook
SERIES DOI: 10.1572/kolbrin
kolbrin.com

Trade Paperback
ISBN-13: 978-1-59772-030-4
DOI: 10.1572/9781597720304

Adobe eBook
ISBN-13: 978-1-59772-031-1
DOI: 10.1572/9781597720311

Microsoft eBook
ISBN-13: 978-1-59772-032-8
DOI: 10.1572/9781597720328

Mobipocket eBook
ISBN-13: 978-1-59772-033-5
DOI: 10.1572/9781597720335

Palm eBook
ISBN-13: 978-1-59772-034-2
DOI: 10.1572/9781597720342

YOUR OWN WORLD BOOKS
an imprint of Your Own World, Inc.
Silver Springs, NV USA
SAN: 256-1646
yowbooks.com
kolbrin.com

This edition is dedicated to the memory of those unknown ancients who labored in the face of future uncertainty, to share their timeless wisdom with generations yet unborn.

— and to —

Those future caretakers who choose to follow in the loving footsteps of generations past.

Table of Contents

Introduction vii
Kolbrin Citation System xiii
Book of Origins (Origins, OGS) 1
Book of the Silver Bough (Silver Bough, SVB) 31
Book of Lucius (Lucius, LUC) 61
Book of Wisdom (Wisdom, WSD) 91
The Britain Book (Britain, BRT) 129
Index 165

INTRODUCTION

The *Celtic Texts of The Coelbook* is an abridged edition of the *The Kolbrin Bible: 21st Century Master Edition*. It contains faithful copies of the last 5 books of this 11-book historical and prophetic anthology.

The Kolbrin Bible is an ancient secular academic work; it offers alternate accounts of several stories from the *Holy Bible* and other wisdom texts. Previously named *The Kolbrin*, the work is now titled *The Kolbrin Bible* by the publisher. This is because the term *"Bible"* accurately defines the work and also has its roots in a civilization that played a critical role in its dissemination.

In the classic sense, the term *"Bible"* comes from the Greek *"Biblia,"* meaning books, which stems from *"Byblos."* Byblos was an ancient Phoenician port located in what is now the central coast of Lebanon.

In their day, Phoenician traders operated the most advanced fleets of ocean-going vessels in all the world. Before their fall to the Roman Empire, their principal trade routes stretched throughout the Mediterranean area, out along the shores of Western Europe and up as far North as Britain.

Of note to this body of work is that the Phoenicians imported papyrus from Egypt and sold it abroad along with wisdom texts of their time. In doing so, they distributed the earliest known variant of *The Kolbrin Bible*, called *The Great Book*, to their various ports of call. Their Northernmost port was in Britain.

In the 1st century BCE, *The Great Book* inspired its Celtic scholars in Britain to write their own collection of creation stories and other folk tales, now called the *Celtic Texts of the Coelbook*. They did it to give hope to future readers who would surely face the same natural disasters as they did.

Regrettably, the number of volumes originally contained in *The Coelbook* remains unknown. This is because much of both collections was destroyed when the Glastonbury Abbey was set ablaze in 1184 CE. The attack on the Abbey was ordered by English King Henry II, after he accused the Abbey priests of being mystical heretics.

Fearing for their lives, the Celtic priests of the Abbey fled into hiding with what remained of *The Great Book* and *The Coelbook*. Later translated into English, *The Coelbook* is now published as the *Celtic Texts of The Coelbook*.

For more information visit www.kolbrin.com.

Your Own World Books Editions of *The Kolbrin Bible*

Your Own World Books first published several print and electronic editions of *The Kolbrin Bible* in April 2005. Each edition is a faithful copy of the 20th Century Major Edition and uses the Kolbrin Citation System developed by Marshall Masters.

In May 2006, Your Own World Books published second editions of *The Kolbrin Bible*. Updated with over 1,600 typographical corrections based on the *Chicago Manual of Style*, the verbiage remains exactly the same. An index was also added to the print and Adobe eBook editions.

The Kolbrin Bible	Books	Comments	Paperback Edition	eBook Formats
21st Century Master Edition	ALL 1-11	Published for scholars, this edition is available in an A4 letter-sized paperback with ample margins for notes. The typesetting is easy on old eyes.	8.268" x 11.693" Easy on Old Eyes Wide Margins for Notes	Adobe Microsoft Mobipocket Palm
Egyptian Texts of the Bronzebook	1-6 Only	Recommended for those with an interest in 2012 Mayan prophecies, Planet X (Nibiru) and factual alternate accounts of Noah's Flood and Exodus.	7.44" x 9.69" Affordable Ideal for Home	
Celtic Texts of the Coelbook	7-11 Only	Recommended for those with an interest in Druid/Celtic philosophy and prophecies. Also contains newly detailed biographical accounts of Jesus Christ with several first-person quotes.	7.44" x 9.69" Affordable Ideal for Home	

Table 1: Your Own World Books Publications, May 2006

Note: This edition does not include the *Egyptian Texts of The Bronzebook*, which were originally written in Egypt following the Exodus of the Jews, ca 1500 BCE, and later transcribed to bronze sheets and stored in copper-clad wooden boxes.

For more information about the abridged and unabridged editions of *The Kolbrin Bible: 21st Century Master Edition,* visit www.kolbrin.com.

Languages of *the Kolbrin Bible*

One of the most commonly asked questions is "what was the original language of the *The Kolbrin Bible,* and who wrote it. The answer is in multiple parts.

Book	The Kolbrin Bible 21st Century Master Edition	BCE		CE		
	Book Title	15th Century	1st Century	1st Century	18th Century	20th Century
		Original	Translation	Original	Translation	Translation
		Egyptian Hieratic	Phoenician Script	Old Celtic	Old English	Continental English
	Egyptian Texts of the Bronzebook					
1	Creation	◆	◆		◆	◆
2	Gleanings	◆	◆		◆	◆
3	Scrolls	◆	◆		◆	◆
4	Sons of Fire	◆	◆		◆	◆
5	Manuscripts	◆	◆		◆	◆
6	Morals and Precepts	◆	◆		◆	◆
	Celtic Texts of the Coelbook					
7	Origins			◆	◆	◆
8	The Silver Bough			◆	◆	◆
9	Lucius			◆	◆	◆
10	Wisdom			◆	◆	◆
11	Britain			◆	◆	◆

Table 2: Languages of The Kolbrin Bible

Languages Used Before the Common Era

The *Egyptian Texts of the Bronzebook* (the first six books of the *The Kolbrin Bible*) were originally penned in Hieratic as *The Great Book* by Egyptian academicians, following the Exodus of the Jews (ca 1500 BCE).

One of several copies of this work was translated into Phoenician and eventually made its way to Britain. This is because Egypt and Phoenicia were both very powerful nations at the time, and their languages were widely used.

Languages Used During the Common Era

The *Celtic Texts of the Coelbook* (the last five books of the *The Kolbrin Bible*) were originally penned in ancient Celtic. Work began on the earliest parts of *The Coelbook* in approximately 20 CE and finished in approximately 500 CE.

Inspired by the scope of the Egyptian texts, the Celts wrote their own historical and philosophical anthology in a similar manner, but in their own language. Viewed as a religious work by many, the Celtic texts offer a timeless insight into Druid folklore, mysticism and philosophy.

According to some historians, *The Coelbook* was also inspired in part by a visit by Jesus Christ to Britain. At the time, Jesus was either in his late teens or middle twenties and traveled via a high-speed Phoenician trading ship to Britain with his great uncle Joseph of Arimathea, who undertook the journey to inspect a tin mine he owned.

These historians further maintain that Jesus studied the Egyptian texts in Britain. This is because the Celtic texts penned following his possible visit contain a never-before published biography of Jesus.

Given the detailed and highly revealing nature of this biography the case can be made that the biographer personally met Jesus, or interviewed someone who had. Additional corroboration comes from reliable historical accounts that indicate Joseph of Arimathea founded the Glastonbury Abbey in or about 36 CE, and that it eventually became the repository for these texts during the 1st millennium.

Stored together in the Glastonbury Abbey under the watchful eyes of Celtic priests, the texts remained safe and were actively studied until the 12th Century, when the Abbey was attacked and set ablaze by minions of King Henry II.

After the attack, the priests fled with what remained of these ancient works to a secret location in Scotland where the Egyptian texts were transcribed to bronze sheets. At that time, the two books were still not joined, and the language of both remained as-is; Phoenician (translated from Egyptian Hieratic) and ancient Celtic, respectively.

In the 18th century, the two books were combined and translated to Old English to form the first identifiable edition of *The Kolbrin Bible*. In the 20th century, the manuscripts were transferred to London and updated to Continental English.

The latest edition of the *The Kolbrin Bible* still uses the Continental English update, but has been edited according to modern rules of grammar and punctuation based on the *Chicago Manual of Style*.

The Seven Major Editions of *The Kolbrin Bible*

The *Celtic Texts of The Coelbook* is an abridged edition of *The Kolbrin Bible:21st Century Master Edition*. Born of great wisdom and love, the overall creation span of the *The Kolbrin Bible* is greater than that of the *Holy Bible*.

To facilitate a historical study of the work, the publisher has divided the creation span of the *The Kolbrin Bible* into seven "master editions" using the criteria of publication era and country.

Master Edition	Publication Era/Country	Description
1st	15th Century BCE Egypt	First penned in Hieratic after the Exodus of the Jews from Egypt (ca 1500 BCE). Published as *The Great Book*, a 21-volume work. The surviving volumes are now published as the *Egyptian Texts of the Bronzebook*. The genesis of this secular work was a new Egyptian interest in finding the one true G-d of Abraham as a consequence of their defeat at the hands of Moses. The work contains many historical accounts that parallel those of the Torah (Old Testament) and warns of a massive object called the "Destroyer" that is prophesied to return in this time with catastrophic results for the Earth.
2nd	1st Century BCE Phoenicia (Lebanon)	The 1st Master Edition is translated into the Phoenician language. The simple 22-letter alphabet of the Phoenicians eventually becomes the root alphabet of the Greek, Roman and English alphabets. Before falling to the Roman Empire, they distribute the work throughout the Mediterranean area, Western Europe and Britain.
3rd	1st Century CE Britain	From approximately 20 CE to 500 CE, the last five books of what would eventually become *The Kolbrin Bible* are written. Now published as the *Celtic Texts of the Coelbook*, this part of the work was first penned in ancient Celtic. During this time, the Egyptian texts of the 2nd Major Edition were studied by Celts as well as the children of wealthy and powerful Romans. Copies of the work eventually found their way to the Glastonbury Abbey.
4th	12th Century CE Scotland	In 1184 English King Henry II ordered an attack on the Glastonbury Abbey, claiming it's Celtic priests to be heretics. Those who survived the arson and murder fled with the surviving Egyptian texts of the 2nd Master Edition and later engraved them on bronze sheets. Stored for centuries in a secret location in Scotland, this edition is also known as *The Bronzebook*..
5th	18th Century CE Scotland	*The Bronzebook* was merged with *The Coelbook*, and then both were translated into Old English. The new anthology was collectively titled *The Kolbrin* by it's caretakers, the Hope Trust of Edinburgh, Scotland.
6th	20th Century CE England New Zealand America	In the years following WWI, the 5th Major Edition was relocated to London, England, where it was updated to Continental English. This master edition remained unpublished until 1992, when a senior member of the Hope Trust distributed several copies of the work. One distributed copy was printed in 1994 in New Zealand by a small religious order and another in 2005 in America by Your Own World Books. The only differences between the New Zealand (1994) and American (2005) editions appear in the front matter, and the American edition added a new citation system and was published in both print and electronic variants.
7th	21st Century CE America	Your Own World Books updates the 6th Major Edition with 2 significant changes. While the Continental English language and spellings remain unchanged, the text is updated to comply with the *Chicago Manual of Style*. Over 1,600 typographical corrections are made. Also new to this master edition is a first-ever index with over 2,700 unique entries. This master edition is also published in 2 abridged editions; the *Egyptian Texts of the Bronzebook* and the *Celtic Texts of the Coelbook*. All editions are published in print and electronic variants.

Table 3: The Seven Master Editions of The Kolbrin Bible

Kolbrin Citation System
Marshall Masters, 2005-2006

All Your Own World Books abridged and unabridged editions of this work use the same Kolbrin Citation System. It is designed to speed collaborative studies between researchers and authors using any of the twenty print or electronic editions published since April 2005.

Book Citation Schema for *The Kolbrin Bible*

There are 2 citation forms: Long and short. The long form uses a whole word to form the book prefix. The short form uses a 3-letter acronym.

Book No.	Master Edition	Egyptian Texts	Celtic Texts	Book Title	Long Form	Short Form
1	◆	◆		Creation	Creation	CRT
2	◆	◆		Gleanings	Gleanings	GLN
3	◆	◆		Scrolls	Scrolls	SCL
4	◆	◆		Sons of Fire	Sons of Fire	SOF
5	◆	◆		Manuscripts	Manuscripts	MAN
6	◆	◆		Morals and Precepts	Morals	MPR
7	◆		◆	Origins	Origins	OGS
8	◆		◆	The Silver Bough	Silver Bough	SVB
9	◆		◆	Lucius	Lucius	LUC
10	◆		◆	Wisdom	Wisdom	WSD
11	◆		◆	Britain	Britain	BRT

Each book of *The Kolbrin Bible* contains multiple chapters. Following the book prefix, each citation uses a two-part suffix to denote the chapter and paragraph numbers.

The first chapter in each book is designated as number 1 and each of following chapters are numbered in ascending order.

The same numbering rule applies to paragraphs within each chapter.

Note: this system does NOT reference page numbers.

Kolbrin Short Form Citations

This citation form is used in the text itself and is recommended for use by collaborative research groups.

Short Form Syntax
Short Citation Book Acronym <colon> Chapter No. <colon> Paragraph No.

Examples:

> BRT:8:20 "The smooth-tongued hypocrite glosses over the misdeeds of others. He excuses unworthiness and sings your praises before your face, in your hearing, but reviles you behind your back. Avoid all such as these, for their friendship is worthless."

> Hi DeWitt:

> Just downloaded the *Celtic Texts of the Coelbook* in the Adobe eBook format, and I'm delighted to learn the citation system is the same one used in your 21st Century Master Edition print copy of *The Kolbrin Bible*.

> Could you give me your thoughts on BRT:8:20 "The smooth-tongued hypocrite glosses over the misdeeds of others. He excuses unworthiness and sings your praises before your face, in your hearing, but reviles you behind your back…"

> Many thanks, Kristyn

Kolbrin Long Form Citations

This formal citation form is recommended for use with articles, essays and books that reference this work using footnotes, etc.

Long Form Syntax
Long Citation Book Title <space> Chapter No. <colon> Paragraph No.

Examples:

> **Celtic Texts of the Coelbook**
> Your Own World Books First Edition
> Britain 8:20

> "The smooth-tongued hypocrite glosses over the misdeeds of others. He excuses unworthiness and sings your praises before your face, in your hearing, but reviles you behind your back. Avoid all such as these, for their friendship is worthless."

> "The smooth-tongued hypocrite glosses over the misdeeds of others. He excuses unworthiness and sings your praises before your face, in your hearing, but reviles you behind your back…"
> —*Britain 8:20*

> [4] Celtic Texts of the Coelbook, *Britain 8:20*, Your Own World Books 1st ed. (Silver City, NV)

Regardless of how you format the typeface style of your short and long citations, always use the proper syntax to ensure clarity.

Marshall's Motto

Destiny finds those who listen,
and fate finds the rest.

So learn what you can learn,
do what you can do,
and never give up hope!

—*Marshall Masters*

OGS:1:8 Life is a song, sometimes a song of sadness, sometimes a song of joy. Now a dirge, then a hymn echoes through the chambers of creation. Often a gay carol or lilting lovesong gladdens the ear of the air. All this is the Song of Life. So lift up your hearts, and rejoice in the singing soul, which will, in days to come, rise on ghostly wings to quit the inner circles of woe, where the discordant notes of mortals intermingle with the melodious notes of spirit music, winging its way to where the stargirt chorus sings in glory.

Book of Origins

Table of Chapters

OGS:0:1 – OGS:0:2	Preamble	5
OGS:1:1 – OGS:1:27	Chapter One – The Worldbirth	6
OGS:2:1 – OGS:2:35	Chapter Two – The Dawndays	9
OGS:3:1 – OGS:3:25	Chapter Three – The Floodtale	13
OGS:4:1 – OGS:4:	[There is no Chapter 4 – ED]	16
OGS:5:1 – OGS:5:6	Chapter Five – Workers in Metal	16
OGS:6:1 – OGS:6:31	Chapter Six – The Tale of Hewe	17
OGS:7:1 – OGS:7:27	Chapter Seven – Tale of Gwinvera	19
OGS:8:1 – OGS:8:21	Chapter Eight – The Firstfaith Bringers	23
OGS:9:1 – OGS:9:37	Chapter Nine – The Battlebook	25
OGS:10:1 – OGS:10:12	Chapter Ten – The Maymen Lore	29

Book of Origins

Preamble

Translated by John Laid Ledylith

OGS:0:1 This task was undertaken and carried out by order of the Tothnaelethan made in solemn accord, assembled as beforetimes at Tanagekil near Sunderstow. One hundred and sixty years after the death of Ardpeth, the last king. Twenty years after the death of Garadon Pankris. Eighty years after the death of Kelwin. One hundred years after the death of Afterid. Thirteen years after the death of the great king who died in the year of the devil's breath. This dealdew, lasting upward of a dozen years, so striking the land that people lost their distinctions, and the long conflict came to an end. Forty-four years after the battle of Strathard, when the Christian king died in his forty-sixth year, going down with a great slaughter before the hand of Kadwilan of the Firstfaith, who died at the hands of a treacherous king, being trapped between the trees by Dinsleir. In the month of September, between the seventh and the tenth day, in the third year of the reign of Ethelbred, which is the seventh year in the reign of Egfrid, son of Oswey, king of the North Saxondom. The fourteenth year in the reign of Ardwulf, king of East Saxondom and the second year in the reign of Ketwin, king of West Saxondom. The fourth year in the reign of Lothir, king of all the Kents, and the fifth year we suffer under the afflicting fires of the Black Bull of the North. It is two hundred and twenty-two years since the coming of the long-sword-wielding warbands and one hundred and sixty-five years since the death of Okther. It is one hundred and thirty years since the last warband came and stayed with the land they took, when Britain ceased to be, during the reign of King Ifor.

OGS:0:2 These are the elect Kailwardens who undertook the work: Humog and Lewin of the Gutradors; Pencluith the Dalradan, a smith of the Shieldmakers; Helaf the Carver, born among the Scots over the sea, of the Shieldmakers; Malkuin, a Chief, born among Kwits, of the Engravers; Enelek the Potter, born among the Kwits, of the Shieldmakers; Ipedruad the Grinder, born at Alcuth, of the Coppersmiths; Fronwin the Swordmaker; son of Klude, a Briton born as a freeman among the Saxons to the West and an engraver of note; Edwin the Elder, a Talesman who writes, born of a Mercian, of the Shieldmakers; and Glason the Inglinger who became one of us.

[This preamble appeared at the back of this book in the 1st edition. It was moved to the beginning for this edition. Also, some of the 1st edition eBooks used "OGF" instead of "OGS" in the citations. The correct form is "OGS" for this book.—Editor]

Chapter One – The Worldbirth

OGS:1:1 This is an unhappy time of strife and change, and the old folk knowledge and skills are passing away like leaves falling on flowing water. We of the Gwidonad are therefore gathered together under the shield of Hirweal for the purpose of preserving the things dear to our hearts. To do this, we firstly discover their biding places, and secondly commit into writing all the hallowed tales concerned with them. Also, as the mortal memories of men perish with their frail bodies, we deem it well to commit into bookwriting the old knowledge once written in our minds.

OGS:1:2 Behind us lie fourteen Earth generations of mankind, and this has been the manner of their naming: The Generation of Light, The Generation of Fire, The Generation of Water, The Generation of Grass, The Generation of Trees, The Generation of Wood, and The Generation of Stone, and all these together are the Blissful Generations. Then followed The Generation of the Spear, The Generation of the Axe, The Generation of the Shield, The Generation of the Sword, The Generation of the Bow, The Generation of the Helmet and The Generation of the Chariot, and all these together are the Homeless Generations. The years before us contain six full Earth generations and whatever remains of this Generation of Change. Each of the past Earth generations was three times the length of the one, which followed it.

OGS:1:3 Men ask, as men always will, how the widespread, wonderful world came into being, and whose were the feet first treading the good soil upon it. This, masters, is the old tale concerning the dawntime of life, handed down from the blissful morning days of Earth's existence.

OGS:1:4 Before time was born, it could be conceived. Before all things seeable by the darting eyes of men were seen by any eye, they were conceived. Before sound was heard by any listening ear, it was conceived. All things now knowable by man were first conceived by none but The Inconceivable One, existing solitary in awesome loneliness. Back in the predawn state there was no feeling, throbbing, loving life beyond The Alone One. There was nothing, in which something other could be perceived and manifested. The Inconceivable One's reflecting mirror was not yet made. Love, the sunlight of life, could not be known, for even One So Great could not yet conceive a state of satisfaction in self-love. The one thing not capable of conception was the realisation of responsive love.

OGS:1:5 So from The Inconceivable One there came a great outpouring melody, the song of conception, the notes winging vitalising consciousness outward in radiating ripples. All that is now existing came out of that, which was harmoniously sung into being, and the sweet echoing vibrations still sound in rhythm throughout the many circles of existence. All life and matter vibrate in response to a divinely originated, orchestrated melody and rhythm.

OGS:1:6 As the sweet notes of the divine, lilting music swelled outward, Heaven was formed from the song-created radiance of immortal light. Rising on a higher note of ever increasing splendour into a great pulsating chorus, it hurled forth a whole string of worlds, scattering them in illuminating brilliance through the black matrix of Ked. It was like a handful of bright pearls being thrown into the darkness of night. In a perfectly timed cadence of melody and harmony the worlds were hurled into separate existence, each finding its proper place in accordance with its note. All life is therefore nothing except a response to harmony and melody, to the spreading ripples and resounding echoes from the first Divine Hymn, the life-awakening song. The only disharmonious notes were those which later emerged from the hearts of sinful men.

OGS:1:7 The songs and poems of men, poorly stirring the unresponsive heart, are futile attempts to recapture some part of the first grand symphony. Men instinctively know they are musicians in the great orchestra of life, singers in the chorus of existence. The Song of Life still vibrates upon the lute strings of each throbbing heart, filling it with responsive vitality. On Earth, it can never be heard in perfection, yet it is here the singing lessons must be learned; for once through the dark archway and in the Court of Splendour, the newly released spirit must introduce itself by song. The good, clean spirit vibrates with a happy, harmonious melody, while the dull, evil-doing spirit rasps out harshly in agonising discord. The first thing the travel-weary homecoming spirit hears is the welcoming notes of the Divine Melody. Happy are they who harmonise with it, sorrowful are those who vibrate discordantly!

OGS:1:8   Life is a song, sometimes a song of sadness, sometimes a song of joy. Now a dirge, then a hymn echoes through the chambers of creation. Often a gay carol or lilting lovesong gladdens the ear of the air. All this is the Song of Life. So lift up your hearts, and rejoice in the singing soul, which will, in days to come, rise on ghostly wings to quit the inner circles of woe, where the discordant notes of mortals intermingle with the melodious notes of spirit music, winging its way to where the stargirt chorus sings in glory.

OGS:1:9   Out from The Inconceivable One came the radiating substances of Dewa, who sits supreme in the invisible Universal Hub, and this is His circle. The outflowing notes became contrasted among themselves, dividing into two, and those that poured downwards became the substance of Mamvar the Lifebringer. From the life-radiating substance of Mamvar came Mamdadeh, who spread life wide over the world. The son of Mamdadeh was Dada, whose name was not spoken in the beforetimes, and he carried the spirits of men in his seed.

OGS:1:10   These are the generations of the ancestral godmen who came from Dada, as they have been known tons, and it is well to know from whence we came, we being of their blood. We stand high among the proud races of mankind, not being numbered among the least, and sad will be the day when men lose pride in their heritage. Yet it is foretold that the day will surely come, at a time when men stand on a strange threshold, with the choice of regeneration or decay and doom.

OGS:1:11   Those generated from the seed of Dada were the three Heaven-sent forebears of mankind, named Magog, Gatuma and Keili. We are told that these were beings in spirit form dwelling apart from the Universal Hub, at the outer reaches of Kewgant, but of this there is now no sure knowledge. It is known only that Magog ruled in the North and East, Gatuma in the South and Keili in the West, but old tales tell of Keili's travels from the widelands of the East to this sea-girt green isle. The consort of Keili the All Knowing, he who guards the memories of men, was Kithwin the First Well Beloved, and they had a son and daughter. The son was dark-visaged Aveg and the daughter Kerirway, the most beautiful of women, who set the standards of womanhood, to which all who desire to catch the will-o'-the-wisp of love should aspire.

OGS:1:12   The son of Gatuma was Gatumugna the Skyfighter, whose son was Tuwait, the Townfounder and Metalmaster, who married Amerith, the Skychief's daughter. Their sons were Nodinos the first earthling, and Magilmish the Wanderer, in whose days the sky chariots came. It is told how, in the glowering dawntime of the world, Amerith flew on swift wings of the spirit from her kingdom in the West to consult with Tuwait the Eastern Father, son of Gatumugna. They met beneath the great lifetree, known as Kalesdrid, which grew at Enok. They lived awhile within the green bower set in the lushlands surrounding the lifetree, and it was for her the ring of youth was forged. This she gave to her seducer and so became as other women, while he lived in youth and strength. It is thus that the ring became known as the Prize of Seduction.

OGS:1:13   Magilmish was a mighty one among men, whose fame spread far and wide, and he was called the Lord of Battles, the Victory Winner, the Mansmiter, the Earth Burner, the Wind Fighter and the Water Spouter, and called Gilamish beforetimes. Those were his names among all the peoples of those days, for not all knew him by name, and some misnamed him. His son was Jovan, whose son was Bethbal, whose son was Amalugad, whose son was Lugad, the Hammerer. The daughter of Nodinos was Efa, born of the Skymother. Efa married Nud, the Underearthman, whose eyes could not bear the daylight, and their son was Gwin the Fairfaced. Efa ran away from Nud and became the wayward wife of Belesetin.

OGS:1:14   The sons of Magog the Great Brooder, were Kelefa and Mamagog the Fertiliser. The son of Kelefa was Helith the Lifebringer, whose daughter was Amerith the Desirable, much besought by the Battlekings. Those who hold to the old tongue call her Asterith and say she was the mother of the first true man. These are not things to be hugged to the heart, for it would be a wise man indeed who knew the nature of the first mortal man after the sinful intermingling.

OGS:1:15 The son of Mamagog was Bele the Bright, first husband of Dona Smiling Eyes, and one of their sons was Lew Dewtears, the bright, happy cradlechild who laughed in the sunshine. It is told that he shed tears of glistening dew, which healed any wound, and unless these be the rainstones, the story is past understanding. He became king of Karguthrin, where tales of his times are still told in the halls. The other son, Lew's brother, was Malvas Anshriver of the dark tears, and it is said that if he cried, any tears falling on bare flesh would raise unhealable weeping sores. The tale goes that Malvas possessed the balebag containing foul maggots of sickness and the cankerworms of barrenness and infertility. Also it held within its folds the balebook with recipes for every dire event and tribulation. His companions were the dread loping wailwoves of death, but now none knows the meaning behind the tale. We do know that Malvas was the forefather of the dark dwarfs. We know, too, that the ancient taletellers dressed wisdom and Truth in garments of frivolity and motley, so only the discerning benefited, while the mindless manyfolk were momentarily amused but then passed them by as things of little consequence. Who, not knowing and looking at the mud mussel, would believe a beauteous pearl must lie within?

OGS:1:16 The sons of Lew by his first wife, Anath, she who caused the building of mysteryful Kamailas for the glorification of men, and who died because of her desire for Thaneros, were Belesetin and Franan. Their daughters were Branwen and that Nertha sometimes called Naniku in the old tongue, who was the first wife of Nodinos and mother of the first full woman.

OGS:1:17 The sons of Lew by Morigu were Kela, Gwinon the Welcomer of Warriors, Leir and Robeth, and the first wife of Leir was Pendora, by whom he had two sons, Mandobrak and Frans, and a daughter Branwin. By his second wife, the Northern Beauty, Leir had Thanis, Wothin and Dylan.

OGS:1:18 The first wife of Belesetin was Efa, who married Nud after being cast out from her homeplace. His second wife was Franwy and his son was Evalak, Guardian of the Gate, and his daughter was Modren whose son was Owin Wiseheart.

OGS:1:19 The second husband of Dona was Manwidan and their daughters were Pendora and that Arinrada who gladdens the hearts of old men. They lived in the days before the misty veil became impenetrable and Evalak ruled the isle containing a forest of fireapple trees, which men now misunderstand. Many meanings are lost to those who have learned the old tales of wisdom in the new tongue.

OGS:1:20 Arinrada married Traith the Whitehaired, and their sons were Athlan the Strong Wave Wanderer, Kolehan the Teacher, and Kornayna the Bull Borne War Watcher, and their daughter was Mebid who married Bramathamlin. The son of Athlan was Elan the Sea Smith of the Floating Forge, who married the daughter of Manwidan for whom he made armour of a mysterious metal, which no axe, spear, sword or arrow could penetrate.

OGS:1:21 The son of Elan was Karunas the Hornheaded, who married Newlyn the Fairmaid, daughter of Bramathamlin, she whom they of the Old Faith call Tanis the Moonmaid, but it was not her desire which brought the first daylight; it was another's. Their son was Laledkin the Larger, whose son was Hewe, Great Chief of the Upright Ones, who married Helen Bloderwed, whose son was Ayed, who married Sibel the Strange Priestess, whose son was Brydin, whose sons were, Brydin the Younger and Belinos the Bookbearer. The son of Belinos was Bladud the Builder, who was cured of a corrupting disease by mud from a swine's wallow.

OGS:1:22 Bladud married Kelwinith, daughter of Molmed the Wise, whose wife was Tishana, whose mother was Sibel whose husband was slain by Kastwelan the Invader, while fighting with the dark men of Filistis with whom they had sought refuge.

OGS:1:23 Bethbal married Anarath and their daughter was Anath. Athlan married Niad, daughter of Vala. The son of Bladud was Elas, whose son was Lokrinos. The son of Molmed was Marsis, whose son was Kamba, with whom Kelwinith sought refuge in Finkera, over the sea of Mertis. The son of Kamba was Humba, who failed to build his boats of ash slats, so they came apart, and he was drowned, whose son was Erigen, whose son was Kratalinth. The wife of Humba was Marva, daughter of Fermadamid.

OGS:1:24 The son of Kolehan was Neptoran, and his daughter was Sowithy, and Neptoran married

Wokelyn. The sons of Mandobrak were Luk the Arbitrator, who plays with the chancechips, and Dianket, who first taught men the use of healing herbs, and that Luktin who was the uncle of Lugad and who taught men the ways of working with wood, and who could fix a spearhead immovably onto its shaft.

OGS:1:25 There is tale at variance with others which states that the daughter of Dianket was Newlyn the Ravenfaced, who married her uncle, which ill-omened marriage caused barrenness among cattle and green-growing corn to lay down in shame. The sister of Neptoran was Sowithy of the Fair Isle, who married Lugad Hardhand the Hammerer, who taught the working of bronze and was the father of our people. It is told how he was shot in the thigh by a dwarf's arrow and how, every year at Samhain, the deep wound opened and erupted a vile venom which dropped off to dry into a grey powder. This wound was eventually healed by the kiss of a rainstone, and it is said that in this way, its holiness was discovered... but surely the drops of venom are the vile rites of the dwarfs!

OGS:1:26 The son of Neptoran was Grakenwid and his daughter was Nanara, who married Kamelognatha, Builder of the high-walled city over the water, who was the son of Ognana and Brigenda. Kamelognatha sought refuge in this land and taught men the art of writing on wood and stone.

OGS:1:27 The tales concerning the doings of our forebears in faith and their generations are not well known among us, for we are a different people having another tongue. Yet though some tell them one way and some another, we have sought out that, which is common to most. In these times of change it is well to have an anchor in the past, but unless it bites into a sound seabed, it is of little value. It is said that the sole message, which can be given to the future is words written in the past, so we write.

Chapter Two – The Dawndays

OGS:2:1 Generations ago, the people living in Britain were unlike those now occupying this bountiful land, and in bygone ages, great herds of cattle were tended on rolling, green plains. Southward grew long-stemmed corn, but in those long-gone days, it was not bartered with blackbearded strangers from beyond the stormy seas.

OGS:2:2 The first folk holding this land were the Kamledis, called Wictarin in the old tongue, but these were dwellers in the North, while southward were the dark, shortlegged dwarfmen known as Oben. They were kingless and chiefless, though it is said by some that stocky-statured Kathlon was once their king. None knows who led the dwarfmen here, though men do say the land spawned them, though the land is good. They were hagridden, forest- fearing river-dwellers who painted their faces and legs, users of evilly poisoned weapons. Theirs were the grim gods of death and darkness, and at their festival times, the dwarfmen sat in sombre caves eating children as part of their evil feasting. They had no priests, only dwarfesses called Chethin, meaning raven-adopted, and there was a great one above the others, called Harada, who lived in a smoky cave called Hegrin.

OGS:2:3 They were ruled by old hagwomen, who prepared hellish brews in firechurns tended by devilish brownswaddled dwarf maidens, for they also worshipped beings dwelling in smoke. The last hagwoman queen of the Oben was Kwasir who had a cave shelter hole at Inswitan, which is the Dwarf Isle, now called Iniseug in the Western tongue. Here they worshipped the Old Yearteller, coming from afar on windfloats, the neighing windhorses of later days. The most hallowed of their rites were those celebrated before the mayflowering, when filthy things were done, for they had no shame. Here, the Children of the Dusk gathered in the month of willows to worship Mamdo and her balebrood, performing vile rites under the command of Blasis, their great mangod.

OGS:2:4 The dwarfmen, both North and South, were skinswaddled, though sometimes wearing nettlecloth clothes of black or brown, and like the cat, dove and dog they mated openly without shame. They gathered toadstools, brockberries, ivy, wayweed and other unwholesome plants, using these with evil moondew to make a maddening brew, which opened a strange door on hellish worlds. They were ruled by cowled sewds and dradwitches, and were unable to number beyond a score. There are dwarfmen still living among us in the forest depths and in caverns under the Earth, though none here has seen one. They quickly take to flight, and though fearing it, will take refuge within the forest. Sometimes a bold one will stay and will greet the wayfarer with, "Hail, man; I saw you from afar but stayed." To which the reply must be made, "Before seeing you I was as one dead, but now life comes again." Then, providing a gift is also given, the wayfarer remains unmolested.

OGS:2:5 In the generations of the dwarfmen, broad Britain was a many-marshed land, where dismal ferns and tangled forests hindered passage from place to place. The Oben were not numerous and their children few, but they were hardy and long-lived. Their caves were painted, even in the darkest depths where daylight never fell, for the eyes of the Oben were like those of cats. They were not skilful hunters but set many traps, and in lots of ways were like children. They were playful when not engaged in dark doings, but their menfolk were not manly, nor their women womanly. They were cunning and devious, not to be trusted.

OGS:2:6 Far to the South were the swarthy swarm of the Frolga, though these were not true dwarfmen but the outcome of intermingled blood. They were worshippers of Nana the Mighty Mother, and were ruled by many feywomen who sat in night councils when the summershiner slept. Into the land held by the short dark Oben, came tall wiry Tothsolars, who were sunfolk. They came through Airana and the country of the Nudlanders, who wore gallitraps, and it was in those days, men began to breed swine, the first beast bred to be eaten, for only the dwarfmen eat dogs and cats. The land was then called Muredin, meaning the Place of Rest.

OGS:2:7 Then into the easterly lowlands came seaborne Baradon with his plowmen, and that part lying between Hilderith and Pretankely they made their own and called it Holbon. Baradon was the son of Indrud who married Hurash. Indrud was the son of Jova who married Elsis, and Jova was the son of he who became the first father of households.

OGS:2:8 Wise, hoaryheaded men have treasured these tales belonging to our first great race, the wise and noble, having its birthplace in great forest-girt mountains bespangled with green, skypointing pinefingers. These are tales of times before men were men, when the big-bellied murkymother ruled the world-covering Netherfolk, sharing the land with giant Endlings.

OGS:2:9 The great gutted one was unaware of the wind-blasted salt waters; living in the mountain-hid, thicket-walled cave places, beyond the corn grass plains of Nonima, she knew only the cold companionship of hooded adders. There in smoke-smothered, gloom-enshrouded caverns, attended by her daughter Eldiwed, she read signs for rock-stooled Balings, plucking dark wisdom from writhing flames.

OGS:2:10 Lovers of the comforting fire warmth, smoke dreamers, seekers of home hearth's consolation, not far ranging war bringers or land openers, the Netherfolk desired only to remain undisturbed. Compatible companions to intangible wraiths, flitting shades and unsubstantial ghosts, they knew full well the secrets of Gorwel. Fearing forest-ruling Pafamba, they begged protection of the Netherogre, but among the life-giving trees, he was powerless. In the smoke-curtained, many-pillared hole hall, unblessed by regenerating sun-ray, the Netherfolk called upon their wan night goddess, their prayers weird yelpings in the ruddy gloom. Their music was the rushing gurgle and splash of falling waters, their song a howling whine.

OGS:2:11 These were of the race spawned long ages ago in dark-mired moss swamps, fern-eating foemen of the poisoned dart. Not for them the swiftly killed sacrifice; their delight was in painful maiming, in the broken humiliation of their betters. Woeful indeed was the yearly fate of the hagmother's spouse on the long dark night preceding the bridal day during the feast of flame.

OGS:2:12 They were wolf-talking howlers of the night, owl-screeching denizens of dim caverns, speech beguilers of wild creatures in closed places. Cowled and cloaked in dull clothing, they were undistinguishable in their habitat, save for the foul, nostril-stinging smell of bodies ointmented with pigfat, soot, blood and clay. All the night, at the dark of the moon, they pranced around stone-hedged, deep-dug, glowing firepits, their kirtles upheld by the never subsiding limb beneath.

OGS:2:13 Bemudded, grease-grimed and grey were the heads of the hagwomen seated around the ashfires, muttering darkly over the rowan omensticks. Casting spells for the hell-spewed horde, they sucked fat dripping portions from the stone-heated pots. Only the poison-speared he-goat leader of rituals received choicer portions than they.

OGS:2:14 Never fighters with sword or axe and shield, the battle-shy dwarfmen were twin-handed dart hurlers. Back-pointing, evil-toothed, barbed short lances were their hand-carried weapons, and no mansmiting metal was theirs to work. Nor did they pin their cloaks, but held them together with animal threads. They had no shields, but were agile and deft in dodging the thrusting weapons of their foes.

OGS:2:15 Into the dark, wild, wooded land came blood-haired Lodmor, son of Kel, wave-borne, encased within the ship bellies of oak and beech. Father fighter of the upright Iberis, the Hearth Hallower, the Wife Maker, the Child Protector, the Wild Herd Rider. Up the flowing waters to Muspel, place of the Netherfolk, came the fair-skinned wanderers. Not with fight-straining eyes, but with hands empty of weapons and guileless hearts, seeking only to live out on the grass-thatched plains. Their eyes fell on sights never before seen, the feast of offal, the fire-smoke dancing, the open coupling before jesting advice-giving onlookers.

OGS:2:16 No sight, this for maidens of the Iberis, no place for wide-eyed womenfolk, not for red-cheeked children's curiosity the pleasures of the dusky horde. Not for hard-hunting men the stone benches of the wolfwenches; the heavy-handed ones who made men of men had come to a land demanding their care, and they were vigilant. Long into the night echoed the songs to Bilew and Blasis, while those of the upper-born race sat sternly silent, their disgust unvoiced. No thoughts of spear-reddening had they, as they gazed upon the revolting antics.

OGS:2:17 Beyond the undistinguishable wall, where ruddy firelight gently kissed the face of darkness, skulkers of the Netherfolk stole the fur-swaddled sleeper, manchild of the lusty-lunged war singer. Swiftly he was borne away in the arms of the son of the day banisher. Righteous rage broke out in the ranks of the Upright Ones. No longer were the war weapons unwhetted, ruddy indeed the dawn over Muspel, but in the bushes and trees about the place lurked most of the swarthy swarm, escaped to howl vile threats and defiance at the grouped warriors and their protected womenfolk.

OGS:2:18 With the opening of the dawn's eye, the brawny warriors were spreadwide, driving the wily foe from his cover. Eager the faces; fierce, close-held the comforting shields, but the foemen were as hard to grapple with as the morning mists. The call to close came many times; the red horn resounding through the thicketed woods, but the dwarfmen were never in front, always behind. Then, as the skychief descended towards its resting place, the warriors came to a clearing before a caverned-cliff face, and there the evil brood were cornered. Grim-faced, the tall ones entered the battle clamour, but axe and sword bit only unsatisfying air. There was a scattering of the small ones, followed by a hunting through darkling glades. Ever the swift, silent, poisoned darts flew and the bitter barbs bit deep, fastening viciously on to heroic flesh. Evil indeed for heroes to thus die!

OGS:2:19 Back through bramble-entangled woods, through high-grassed glades, came the weary warriors, the long, thirsty swords still alert and eager for the blood of barbed-dart throwers. That night, they camped where they had left their guarded womenfolk, and with the dawnlight the sentries discovered a dwarfman. It was Kamwird the Wrinkled, and he brought back the manchild and the heart of his abductor. "Tatish, peace" cried Kamwird the Wrinkled, before the long, sharp-pronged spear of Thunderwolf, "Let be; let us bide together." Sad tears, the dark eyes shed. "Peace" said the swordsheathers, "Defile not the ankitel. Peace be." The Hardgripping hands familiar with spear, axe and sword were extended in friendship and the vengeance-smiting and bloodflow ceased.

OGS:2:20 Then to the stockade came the small ones, emissaries for peacemaking. Magas and Shine, dwarfmen of Himy, Mooney, Meany and Shindy, with Lum the leader, brownclad, hooded, kirtled, belted and entassled, russet-skinned and ruddy-faced. Then came wise Killen to the peacemaking, tall towering, sinewy and stern, he of the generous hand. Thus was the way opened for the fairfolk to enter the land.

OGS:2:21 Lodmor led his people through the forested land to the white, dusty, hawthorned plains, and they settled there in peace. There they raised noble sons, white-browed, blue-eyed, slim womaned and dutifully wifed. Russet battleaxes were laid aside, the whetstone no longer caressed the sword. Brawny arms drove in the firmly held alder piles, raising the ash-held rafters, spreading above them in the thick-led fern and corded grass. Laughingly, the children played, the merry maids singing, the building blows of men echoing in the clearings. In from the moors to carry timber and stone, came Sons of the Nightcrow, blue-skinned people, dark-cloaked, mossy-haired men akin to the Oben, worshippers of The Ever Broody Mother.

OGS:2:22 The son of Lodmor was battleblooded Killen the Northrider, whose mother was Elvira, Maid of the Morning, and while Killen was yet young, dwarfmen came to the high stockade, emissaries seeking allies.

OGS:2:23 Killen sat with his father, listening to the words of the dwarfmen. It was agreed the dwarffolk should live under the shield of Lodmor, and they would labour in return. Then Killen gave them sticks for hoeing and digging, long stones for planting. Leeks, beans, flax, barley and wheat were unstintingly given, along with woven haircloth. In wooded glades cleared by tree-encircling fires, the sowing commenced, the bough bowers were built, the swine enclosed.

OGS:2:24 Not all the wide-ranging warriors thought as did Lodmor, for some said "Let us make masters for this dark brood of dwarfmen. Let us sever the haglings from their Ever Broody Hagmother, the smoky hellhag of dark caverns. Let us pen them as cattle."

OGS:2:25 To enslave was not the nature of the Upstanding Ones. Blood had been ransomed with blood and no score remained unsettled. No woman of the dwarffolk was beridden.

OGS:2:26 When the time of mayfeasting was at hand, Lude came, the dwarfchief, son of Frokith, with him his daughter, the night-haired Rada. The dwarfmaiden came well attended with young hagwomen, her skin like half ripe rose seed. Small-faced, bedimpled, bird-eyed, full-haired to the knee, brown-kirtled, fur-shod and cloaked with acceptable grace, she came as a worthy bride offering. Hers was the bracken bed, fragrant grass mingled within.

OGS:2:27 For three days Killen the Battleblooded Northrider, the Weary Wanderer, the Forest Fighter, remained silent, his thoughts remaining within himself, but then he welcomed the trothplighter. He welcomed the dark maid, the non-beridden one of the dwarfmen, for she was not unworthy of a true man.

OGS:2:28 Spake dark Lude, "This woman, the safeguarded daughter of a chief, has never been any man's plaything. Not for her the bed of sand, the dance-ending gift, this is a true lady of the Elfingers. Of women in the land, none is above her; none exceeds her in beauty or virtue, if these you value. As man speaks with man, chief with chief, match gift with gift, let this land be ours. Give me a tall, corn-haired maiden, full-bosomed, fair-skinned, sun-faced, to enliven gloomy lives."

OGS:2:29 Spake one-tongued Killen, "Not for me the words of hidden meaning. No maid of light shall be given to man of darkness, though dwarfmaidens are not denied to men of mine. If night mingle with the day, the light is lessened, so the day spurns the night. The night is not guardian of the light, so what cares it? Does darkness put out the firelight or fire dispel darkness? Can they mix? No milkskinned maid shall go at my behest."

OGS:2:30 "This I declare, for even I cannot forbid the trothpledge of one who loves. If there be a milkskinned maid who would freely choose to go, then let it be. She may bide as a bride of yours, but surely it is known no milkskinned maid would sever herself from our race, for return with a dark brood is forbidden. No dark brood do we accept; our men with your maids go, but what come of it is not one of us, no acceptable issue of ours. We father no dark brood, nor twilight offspring. What do we choose to father our herds, the best or the worst among bulls? Are not men many times greater than cattle?"

OGS:2:31 No milkskinned maid came freely forth; the dark dwarfmen chief was left unwed. In stockaded homes, the tall Upright Ones slept secure, no maid crept forth to mingle with the murky ones of the night. Yet when the fullsailed nightscanner shone above, with weird prancing, the Nethermen danced in the downshining light. Round and round, rapidly moved the dancing feet, the earthen mound quaked, the singing rose on the nightbreeze; flute music mingled with the tree sounds. Faster flew the nimble feet beating down upon tight-packed earth, wilder whirled the dancers to their coupling climax. The earthwatchers drew a curtain of cloud over the eyes of the nightshiner. No corn-haired head rose from its resting place.

OGS:2:32 Many the moon-bathed dances, oft the wild prancing, but less and less the dark broods numbers, further back into the forest and cave went the dusky-skinned ones. Oft in the night darkness, fair maids were snatched by brown-cowled dwarfmen, to breed twilight broodlings in secret places. Woeful were the enforced couplings and woeful the issue. Not for milkskinned maids, the free sinful coupling of the foredoomed dawnrace!

OGS:2:33 In five generations, the Nethermen were gone, only in the dark depths of cave and forest could they be found. No longer were the milk-skinned maidens molested at night. The night offerings were put out; the dwarfmen came and supped; honey, bread, milk and sowflesh were taken in gratitude. The race of Nethermen passed into the shadows of time, only twilight offspring roaming the land, tawny-faced, blue-legged, weirdly-painted, brown-cowled, rope-belted, builders with stone.

OGS:2:34 No longer dwellers in dismal caves, or hunters in dark-mired swamps, the Alfing built slime-covered bough houses and raised high, upward pointing stones. Still soot-besmeared, pigfat-ointmented like the darkside of their forebears, they were also feathered and quill-ornamented. Being twilight-fathered, they faced no man courageously, coming to the attack like ground-slithering snakes, striking venomously from secret places, still forest skulkers. None could recite his lineage, for no man knew his father.

OGS:2:35 These were mother-lap-reared half folk, speaking with the tongues of their fathers, their words like crackling, spluttering green twigs burning in the fire. Brown and green clothed, bebangled, stone-hauling Idunings toiling for their black-bearded masters for unknown ends.

Chapter Three – The Floodtale

OGS:3:1 Over the sea now called Basabrimal, came a far-ranging race from Krowkasis, the Motherland where Gatuma ruled, where skyreaching mountains rise out of a wide, green, dark-soiled plain. They were horsefighters, known among themselves as the Wildland Cultivators, and they landed at the place beforetimes called Haltraith, in the land of the Horsefolk, now held by Engling. They built the wood-walled town called Hovenlee in the new tongue, near where the great sea king sleeps beneath his mound.

OGS:3:2 They took their land from the herd-keeping Frolga and ranged wide from shore to shore, renaming the water-encircled land, the Honeyladen Isle, for never before had they seen honey in such quantities since leaving their own land. There were folk here before the fleet-footed Frolga, but they were magic-dealing dwarfs living in holes sunk in the ground, covered over with wicker and earth. It is said they knew and understood the speech of all wild creatures and often talked with them as brothers. They were friendly and frolicsome, and before them only, the bowed Yoshan roamed the land.

OGS:3:3 In the days when the Wildland Cultivators came and swallowed up the Frolga, there were bears, wolves, wild cattle, boars, oruks, deer, elk, lioncats, man-eating water lizards and beasteaters that dwelt in lakes aplenty. The Frolga were not small, but lacked fighting skill; they were spearmen and without bows, but skilful stone slingers.

OGS:3:4 Behind the Wildland Cultivators came the Uksening, but being boatless, few came to this green land, most turning southward to Amorika. Those who came were workers in wood and metal, and it was they who built Kelnahilene, which stood even in the generation of our grandfathers' fathers.

OGS:3:5 In the generation when Glenapton was king of the Wildland Cultivators, a North-spawned horde came down upon the flatlands, led by Beledon the Thrummchinned, who gained kingship over the land once called Keningwed. Kolwader, the son of Glenapton, married a daughter of Beledon, and Frewil, son of Beledon, married a daughter of Glenapton, and there was peace.

OGS:3:6 It was in the generation of their sons that Benlanda, son of Bamlod, king of the Parsis, took the land, and all Britain moved southward.

OGS:3:7 The southward moving folk established the places of their responsive gods where once other gods had been hallowed, and they took the place of Madrad. They took the lands of the cattle-herding Basgala and the seatrading Taning, and out in sky-wide Senmag, they built the great hall of Karkilgule, with material carried from the Land of Illusion during the cold half of the year.

OGS:3:8 In their generation, people of this blood, the blackbanded Kelglain, built the wooded town of Maroliven which stood until the coming of the long-sworded Helwaren. Its burning was a vile act of spite following their bitter defeat at the harsh battle of Belishmer, when king Faidlimid was slain and honourably buried at Kumbirgels by the British battlechiefs.

OGS:3:9 It was the Wildland Cultivators who gave the floodtale to our housebuilding forebears, but the generation of its happening is lost. In those days, men were inclined to the ways of peace, and harvest followed winter without change; but it came about that looking up into a darkling nightsky, they saw a strangely formed moonchariot overhead. It passed away into the rosy dawning of a new-born day, but then at the night end of the skyroof appeared the dread figure of Awamkored revealing itself to the eyes of wondering men. It crawled out into the brightness.

OGS:3:10 The foul breath of the nightcomer newly sprung from the dark depths of its unearthly lair, spread across the brightening face of Heaven, like an evil grey veil, and even the ever fearless sun withdrew to gird himself in red war armour. The fastbeating hearts of men first shrivelled with despair at the fearsome sight, then rose while their throats responded with glad cries as the moonchariot came back over the dim horizon. There, riding the battlebar, flaming sword held high, was the bright, beloved figure of Lithalun, her fair hair strung out behind as she flew towards the hellfigure.

OGS:3:11 They met in an awful, hell-echoing clash, with the noise of ten thousand rolling thunders, and men bold enough to look were stricken with blindness, and uncovered ears were deafened forever, Cold moontears were shed by the fang and claw-torn champion of mankind, while the hellish Awamkored drooled white cinders, which, if they touched the skins of men below, raised evil weals.

OGS:3:12 The unearthly foemen fell apart and hurled great self-created rocks at each other, and onlookers below dashed for protective shelter as they howled down out of the sky above. The very Earth, herself immovable, was sickened with fear, and her bowels became loosened with dread; her belly trembled before the awful sight. Men, looking anxiously to their lord the Sun, were dismayed to see his constant change of war garb, from red to blue, then to yellow, then green, then brown.

OGS:3:13 Good Mother Earth opened her groundmouth and roared earcracking protests, while her whole comforting body shook in fear under the gloomy battle shadowform above. Men and beasts were drawn together in a strange brotherhood of fear, none doing harm to another.

OGS:3:14 Those hardy enough to maintain a watch on the combat saw the flashing chariot of Lithalun crush the writhing body of the nightcomer, and then saw its vile black blood, thick like resin, fall upon the thankful bosom of Earth. Where the blood fell, flames sprang up. The fear-heated, blood-despoiled body of Mother Earth was cooled and refreshed by the soothing moontears of Lithalun, shed in womanly relief as she drove back towards her hidden abode in the recesses of Heaven.

OGS:3:15 This is the tale of the skyfight, but whether it happened before or after the generation of Hestabel and the floodtale, none now truly knows. It concerns the Doomdragon, which has come more than once and will come again, and the last music mankind will hear is the shrill throbbing notes of the Doomsong.

OGS:3:16 This is the floodtale, which has come down to us from our housebuilding forebears, and it happened in days generations ago, when men were widely divided.

OGS:3:17 Out into the grey, watery wilderness, where now the restless Western waters roll and heave, there was a place called Tirfola, meaning the Far Western Land. It was a country of high mountains, higher by far than those known to us, and low, green-grassed hills swept down from them to brown, fertile, plowed lands at the sea edge. The folk of Tirfola lived in fine houses, though the roofs were flattened, built on cliff shelves and places high above the fertile valley floor. Ladders went up the side of the houses, for they were entered from the roof; the ways of other people are strange! They hunted the roving deer in open-gladed forests where there were no entangling brambles, and fished in quiet pools of gay, splashing rivers. They plucked the plentiful herbs, which grew in manifold variety, there being some for every known purpose. It was indeed a land of peace and plenty.

OGS:3:18 The day came, as come it always must whenever peace and plenty abide, for then, Earth displays a defect in her instructiveness, when the soothsayers saw kolkers in the night skies, but they were unable to agree among themselves as to what these portended. Some said this, and some that, while the wiser ones listened, saying nothing.

OGS:3:19 The day came when sleeping Earth awoke to a great silence and stillness, not a breath of air strirring the anticipating trees, and no bird left its perch and every animal remained quiet within its den or in the field. All was hushed and motionless, waiting. Then, the soaring sun brought low-moaning winds which stirred the trees and grasses to rustling, murmuring life, but all living creatures huddled closer together. The skyroof above was darkened and lowered; it was ruddily-hued and gave out sharp, whipcracking sounds, as though it would break asunder, with now and then a shrill, long-drawn cry. In heart-thumping procession, awesomely-figured skygods never before seen, passed overhead. Men lived through two fearstruck days of dread, not knowing what to expect, during which time there was no true night, one heartstopping sight after another passing before their horror-filled eyes.

OGS:3:20 When darkness did fall, it was not the restful nightdarkness which soothes workweary men, lulling them to revitalising sleep. No indeed, it was that form of darkness known as the smothering cloak of Thunor, though never before had it spread so wide. Water streamed downward from the fountainspouts of the sky, not as rain falls but as water drops out from a pail upturned. Neither was it the pure, true rain; it was tainted with bitter blood from some strange battlefield in the vast skyspaces and contained broken pieces of the rainbow. The skyroof itself was borne down to the very surface of the seething waters, and Mother Earth cowered beneath it, as the shrinking fieldmouse cowers before the harvesters' footfall.

OGS:3:21 A vast, black cloud was drawn like a curtain across the skyroof, stretching from horizon to horizon. Rising above it were strange billows of flame and smoke; though what the fire consumed, it is not possible to even guess, for all know water does not burn. Then all things ceased movement, all was silent and still; a heavy, ill-boding, brooding silence, the stillness of hearthammering fear.

OGS:3:22 Then, with awful suddenness came a high wave wall of dark, white-fang-edged waters, sweeping swiftly along in fearsome irresistibility. It carried everything before it as a broom sweeps the floor, and accompanying it was a high born note, long-drawn out. Behind it, upon the seething waters, all the fruits of the land, house debris, trees, bloated dead animals and humans floated upon the wild, wide waters. There was an earthy-brown, foamy scum, which drifted strangely over the surface, not sinking, yet not like oil, for it was gritty, it was irregular and held together, it was like the scum on a fuller's tub.

OGS:3:23 There was a great downpouring of rain, which stopped after seven days, then the skyroof rose back into its proper place, and our fearstruck forebears saw once more the blessed light of day. They stood upon their drenched mountainsides and saw great trees, the like of which had never before been seen, float past. Hell-formed, hideous things came up from the depths and, swelling, burst on the surface. There were fearful sea monsters and great whirlpools, terrible things from unknown places. Wild creatures were washed about, dead or dying. The surging seas tore between the high mountains in great rip tides of dirty water. Standing on their hilltops, our frightened forebears saw the swimming house, made fast against the sea, come up to the land, and out from it came men and beasts from Tirfola.

OGS:3:24 It was built as a house on a high platform, standing well above the waters. When they had landed and made themselves secure, the black-raimented strangers built a tall tower of stone upon which they kept an ever burning fire, to honour the gods who brought them to safety. It was said that, if the fire ever went out, the waters would rise again.

OGS:3:25 Upon the surging waters was another wave-tossed craft, the great Brimcofer of Hestabel, the Wildwave Wanderer, Slayer of Niktoran the waterbeast, Worker of Strange Metals, who married Newlyn of Warnwilt, daughter of Manwidan, far famed for her beauty. For her hair outdid the yellow of the celandine. Her skin was softer than down and whiter than the mayflower. Her lips were the red of strawberries and her bosom soft as the windflower. She exuded the sweet perfume of new-mown hay. The son of Hestabel was the temple-protecting, three-spirited Esures, who made his home in the Great Oak where to this day he is worshipped as the god of beer and greenery. The tale tellers are not at ease with Hestabel and Esures, whether they were gods or men, but in some men the division is not clear. Perhaps gods are made by the regard of men.

[There is no Chapter 4 – ED]

Chapter Five – Workers in Metal

OGS:5:1 There are, in this land, two tribes of smithworkers and metalforgers, and one is the Merkings who remain among the Kwicta, and they tell a tale of a flight from the West where their forebears lived in painted abodes cut out of rocks. It is now the Land of Manan and closed to men by the waters above, for it burst asunder at the bowels, streaming out through Linleon during a great night of darkness. So it is that these others who work with metal worship spirits who dwell beneath the sea. They do not worship gods as the Kwicta do, and still cast food upon the waters; but they do have god-beings which are less than gods, and worship these, calling them, Haspa, Yelpa and Tiz. They acknowledge Blasis and leave offerings to Nana.

OGS:5:2 Oxen are sacred beasts to them, and they do not eat the flesh of geese, believing them to contain the souls of women. Yet they eat the flesh of boars, though believing these have been entered by the souls of men, but they do not eat this except with solemn ceremony. Once, though no longer, their chiefs were not succeeded by their sons, as now, but brother succeeded brother by the mother, then succession was by the mother's daughter's son.

OGS:5:3 In the days before Umpopal was the Great Chief, wives were the property of all men of the household. It was not until after the coming of those who followed Lugad the Bronzefinder, that many changed their ways. After Lugad came, the dead were no longer buried in the old manner, nestled in boughs and stones. They were laid out straight, heads to the West, with their comforting objects and oak boughs, as is done today.

OGS:5:4 These other metalworkers learned their craft from Yasus, otherwise called Hestabel, though some say they were two, and brothers. He came boatborne with the other children, Ree and Mag called Maya, who became his wives, for their father had cast them afloat at the time of the land sinking. This is not a tale known to us, and not being ours, is not well understood. They were fortunate to escape the underwater dwellers who lurk in the depths to snatch seafarers down to destruction. We have heard many tales of our times concerning the Brimkrakan, which drags seacraft down to destruction in all the four seas of Britain. Yasus was saved by the People of the Bear and became their chief, but they married among the dark Feymin and became as they are today.

OGS:5:5 These people were disliked because of their ways, but were not shunned. No king ever molested our forebears, for they threatened no one and served all alike. They went freely from place to place with their hearths, were law-abiding folk and not land-hungry. Our people held safe the secrets of metals, though later they were opposed by the Sons of May when they came, for these feared the knowledge held fast.

OGS:5:6 Though given high estate among the Kwits, our people do not make swords for the Black Brood of the North. It is the same Kwits who have given land, which the wanderers do not need. Our people first came to this land through Pokatha and even now have great houses at Karboska. The others came across the water from Eblana, but the generation of their coming is unknown to any here.

(This chapter is from parts reconstructed. The two tribes of metalworkers were the Sons of Fire and those who were called Merkings.)

Chapter Six – The Tale of Hewe

OGS:6:1 Great Hewe the Strongarm, Chief of the Wellborn Ones, was brightbearded, blue-eyed, but not overtall. He was the bronzebound ruler of warriorful Hefa, a place lying out in the shallow seas eastward of Britain, with a many-moated white castle and high coloured walls. This was the seat, from which he ruled oft-flooded Edyfrabandy; gaining control not by the sword but through marriage with the corn-haired daughter of Kwetana.

OGS:6:2 Hefa lay off the bay called Arkist, over the sea called Mortosh, and the people thereabouts were the Kudira. They were warwise and learned in other ways, but their week was too long by two days. After the arrival at Solmanth, to which he came peacefully as a bridegroom to his waiting bride, Hewe became king of the Kathon, and he taught men to plough and till the soil. He crossed to the Summerland where he set up a great school of learning, and there was first taught the writing of books in the trees. The brother of Hewe was that Taran who took men of Hefa across the sea to Ladore.

OGS:6:3 The fightingfolk who came with Hewe were outstanding among others, being fair-headed, light-eyed, soft-spoken, tall and slim, upright, big-muscled, honourable, brave and musical. Yet they were not of the Firstfaith and spurned the Old Faith, nor were they with us, but they were akin to the true folk of this green isle and kindred to the brave ones across the landbound sea. They were not stonebuilders, though they rebuilt skybound Morkoravit, the great gate hall which the Dark Ones call Shindekra even to this day. This is the hall of the horse stones.

OGS:6:4 This is the tale of Hewe, the strongarmed wielder of the mansmiter, child of the Arayan, which was given to us by our housebuilding forebears, but the days of this generation are lost. It concerns the Erim, with whom he fought, who were the Feymin of other times.

OGS:6:5 Hewe of the sunfilled heart, lithsome as the willow, sturdy as the oak, fair-skinned, blue-eyed, straight-tongued, peace-minded, not strife-seeking, yet warwise; this was he who led the Glorygleamer Folk. He gave merry life to the green-grassed heart of Britain, flower-meadowed, sparkling-streamed, water-veined. He brought to these sand-bangled shores the high-hearted race of iron-muscled horn-handed freemen.

OGS:6:6 He, the son of woodgirt fields, first turned the sod of Britain in hilltearing brown furrows; upon the high slopes, he made the soil to be uplifted, overturning it upon the winter-held grain. He first brought the long ox-drawn fieldrakes and carried fertility to the pasturelands. Winters were no longer times of hunger, for now, all ate without stint from hide-lined cellars filled with fire-dried corn.

OGS:6:7 Cabbages and onions, peas and gulegift, forest gleaning of womenfolk, grew in tended soil, staked plots in the forest glades. Cattle gifts of cheese and curdcake, fire-dried flesh of summer-fattened beasts, nuts and brown herbs were the winter fare. Men wandered freely from place to place, wood-wending paths directing their feet. Patient beastback bore the handiwork of men in bursting hidebags. Never were the ever welcome wanderers waylaid with evil intent.

OGS:6:8 On stout hewed house pillars, sheathed swords slept in silent companionship with decorative shields. The old ones slept beside glowing hearths; contented the womenfolk, happy the children, peaceful the hefty, wide-handed, brief-bearded men. They had found Kastira and were content. Warm-clothed against the winds of winter, hide-headressed, black-cloaked, long-tuniced, breast-belted, kartak-ornamented, they lacked little for content.

OGS:6:9 The summer pourer of the rainbow smiled over fertile, flowering pastures, playgrounds of mirthful maids. On green carpets, the young ones skipped to the maiden wakening dance, flute-playing youths and clapping singers gathered around the herbrew pails. Oft told the old tales, oft sung the songs of yore.

OGS:6:10 Not for these, the earth-holed house, the bewattled roof covering. High-raftered, the roofs over the eating hall, broad-beamed, the guest hall, high-raised the host hall. Sturdy-timbered, the roof-holding posts, hide hung shielding the slumber rooms. Bracken bench beds gave restful repose to toilers of the day.

OGS:6:11 Twelve was the number of the councilmen, wise the judgements given by the wisp-haired, hoary-headed, bronze-bangled ones who sat on the oak trunk seats. These were the times, when days received their names and weeks their numbering. The coming of the moon was made known, and daylight was divided into four parts. The three parts of night were named and the two times of eating. Men knew the four divisions of the year, and their names were known.

OGS:6:12 Much-landed Hewe taught the mating of the Golden Faced Skyspirit with the Lady of Life; their son, the Godling of Greenness was never unknown in this seanecklaced land. He was the nevertiring teacher of Truth, but this was not he whom the Britons worship, that one being not a man but an invisible spirit.

OGS:6:13 Before Hewe, folk saw at night only by the ruddy illumination of firelight, or its child the flaming fire-brand, but he gave them fatlamps feeding on the floating residue of flesh. Not yet light from the bee. Not yet were the fiery forges set up in this land by brawny, brown-eyed smithmen, their squat four-wheeled workwains ox-drawn through forest ways.

OGS:6:14 Peaceful the lush, green land; peaceful all that dwelt between surging seas. From Partain, the fine bright bronzework, the big-bellied pots. From Longaset, the hides and hornwork, the work of strange smiths. From the Liky, earth-hidden things borne away in far-faring boats. From Setnaspor, the hard sharp stone tools, the ripe corn cutting knives.

OGS:6:15 Yearly, from the Erim at Haroganos came the tribute of murkymaids, mothers of the studbrood, workers with hillside herds and forest feeders, gatherers of wood and fruits. Never had the tribute been withheld, well were the Erim instructed. Inawk the Collector, chooser of bright-eyed murkymaidens, came always with the best, fitting ones for mothering the studbrood.

OGS:6:16 What of Wenda, non-beridden daughter of Orma, trothpledged to Lopik the Blackbannered Chief, she of the flower-garlanded, throng-gathered-unbraided hair? Small-breasted, small-handed, delicately wiry-bodied, rowan-cheeked, sombre-eyed. Who spoke of her to Inawk, who told of her beauty, her ever smiling lips, her wit, her wisdom? She was unfound among the gathering. The hagmaids gazed long, at Inawk's behest, into the full moon-enlightened waters, but she was unseen there.

OGS:6:17 Orma was taken and all the hagwomen, every maid and every youth. Neckbound, they were brought to the studhall, unharmed, they were fed and bedded. In the nightdarkness the wolfwretches came, evil weapons struck silently, sleepers died, vulnerable backs took fanged barbs. Dektire, child daughter of Ardan, was snatched for foul bewitchment, a sacrifice to Galo, victim of the bloodletting hagmaidens.

OGS:6:18 Through the wide pastures the hawk banner bearers sped, forests echoed the horn blasts. The brand-bearers cries were heard afar. Large the council-called gathering in the field of the stonecircle, and when the shaft cast was counted all cried out for blood.

OGS:6:19 High-spirited, stallion-mounted Hewe, swiftsmiter girded at waist, bright bronze mace in hand, raised the winged warbanner, and harsh the heartgripping warcry from a thousand ensavaged throats. Bright the gleaming bronze blades, the slim, sharp spearheads, the weighty manmaulers. Forward the hefty oakhearted warriors, eager-eyed for battle.

OGS:6:20 Tall, appleash-wooded the hill summit where the folkhorde of Brim stood, no timbered-stockade builders these wood skulkers. Sharp-staked, wildly-pitted the approach, low stone-walled the last defence of the earthruiners. The summershiner was halfway down to his trysting place with Earth.

OGS:6:21 Fast flew the hellballs of stone, the soft-singing death bringers flung by the foulfighters. Lopik, the loudmouthed boaster, shrieked loud against the shieldsheltering stalwarts, fast flew the hook-toothed blades with poison sting of death. Safe were the throwers from the stallion-led horse charge. Never ceasing was the downfall of slingshot stones.

OGS:6:22 Loud were the shrill shrieks of the wildhaired hagwomen, black garb besmirched with sacrificial blood. No tongue of man used they; wolf yelps, howls and cat cries tore the air. Then the shields lifted and came forward, the bright blades gleamed redly, the painbringers arrived among the Erim. Heavily the bloodied manmaulers fell, smashing through shield and bone, wielded by oaklike arms. Loud the cries of the Erim. Long, linden-shafted red rammers thrust forward; the barbed dart was of no avail.

OGS:6:23 Within the wood, wicker-shielded Lopik, tree hid, stood to thrust the poisoned barb. As the skulking stoat springs upon its prey, barefanged to kill, the foulfighter leapt upon the battle-wearied warrior, brother of Dektire. Deep sank the evil barbs before the ash shaft broke, but Lopik was within reach, carried forward by furious thrust. Loud the thud of the full-falling battlehammer, biting deep into the incrushed brow, unavailing the leathern protector. This was a vermin slaying. Gone were the hagwomen and nethermaids to their gloomy abode.

OGS:6:24 Far through the forests ranged the vengeance fighters, many the bloodied bodies of Erim left behind. Then in wooded glade, battle-weary eyes beheld a maiden figure; Wenda, not overfearful nor overbold, small beneath the tall trees, hooded, caped and kilted. None stood with her except a two-tongued hagwoman cowering against a tree trunk. Silently, curiously, the sleepless, weary Erim fighters gathered.

OGS:6:25 Here was a self-given peace pledge, a ransom for fainthearted fighters, a deed not unworthy of those, to whom she came. No gallant, generous heart could not accept. Tiny indeed was she before the great Hewe. Here was no studmother, but one worthy of being a true wife. No man indeed he who would accord her less.

OGS:6:26 It was Lir, grandson of Wenda and Olva who built the first house on the place where walled London now stands.

OGS:6:27 These are the sayings of Wenda the Wise: "The woods are havens for the heavyhearted, for trees soak up sadness. The lofty trees, sheltering sheet of forest dwellers, whisper soothing words to the worried. The only true friend is the tongueless tree."

OGS:6:28 "The most painful ills are the heartsmiting ones; therefore, never leave it unshielded. A high-sounding title is a poor wood waif, unless it is parented by eminent virtues. The treetops bow in homage to the winter winds, forest creatures are lean, and sheep no longer graze on the summer pastures. Woe to him, say the whistling winds, who sacrifices his honour for worldly gain."

OGS:6:29 "The chill arrows of winter cleave the fall air; within the home a warm fire, and low conversation is pleasant, but much talk unguards the tongue, and to dishonour a confidence is the sign of weakness."

OGS:6:30 "The brow of the hill is white with snow, and wild birds search diligently for food. Squirrels sleep soundly, dreaming of nut hoards. The wind whistles through the walls' wickerwork. Then call to mind that when winds of adversity blow, the fire of friendship comforts, but prefer to be a firetender, not a fireside squatter."

OGS:6:31 "Having no feelings, the fish is chaste. What claim to virtue has a woman chaste as a fish? As a benchbride's love flowers in dark corners, can sweetness be anticipated from its fruits? The woman surrendering to a true man has become a conqueror. No lover of children the benchbride, or she would not act as she does. The benchbride's love is consummated in darkness, for darkness is the befriender of shame. Tarnished or inferior love sold cheaply, that is the benchbride's bargain."

Chapter Seven – Tale of Gwinvera

OGS:7:1 Because they are incomplete, four tales, of 'Helen the Sunfaced', of 'Lavid the Fool and the Warking', of the 'Three Spearkings' and of 'Helen Blodawed and the Golden Chariot', have been omitted. This is the tale of Gwinvera as it has come down to us, and to we who reconstruct it, the task is not easy, for the pages are torn in several parts.

OGS:7:2 The tale is told, how, back in the bygone days when gods walked the Earth, they made the first woman in this manner. They prepared a vessel shaped by the future desires of men, placing into it these things: The gleam of sunlight mixed with the yellowness of ripe corn, this became her hair. The cold clear dawn dew mixed with the hue of the violet, this became her eyes. The pale radiance from the moonbeam mixed with down from the neck of a swan, this became her brow. The red from the cherry mixed with the colour of mayberries, this became her lips. The whiteness of the snowflake mixed with a mayflower's purity, this became her bosom. They took the sparkle from running waters for her smile and the cooing of a dove for her voice. The heat from the fire to fill her passion and the edge from the sword to arm her tongue. From the core of a flint worked keenly they made her mind and from the fall of a snowflake they made her touch. To this they added a blended mixture of extracts from the playful cruelty of the cat, the dancing lightness of the sunbeam's notes, the flutter from the wings of a butterfly, the song of the nightingale, the industriousness of the bee, the gentleness of a mouse, the softness of a rabbit and the shiver of an aspen tree. If this were a godmade woman, then Gwinvera was a product of their hands. But did these gods not try to keep this woman for themselves, as being something too good for man? But man, in his brave audacity, stole her, and she became the great woemaker. Truth is embedded in the old tales for the wise to find and use as they will.

OGS:7:3 When the mother of Gwinvera was in childlabour, her father, the Battlechief Kumwa, was at the festiveboard, and as was the custom, he called upon the soothsayer to foretell the future. The soothsayer told his lord that the womanchild now approaching the veil would grow to be the most beautiful woman in the land, but would be the death of many men, including her own brother, the Warchief's only son. These words ate at the heart of Kumwa.

OGS:7:4 He asked the wise soothsayer what should be done to avert disaster, and the crafty one answered that he would seek advice among the stars. Not all soothsayers had a temple of truth in their hearts. It happened that the voice of Helva, son of Kumwa, lived in the ear of the seer, so when the report was given at midmorn the following day, it was a lengthy woeforetelling much disturbing to the heart of Kumwa.

OGS:7:5 What was the outcome? The soothsayer spoke long, and Kumwa's heart ached for his only son and for the mother, but his duty was to protect his son, the heir born of his youth, and he could put his daughter to death according to the manner of the times. As a highborn woman's blood could not be spilt among green growing things, for this would blight the land, and only a simpleton could not be hurt by the deed, Gwinvera was given to the Battlechief's fool. He was to take her outside the boundary of the land, and there drown her, his payment for the deed being the wishgranting urn called Helwed, no small reward.

OGS:7:6 The kind-hearted fool had little liking for the deed, his heart was heavy and the assbacked-carried cradlechild so contentedly lovely that the fool's load of sadness grew increasingly heavy. So they went on, the kindly fool and the lovely young one, until they came to the great, gloomy forest of Keliabans lying beyond Dunmerkil. The fool and his assload kept on through the forest, for thought he, "Where else can I go, as well here as any other place. It is in keeping with my heart."

OGS:7:7 Deep in the forest, just before the stars opened their eyes, they came upon a small, streamtraversed glade, and there, nestling among the woodweed was a tumble-down half house. The fool blew the wayfarers' horn and there came a small, shy forestman, first cautiously peeping around the doorpost, then timidly approaching. Had it been anyone other than a gaudy-garbed fool, the small one would have fled, but these forestfarers were taken in and made welcome in the humble hut.

OGS:7:8 Later, the forestman's brothers came back from their foraging and there was much lively chatter, for among such folk, the fool did not feel out of place. He stayed for three days, and it was agreed that the forestmen should take the little one from him and take care of her. What else could they do? For forestmen are gentle and kindhearted; were they not they would never have been confined to the forest. What else could the fool do, if he could not bring himself to put the little one to death? What better place to leave her?

OGS:7:9 The ugly forestmen raised fair Gwinvera with tenderness; they were wise in their way, and because they did not want her to become vain and immodest, or perhaps because they did not want her to discover how different she was, there was nothing in the forest home, in which she could see her face. Knowing about the soothsayer's foretelling, they let her think she was ugly too, or was it because they really wished her to be one of them? Did they not know that love closes the eyes to defects? Her own loveliness was unknown to Gwinvera. Her playmates were the wild creatures of the forest; fawns, rabbits and squirrels played outside her door, and the wise badgers came to protect her at dusk. Wrens and robins were her constant companions. In summer she bathed in sparkling rillwaters and garlanded herself with wildflowers; woodbells and primroses grew everywhere. In winter, she sang through the berrybearing glades and gathered fallen kindling wood under the great trees. She slept on a bed of sweet moss under cosy coverlets of fur. She drank the pure stream waters flowing through the cooking place and ate fish and the plentiful forest fruits. Her garments were woven from fine forest flax and soft down; her mantle was made of white winter fur. Her long, bamp-braided hair took its colour from the water marigold. Yet in all her forest-bounded childhood, Gwinvera never had a companion of her own age or saw any mortal being other than the forestmen.

OGS:7:10 It happened that when the forest maiden had grown to young womanhood, and it was midwinter, huntsmen from the woodcastle of the king came into the naked forest, seeking boars for the yulefeast. They came upon the rough forest home of fair Gwinvera, and she, not knowing who or what they were, acted like a frightened wren. They did her no harm, not knowing whether she were mortal or spirit, but went away marvelling that the gloomy forest could contain such beauty. Such a tale could not long await the telling, and men argued among themselves as to whether a woodspirit had been seen or a mortal. Woodsylphs were known but rarely sighted.

OGS:7:11 It happened that the tale came to the ear of Helva, and he, lacking neither courage nor curiosity, wished to lead men into the forest to hunt the maiden, be she spirit or mortal. But first, as all wise men do before going on a quest, he sought the advice from the soothsayer. The soothsayer, gazing into his scrybowl, saw the beauty of Gwinvera and knew who she was, and knew, too, that never could Helva venture into the forest, nor would he be safe while Gwinvera lived.

OGS:7:12 Now, though the fool who had taken the lovely maid to the forest was dead, he had, before dying, unburdened his heart to the mother of Gwinvera, and she had kept the secret locked in her breast. Now she decided to go to the forest and warn her daughter, lest any harm befall her, for she doubted not but that there would be a hunting through the treefast depths. Making suitable excuses for her absence, she disguised herself as a woodman's wife, and with a young attendant who had been one of the boar hunting party, set out for the forest.

OGS:7:13 The soothsayer with two companions also departed for the forest, all being disguised as men of the peddling tribe, and because those with him were experienced in forest ways, it was the soothsayer's party, which arrived first at the hutted glade.

OGS:7:14 Gwinvera was alone, for the forestmen were hewing in the ground, and these being the first strangers she had seen, she took fright, evading them among the trees, from which shelter she nervously peered out. While the soothsayer tried to entice the maiden to tarry, the youngest of the forestmen, having hurt his hand, came into the glade. The soothsayer's companions seized him, and the maiden's concern overcame her fears. Rushing to his aid, she was taken also, but no harm was done to her, for those with the old man were disarmed by her beauty. He, seeing this, put on the face of guile and acted as would a true peddling man.

OGS:7:15 They bartered the usual ware of pedlars, cloth, brooches, beads, pins, salt, earthenware, dyes, knives, sweetmeats, cords and flints, taking soft pelts and fruit of the ground. Before leaving, the soothsayer gave Gwinvera, as a parting gift for a lovely maiden, a sweetly perfumed ointment and a mouthwatering cake, both infused with deadly poison. The cake she left, small and tempting though it was, she wished to share it, but the perfumed ointment she could not resist, and it was a womanly thing.

OGS:7:16 Barely had the forestmaiden used it when the forestmen returned; they were early, but heavy rainclouds threatened. Delightedly the new-bought wares were displayed one by one, but surprised joy diminished to silence as Gwinvera grew more and more tired, her head at last falling on to the table. The forestmen picked her up and carried her to the bedplace. As they did so, there was a knocking on the door; it was the mother of Gwinvera. They let her in, and the thunderstorm broke full overhead.

OGS:7:17 The speech of the forestmen was not easy on the ears; their chattering was overcome by the downpour, but the mother of the sleeper knew what had happened. The cake, she threw on the fire; the sleeping maid she took in her arms, carrying her out into the thunderstorm. Behind the hut she stripped her, and with moss and mud, rubbing hard, removed the ointmentation. Round and round the glade she walked the small-kilted maid, around and around, never stopping. Talking, prodding, lifting, smacking, stumbling together, falling and getting up, slithering on rainwet moss, bedraggled, muddied and scratched, on tirelessly until final collapse.

OGS:7:18 The forestmen helped the exhausted women inside, and the elder made them make hot brews for the still sleepy maiden. Her feet were placed in a wood tub of hot water, and she was seated by the fire. Later, the two women were bedded down together, and in the morning, the forestmaiden woke up well.

OGS:7:19 They broke fast with goat broth, but the mother of Gwinvera could not dally overlong, nor could the maiden remain with the forestmen, for surely the huntsmen would come again. So a graveplace was made, ringed round with stones and a mound raised, but no maid slept beneath the mayberry bush. Gwinvera left the forest, her long, fair hair beneath a leathern cap, coarse cloth covering her body. A distant herdsman's home gave her shelter.

OGS:7:20 It happened that the herdsman had two sons, one a hefty, hard-handed, wide-strider, fond of brawling; the other a small-handed fireside dreamer, deft but not overstrong. The first was named Bagut and the other Daran. It was only days before Bagut was smitten with the beauty of Gwinvera, but she, knowing not the ways of men, treated him with friendliness and kindness. He, thinking she was being coy and teasing him after the manner of irresponsible women, tried to take her when she was gathering eggs at the hayrick. She fled to the house and the goodwife and Daran within.

OGS:7:21 Bagut became moody; he sulked the day long and neglected his work, and when once he came on Gwinvera alone, he was overcome. He told her that unless she gave herself to him he would be riding towards the woodcastle on a moneymaking errand. She said, "Then having no love for me, what ails you?" He rode away.

OGS:7:22 Now, it happened that the soothsayer had looked into his scrybowl and seen the graveplace in the forest, but looking again, days later, he saw Gwinvera seated on a tussock carding wool, and he knew she lived. He sent men to dig at the graveplace, and it gave up its secret. Forestmen were brought in and put to the mouthopening test, but they knew nothing of where she was and could say nothing to lessen their suffering.

OGS:7:23 So when Bagut arrived with his tale, the soothsayer knew who was being described as having hair yellower than broomflowers, skin whiter than driven snow, hands fairer than blossoms of windflowers, eyes brighter than a falcon's, bosom more snowy than a swan's breast and cheeks redder than mayberries. Men were sent with Bagut to capture such beauty.

OGS:7:24 But beauty had flown, companied by Daran, and sought sanctuary with Pentercil, King of the Howan, Child of the Landholdingers, and this was the cause of the bitter war, which made men scarce in the land. For Helva assembled his warbands and entered the lands of Pentercil, who met him at the place called Rathkelder even today.

OGS:7:25 We have reconstructed the tale as found, but here some part is missing, though account of the battle remains.

OGS:7:26 The chariot clove through failing ranks, through the drooping spears of the weary spearmen, through the ground-resting shields of the swordsmen, through the gasping forefighters, through the bloody-bodied lines of the axe swingers. Behind the tossing, red-eyed heads of the white horses, gold-guilded reins loosely held in one hand and small bright ash-shafted spear firmly held in the other; golden hair unbraided streaming behind her, held back from her face by the golden headguard; her brilliantly brooched cloak flapping like the wings of some heavenly battlebird, Gwinvera sped towards the still standing bodyguard about Helva. No arrow touched her, no slingstone came against her body. She was like a battlegoddess.

OGS:7:27 On the slope between reed-bordered river and tree-crowned hill, the warbands of Helva made their last death-awaiting stand. Then it was all over, and the battlefield foragers did their work. So the tale of the delicate forest-raised maiden who became a rage-driven war goddess, and of Daran who became warwise in one night is one oft told in the feasthalls.

Chapter Eight – The Firstfaith Bringers

OGS:8:1 Once, wherever there was grass, there too was the Old Faith, for it could be contained within no particular domain. They who believed the things it taught were little-minded men, unthinking receptacles for strange tales. With the Firstfaith came better men, adopted sons of Britain, Pritan and the axe-wielding Baruts, and it was he, who named this land the Great White Goddess of the Cowfeeding Pastures. The Baruts learned the sealore from the Chaisite who first ventured out upon the saltwaters, but their homeland is not known. Some say it was Rimvady, West of the Lodgrains, but no man knows for sure. The Lodgrains who bowed to the Great Milk Giver came later.

OGS:8:2 The Firstfaith came only as a babe, it was here that it grew to maturity, schooled at Inisgwin. Those of the Firstfaith respect trees even today, few though they are, but the true nature of the Greengod who gives life and fertility to all green growing things is unknown. They called trees the flutes of The Great Holy One, yet did not believe as we do that trees contain within themselves part of the lifegiving force of mankind, pouring out good and absorbing its evils. They did not understand that without trees to mediate for man between the lifeforce and the deathforce, he could not live. Yet now even we are wiser, knowing the Greengod of Life is not in trees alone.

OGS:8:3 They of the Firstfaith made sacrifices at most of the proper times, but instead of leaf crowns, they wore masks in the likeness of sun and moon, believing them to be the rulers of omens. They worshipped in error the malignant horned star and her escorts, fearfully seeking to turn them away. Instead of the wertmound they used gulerinth to set up the sun measuring daypole, but this offended the shadows. They failed even to do this properly, setting up a new pole every year instead of every seven.

OGS:8:4 They did not treasure the soil from the pole circle, as we do that from the mound. The Sons of May, instructors in the Firstfaith, were not all-wise, seeking signs of the future, otherwise clearly seen, in ashes, birdflights and bloody twisting entrails. They knew the making of a draught of forgetfulness from herbs and the draught of sorrow from berries, also the making of dradsboon which lightens the heavy heart.

OGS:8:5 They did not, as we do, judge wholly by known laws, but oft made trial by using a magic collar. This was first dipped in water blessed with coldfire, they then believing it would choke the guilty one. This is not for us, for are we not told man cannot avoid the responsibility for formulating laws to try his fellowmen, and rules to govern his life? These things cannot be thrown back onto higher authority.

OGS:8:6 They hold one day in seven holy to The Creating God whom they worship in a transparent temple where the sun falls upon the heads of the worshippers. So there are many differences between the Firstfaith and the Gwidonad. We worship in holy places built of stone or in caverns, using open spaces only for the Midsummer Festival.

OGS:8:7 In the Firstfaith, the womanly maidenwed was always preserved for battlechiefs and the Sons of May, who could claim it without dispute except among themselves. With this, we are not in accord, for women are not to be lightly treated, and a maid-enwed is something kept for a husband, a woman's pledge of purity and to the wellbeing of the race.

OGS:8:8   The Sons of May were not lacking in courage, for they were ever in the forefront of battles, though they were mare-riders, never mounting upon stallions. Every one of the Sons of May had to be trained in the use of spear and sword even as we, but they had to know many songs and long lineages and be wordmakers. They had long unmusical songs which were given out with many gestures. The Sons of May could claim no tribe as their own, for they were tribeless. They could not avenge any harm done to their kinfolk, and were any one wronged, his kinfolk could not avenge him. This was not because any one of the Sons of May was ever renounced by his kinfolk, or they by him, but because of the power of his Maydom.

OGS:8:9   Whatever his circumstances, like us, a Son of May could never refuse hospitality. In battle, he always kept his face towards the foe. Like us, he was always respectful in the presence of womenfolk, never raising his voice to loudness or speaking lewdly. This is in accord with our laws. The bride price was forbidden to the Sons of May.

OGS:8:10   Like us, the Sons of May had to prove their manliness, and if one had not done this on the battlefield, he was put into a forest unarmed and hunted by armed men, which is not our custom. If any man defamed one of them he could be challenged to combat on the grovefield, by their combat champion.

OGS:8:11   The Sons of May dressed differently to our Koles, though now all this has passed away, never more to be seen by the eyes of mortal man. They wore a garment of crossed green and brown thread, sometimes with yellow, blue or red interwoven, and this reached halfway between knee and ankle; two necklaces of gold bound together and a headdress of white bound about the head; an apron of finely tanned leather and a cloak of coarse linen; gold, low-hanging earrings. For their rites, they wore a white undergarment with a fur-trimmed overfrock fastened with gold brooches. Upon their feet were sandals of fox fur. The chief among them would wear a diadem of gold set with smokestones and rainstones. All shaved the hair in the front half of the head, so they were called 'bigfaces.'

OGS:8:12   The Sons of May preferred to live in forests, but not in the depths, if possible, beside a lake or water, though no lake was holy to them, as some are to us. They had holy trees, and like our trees of power, these had to be beside a well or drinking pool. They had talking trees, but we do not understand these.

OGS:8:13   Then more wells and pools contained the essence of Krisura, and those drinking hung some portion of clothing on the welltree. Because so many failed to make the rounds of the waters, much of the power has now gone, or perhaps it is because the waters have become metal poisoned. Who knows?

OGS:8:14   In Britain, the two folkbeliefs of Keltica met and merged, and though beforetimes they had been mutually hostile, later they could no more be separated than milk and water shaken up together in a jug. So throughout the land there were now two peoples, those who came before the Kelts and were children of this land, and the people of Keltica who travelled much on water and lived near rivers and lakes. The small-statured dark folk favoured the deep forest and high hills. Different from both were the Painted People, who lived largely on herbs.

OGS:8:15   The language of the pre-people was rarely spoken, being the tongue of slaves and wayfarers, men who wandered. To the West, the people spoke the tongue of foreigners; to the East, they spoke Brythonic and to the South, Lemany. In the South, below the white lands of Albany, there were marshes.

OGS:8:16   Among the dark strangers who came to these hospitable shores were men from Greece, who, because they were exiled by their king, though for what we do not know, sought refuge in this bountiful land. They came in high-prowed craft, long-boarded, roofed over the centre, with many long-bladed oars thrust out through hide-bound rowing outlets. The emblems they bore were the Red Eagle and Snake, and they called the far away place from whence they came Filistis, which means Ruddily-Hued Land, so-called from the colour cast by a huge cloud through which their sun always shone. They spoke a wildish babbling tongue, so difficult that unless spoken slowly could not be understood even among themselves.

OGS:8:17 Their god was a huge, many hued stone, which, when placed on their strange altar, kindled the wood of the offering by its own power, when light fell upon it from the Eye of Heaven. Men who have seen it say that the stone comes out cold from the midst of the fire. They wore garments of woven cloth and leather fastened with metal work, open shoes on their feet and flat hats marked with red and purple. These colours have some virtue among them, which we cannot understand.

OGS:8:18 They built five busy trading ports in Britain, the largest being Donardkath, with a great haven for seacraft. The safe haven was encompassed by a high embankment, and beyond a lower one, and a ditch enclosed their fields and cattle. The only one of these safe havens remaining is Karkol; all the others have gone.

OGS:8:19 These Greeks were men of many skills, they knew things unheard of before in this blessed island. Thus, when they first arrived, Kaswalen, king of the Welsh, hastened to make them welcome. He willingly granted them all the land thereabouts for their own use, so they were not humbled vassals, but men who lived in free alliance with the people. When the land-giving pact was solemnised, at a great glen gathering, the daughter of the Greek chieftain, Jezel Bethamin by name, renamed Thespendu, was betrothed to Kewen, Son of Kaswalen, to pledge the alliance. The Greeks took wives from among the Keltic women, for they had only two Greek women among them, the other being she who became Raith, the sister of Thespendu. She was a holy maiden pledged to their god, and at all times she was guarded by two strangely armed dwarfs. It was told of her that her soft touch cured the sick, and her holy hand healed all but the most grievous wounds. It was said that Kaswalen sent his hunchback servant to be healed of a sickness, and that he returned walking tall and straight as a young pine tree. A foolish woman who fell through the roof while thatching and split her stomach open on the loompost was healed by washing in water made holy in the hand of Raith.

OGS:8:20 The last High Priest of the Firstfaith was Ifananud, called Krisnakel, better known among the strangers as Kelwine. It is said in truth that he was the wisest of men, and his is the protecting spirit, which hovers over the twelve green pastures of Britain. He is buried in the West at Kairhen. He was the son of that Owainbartha who died of shame and Olwin Keesabeg, his wife, at that time the most beautiful woman in Britain (daughter of Tisheala and grand-daughter of Merilyn), who ran away to Dunvarmod. We are told, and what brave Briton doubts it, that when she fled from Karsalog, all the sparrows left their nest-building to accompany her, and songbirds flew in a protecting cloud above her bronze-bound chariot. It was on that tragic day that the Great Protecting Spirit of Britain left the Holiselder with all his retinue. Since then, he has never returned, and the once far-famed place is now the dead and dismal abode of a dradwych.

OGS:8:21 The wheels of life turn and turn, and the pride and integrity, the honest dealing man with man, the cherishing of womanly ideals and the code of conduct for man and woman, will return to those, in whose veins flows the blood of Old Keltica. Great Gods, old and new, hasten the day! (There is but One God, but men view Him differently, through their own deceptive eyes, in many aspects, and He appears to them to be many).

Chapter Nine – The Battlebook

OGS:9:1 When I was a lithe, black-haired young warrior rejoicing in the springtime flush of man strength, Aristolio was a veteran battlecaptain. This was the spirit-strengthening war code he taught long ago in the glorious fighting years of my virile youth, in a far off, fertile Motherland within the warm central sea.

OGS:9:2 He rightly told us we need not over concern ourselves with the strange ways of the High Ones of Heaven. Let the hidden gods fight their own sombre battles in their wonderfully mysterious ways; for men, the grim earthly battles closer here below are sufficiently bitter. These we thankfully win or grudgingly lose, according to our courage and fortitude, our discipline and training, our skill at arms and tactical cunning.

OGS:9:3 Such needful qualities and essential skills, we learn from our own war tutors, though some befitting things, they do not teach, and wars are not won by material armaments alone. To complete the equipment of a sturdy fighting man, something more is required, and to this end, these instructions are given.

OGS:9:4 There are four codes to live by, each befitting the peculiar circumstances of the time. They are: the code of the warrior, the code of the citizen, the code of the kinsman and the code of the individual. There is the code of women, but that is something exclusively theirs and something, which all true men uphold.

OGS:9:5 Among all men, the bloodied warrior is the most important, for he alone is the guardian protector of the things, whatever they may be, all men value. None can have and hold any cherished belief or valued possession except by the grace of the sharp-edged weapon in the strong right arm and the sturdily protective shield on the left arm. He pledges something no other man can exceed in value - his throbbing lifeblood.

OGS:9:6 Each grim warrior is a loving and compassionate mother's son, and his war training starts in her protective arms. She never neglects him, and every care is given to ensure his contentment. A nervous mother conveys nervousness with her breastmilk; she withholds from her man-child the basic warrior nourishment. As he grows beyond her tender arms, she must see in her small man-child the bloodied warrior of the heroic future years. He must not be pampered; he must be taught confidence and self-reliance with his first faltering steps. She must bear in mind that in the foreranks of the battlearray, every man stands supported or betrayed by his mother, according to her handling of him in the forming first years of his growing.

OGS:9:7 The questioning man-child grows towards the restless youth, and the foundations for the fullness of manhood are laid down firmly or otherwise. The youth takes weapons, and, having been battle-blooded, becomes a man. The man is not only brave, he is heroic, for courage resides in all men, no matter how mean-minded. He is well knit in body, he stands tall and his eye and hand are steady. Straightforward, keen looking, stern-faced, he stands steadily still and moves with each foot striking the ground as though to assert his mastery of it.

OGS:9:8 Every movement is deliberate; his speech is slow and his voice strong and low. When he laughs, he does so heartily, the walls resound in comradeship, but he laughs rarely; more often he smiles, though his smile is not readily swift. He carries a battleharness just within his easy capacity, and when arrayed for action, he clothes his body just sufficiently for its protection.

OGS:9:9 Every War-readied warrior must struggle to gain absolute mastery in the use of his chosen weapons, by self-driven application, though of greater importance to victory is complete control over himself in battlestance. His body stands poised under the alert controlling mind, ready for any happening; he is never caught off balance in an awkward stance. Yet though this, the clashing fray, climaxes his life, it is only a thin, compressed slice of his alloted lifespan, for the battle is not lost in its own time and action; it is decided in the preparation, which went beforehand.

OGS:9:10 Many ask, "For what does the warrior fight?" It is not for fickle wealth and encumbering possessions, for these the grim warrior rarely gains, and what puny things they are against his glorious life! It is not for illusive freedom, for of all men, apart from slaves, he is the least free. It is not for his gods, for they if they be godpowerful, require no champion, and if they do are unworthy to be gods. It is not for mocking justice, for the disciplined warrior obeys unquestionably, even when the command is unjust. It is not for any fair city or cherished family, for so often these betray him.

OGS:9:11 This was the answer given when I, in my questioning youth, asked the same question of the Battlemaster, and I still have none better. A man fights because it is the inbred nature of men to fight, and this is true, for it is only through strife that he becomes a man. A man lacking the human fighting spirit would be as unnatural a creature as a woman shunning motherhood. This goes against human inclination; yet true men do not despise these, for the nature of men and women is wide and varied and there is a place in life for all.

Book of Origins: Chapter Nine – The Battlebook

OGS:9:12 A warrior is a man responding gleefully to the stern demands of manhood, even as a mother is a woman lovingly responding to the demands of motherhood. The two are akin, for what motherhood is to a woman, war is to a man. Without motherhood, men would lose respect for womanhood, and without war, women would lose respect for manliness.

OGS:9:13 All battles are not bloodbattles; there are other battles just as hard and demanding, and the blooded warrior who ignores them in unpreparedness is top-heavy and unbalanced. There is a just as deadly, if less obvious, war than any between kings and nations, and that is the war of life. Here the warrior faces his most deadly adversary, which is himself. Man arms his own foe in the battle of life and sends recruits to its ranks.

OGS:9:14 The first rule of the warrior is obedience, and every warrior is a subordinate. The young cadet warrior, unblooded by battle, is the subordinate of every blooded man. Keenly young, abounding with high spirits, overflowing with energy, he is animal-lithe, ever straining at the leash, baying to go, unwitting of caution. He will seek his outlets among companions of his own age, for in the presence of older men he must exercise the disciplinary restraint of respect.

OGS:9:15 It is never unmanly to show respect for age and wisdom; in fact, it indicates the triumph of discipline. Disrespect for those to whom it is due signifies character weakness, which is an unmanly defect. Young, fullblooded warriors are not wilful women or wayward children, they are men who know their exact standing. Therefore, cadet warriors will always defer to the greater skill and wisdom of their superiors and show proper respect for men of high rank.

OGS:9:16 The disciplinary warrior code need not be detailed, for it is written in the hearts of all true warriors and is a piece of essential equipment. A warrior is the protector of all women, even of the womenfolk of his foe, and he will not rape or abuse any woman or child. To strike a woman in the heat of battle or to attack a child is unmanly, and those who do so are a reproach to better men. He who strikes the weak and afflicted, the unarmed or unprotected, shall not be numbered among those in the ranks of true men.

OGS:9:17 A man's estate is decreed according to his manliness, and honourable warriors are men of high estate. If they serve for gold alone and not with high intent, if they serve mercenary men of low estate who manipulate them, then they, too, are warriors of low estate. Peace will come to the world only when warriors unite to impose it. That is the bad dream of rulers and men of cunning in high places.

OGS:9:18 There is no debt to life placed on a man if he kill in a just war or for his homeland, or for essential food or in defence of the sanctity of his family. Nor if he slay the adulterer who defiles his household, even though he become a martyr to marriage because of the laws of the land. It is unlawful to murder, which means killing for gain or deceitfully or striking behind the back. For true men, included in murder is that, which causes sorrow and suffering, which drive to death or robs the needy so they die, or takes away from a man his livelihood wilfully or unjustly, so his family perish.

OGS:9:19 These are the things that were taught to Golahan of the Bitterbiting Sword: No matter how grievous the crime of your comrade , he remains a comrade, and even though you condemn him at law, nevertheless, let the comradeship that was, help to mitigate his lot, no matter how undeserving he maybe. If all that happened was that your comrade could not withstand some temptation, do not disgrace or desert him. Say instead, "It is possible that had the same circumstances befallen me, I might have been in the same boat with him."

OGS:9:20 A knight is a man who serves the cause of duty, loyalty and good, and upholds the virtues of ladyhood. He is a man among men. Resolute but quiet, he speaks little, but what he says carries more weight in the scales than an outpouring of words by others. Therefore, I say to you, be a knight at heart, and let your armour be what it will, for you are a better man than one bearing impregnable harness.

OGS:9:21 A knight does not allow himself to become prey to melancholy and self-doubt; if you are convinced that you are a worthy knight of The Supreme Commander, you have true cause for rejoicing. A knight is one who acts when action is called for, and he remembers that proper deeds without and proper thoughts within strengthen him in times of testing.

OGS:9:22 Loudmouthed men are to be despised, as are those who deal with ladies as they do with the common woman. The true knight deals with them rightly. A knight is never rowdy or boastful when he has been drinking mead or ale, nor does he ever become unsteady or lack self-control. He is never quarrelsome when in his cups, for this displays a small heart. Because you serve loyally and uprightly, do not think that you will escape temptation and trial. You can call yourself a true knight only when you have overcome many temptations and trials.

OGS:9:23 As the waters to fish and the air to birds, so is fear to the coward, and sadness to the melancholy. Avoid the companionship of those who would contaminate you, and avoid hypocrites as you would the plague. They will fawn upon you, but this is the homage weakness pays to strength. Do not seek their praise nor expect life to be bountiful because of your goodness. Water loves the swimmer no more than the non-swimmer.

OGS:9:24 Put no trust in yourself until after the days of testing. Never judge your comrade until you have stood in his place. Never take heed of the tangled-tongued ones, for they who talk in tangles will surely lure you into a delusive net. Give careful ear to the words of the wise and to the tales of the wordmasters, and always be a transmitter, not a transmuter, of traditions.

OGS:9:25 A knight is steadfast, never the prey of passion swept along like mindless beasts by every vagrant wind of impulse. He is the champion of true love and knows that human love-longing serves to initiate the Soul spirit into the higher love that ultimately unites man with God. He honours the ideals of true love and shuns the lures of low love, which pander to the baser passions.

OGS:9:26 The man of knightly ideals aspires only to the love of a true lady. He avoids the available woman who has been the plaything of promiscuous men and is consequently the end product of careless, clumsy, self-satisfying use. The man who gives his heart to such as these is to be pitied by all true men, for he wallows in complacent, but shallow satisfaction.

OGS:9:27 Learn to be careful of every move, and consider it, just as the swordsman has to consider every stroke. He never rains blows haphazardly, but remains alert to drive home the deadly thrust. There are sword-thrusters and sword-smiters, and each must master his own technique, for proficiency means life. He who remains coolheaded and calm amid the cut and thrust of battle is a master of men.

OGS:9:28 The young knight goes into battle saying, "May I die like a true knight", but the battlechief says such a wish is wrong, for your desire should be rather to live like a true knight, and it will follow naturally that you will die like one. It is a lesser knight who desires to die for a cause, for the better men resolve that the foeman shall die for his cause.

OGS:9:29 A knight must learn the wisdom of the wise and strike it on the tablets of his heart, rather than having it as a babble on the tongue. He must know the difference between the indolent man and the cautious one. The difference lies in their use of the period between the action becoming necessary and doing it. One uses the interval for planning the action required and weighing its merits and demerits. The other, through shiftlessness, delays action until he is forced into it, and he is then found unprepared.

OGS:9:30 A sober man was leaving a market town to journey home a few miles away, and he met a drunken rake, and for safety, they journeyed together. As they passed by a wooded place they were waylaid, attacked and robbed. In the town there was a pedlar who, next market day, met the drunkard and asked him whether it was safe to travel the road, which the drunkard and the sober man had travelled previously. The rake assured him that there was no danger. When the pedlar questioned his cuts and bruises, all the drunkard could say was that he must have gotten them while he was drunk and incapable.

OGS:9:31 When the pedlar put the same question to the sober man, he was warned about the footpads and advised to travel in the company of armed men. Thus it is with those who journey along the road of life. We meet two classes of advisers, from which we can obtain advice. One, like the rake, tells that life is full of pleasures, and there are no dangers along the road. The other cautions us against the dangers and pitfalls and urges us to travel well armed with prudence, discrimination and the virtues.

OGS:9:32 Have a warm and compassionate heart. As frozen water cannot cleanse the body, neither can a frozen heart wash impure stains from the soul. The knightly man treasures nothing so much as his honour, which marks him as a man of high estate. Honour may be an attribute of the poor man, for it is not dependent on riches or station.

OGS:9:33 Earth is an apple orchard with fruits delightful to the eye, which waft fragrance to the nose from afar, but at the core, its fruits have the maggots of bitterness and decay. Yet the orchard is good and senses its purpose, which is to produce fruit. It is not in the hashish fields of the hermit's contemplatory life that men develop their souls. This is an escape for the weak and timid from the stresses of life. Those who are simple seekers after the smooth path become drowned in a sea of unproductive felicity.

OGS:9:34 You can pray, "God help me," when you have expended the last ounce of your strength, for He did not place men on Earth to play but to work. Duty, obligation and responsibility are the manmakers, and these are slighted in the times and places where men are less than men. Always reach out beyond the frontiers of your limitations, for if you believe a thing to be impossible, then you yourself have made it so.

OGS:9:35 Conscience is the eye of God in man, and the prudent man lets nothing be seen which is unworthy, unwholesome or unmanly. He is always circumspect in speech, for only those who can unring a bell are able to recall words spoken in haste. If Earth were devoid of evil, how could we know what was good and judge the weak from the strong? How would we know what to strive against to progress?

OGS:9:36 I am a man who has written many worthy things, and I have faithfully copied that which has been given me. Yet sadly, my efforts have brought me down; my clarity of vision has undone me. I have lived in a generation, which scorns truth and cannot bear the stress of the search. It derides the simple things and seeks only after vain pleasures.

OGS:9:37 All men fear a mind, which sees more clearly than their own and they destroy it in self-protection. All base men fear the tongue of truth, for it strips them and exposes their nakedness to mockery and scorn. To think is to be misunderstood by those who do not think. To voice new thoughts is to invite persecution. To have visions of greater things is to be hated by the visionless, and to be a maker of new things is to invite the scorn of the mindless.

Chapter Ten – The Maymen Lore

OGS:10:1 These are words of wisdom, happily told, of the teachings of the schoolmen who came from over the narrow sea. They journeyed from Durain and were children of Dardanos who was the first man to place a horse in harness. Kostain was his son who married Lengilwin of the high brow.

OGS:10:2 The teachings disclosed strange things, but they were the lore of the land and served well when interpreted by the wise. Before times, they were unwritten, for that, which was entrusted to perishable wood lost its power, and understanding came with the flow of words from the mouth.

OGS:10:3 Every thought leaves an impress upon the Spirit of the Shadow self for good or evil. With every impress of evil, there is further corruption and distortion of the Spirit Form. With every impress of good, there is a strengthening force, which beautifies the Spirit Form, and so it resides within in joy and content.

OGS:10:4 There are seven Spirit cankerers, which are: meanness, theft, hypocrisy, fornication, cowardice, lust and envy. Earth, enveloped in ocean and mantled in air, is the school wherein man, conceived in the likeness of The Divine, plays his part as a pupil.

OGS:10:5 The natural world is that, which continues and develops from the creative impulse. The supernatural is that part of the natural not yet comprehended by men. The Great God Above All is a Being composed of the collective souls of men departed to godhood. For it is written in times of yore that God died in the effort of creation, but a New God is being reformed. The whole of creation and life, as it manifests, is the effect of the Old God being transmuted into a New One.

OGS:10:6 It is also written in the books containing the words of the Maymen, that nothing can create itself or spring from nothing. All things must have something pre-existing to themselves, which brought them forth. This is the law, which teaches that there is a God and only this God was unpreceded by anything. That, which is preceded by nothing is God. The Maymen argued the existence of God by calling upon the natural state of things as witness.

OGS:10:7 There are seven absolute values, which are: Love, Truth, Beauty, Wisdom, Goodness, Creativity and Justice.

OGS:10:8 An animal, not having a Soul Form, lives only for the day, and if it lived a thousand years would not be aware of anything out of place. But man, did he live for that time, would be intolerably bored; nothing would give him pleasure, and he would dread the future and hate the present.

OGS:10:9 If man were a mere mortal struggling for self-existence, how can we account for his sense of moral obligation, his power of pity, his generosity, his ideals and aspirations? What other creature manifests these? Can these be qualities engendered through earthly life? Are the highest aspects of loyalty, the most devoted love, the noble self-sacrifices, no more than the waste products of evolution?

OGS:10:10 The soul is supreme above all. It should be master of its own forces and never permit itself to be led by its servants - the senses. The purpose of the moral restrictions and discipline imposed by religion is to give it mastery, even as bodily discipline and proper care result in a healthful physical existence.

OGS:10:11 The soul is awakened by love, by happiness and sorrow. The soul acts upon the body, but the body does not act upon the soul, for mind commands matter. The soul, awakening to conscious realisation, becomes one with the law and is no longer the slave of external conditions but the heir to truth. It is capable of rising above the illusions and uncertainties inherent in matter.

OGS:10:12 The last part is rewritten and reconstructed, but the original sense is conveyed. There were originally over eighteen thousand words in this book.

SVB:1:12 Scriptures come in many tongues, they serve different purposes and vary in value, but each suits and serves a group of people in a particular stage of spiritual development. The lessons of an infant are as essential to its future as are the lessons of an older child. Each scripture gives a glimpse of the light, a spiritual revelation from a different viewpoint, but in each case the light is the same, for there is only one light of Truth.

Book of the Silver

Table of Chapters

SVB:1:1 – SVB:1:15	Chapter One – Interpretations	35
SVB:2:1 – SVB:2:14	Chapter Two – Teachings of Elidor - 1	37
SVB:3:1 – SVB:3:23	Chapter Three – Teachings of Elidor - 2	38
SVB:4:1 – SVB:4:32	Chapter Four – Teachings of Elidor - 3	41
SVB:5:1 – SVB:5:38	Chapter Five – Teachings of Elidor - 4	44
SVB:6:1 – SVB:6:28	Chapter Six – Teachings of Elidor - 5	48
SVB:7:1 – SVB:7:26	Chapter Seven – Teachings of Elidor - 6	51
SVB:8:1 – SVB:8:41	Chapter Eight – Elidor Speaks to His Disciples	54
SVB:9:1 – SVB:9:9	Chapter Nine – Elidor on the Sacred Scriptures	58

Book of the Silver Bough

Preserved by the hand of Gwinder Apowin

Chapter One – Interpretations

SVB:1:1 With scriptures such as these, no matter how pure the original inspiration poured out from the Divine Spiritual Fountainhead, they still have to pass through fallible human hands. This could lead to differences of interpretation and discord among the readers, things most undesirable, where harmony and unity are to be the rule.

SVB:1:2 To avoid all such differences and for the sake of accord and unity, the interpretation of these scriptures must be restricted to conform with the following rules: The interpretation must accord with authentic traditions. It must accord with reason and experience, faith never contending with reason, though it is realised and acknowledged that the nature of life, being as it is, many things have to be accepted and undertaken without logical explanations. The continuance of life beyond the veil of death may not appear to accord with worldly experience and reason; yet it does, but there is a law prohibiting any assurance of this. Such things have to be accepted; therefore, worldly experience cannot be taken as the yardstick in this instance, as in many other instances.

SVB:1:3 Apart from worldly experiences, there are spiritual experiences, which cannot be known and understood by the many. What is told of these must be accepted in faith by those unwilling to devote the time and undergo the austerities and discipline necessary to know at first hand. Only another Twice Born One is in a position to disagree about such a matter, and therefore, all others should be content to leave it in their hands.

SVB:1:4 Higher points of doctrine should be left to those competent to deal with them, but when lesser points are in dispute, then the outcome must accord with reason, and if any one explanation is to be accepted, it must be discovered rationally. All differences of opinion are to be settled by a majority of those competent to judge, and all reasons for supporting, or disagreeing with, any decision must be placed in record.

SVB:1:5 Whenever there is a meeting among brothers, they should assemble in good order, with goodwill and harmony in their hearts, and they should likewise disperse. While things are done in this manner, there will be prosperity and progress, though if any outlandish doctrines are introduced or any dividing disagreement permitted, prosperity and progress will depart. They will remain while the teachings are esteemed and the doctrines hallowed, while the leaders are held worthy of loyalty and the brothers of comradeship. Progress and prosperity will not depart while the brothers are upright and steadfast; while the maiden sisters are modest and virtuous and the married sisters are decent and decorous; while the elder brothers are wise and diligent in preserving all that is good; while the elder sisters are careful in all they do and considerate for the welfare of the younger ones. It is for the old to keep watch and ward, and for the young to dare and do.

SVB:1:6 The harshness of the ordinances should be mitigated with loving kindness, and when brothers or sisters are seen to be falling into the ways of wickedness, they should first be warned. After being warned, they should be reminded, and only after this should they be disciplined. Let some able and discreet person take them in hand and counsel them.

SVB:1:7 When two disagree as to the teachings, this is to be the manner for reaching a decision: One shall say, "This is my opinion," while the opponent says, "No, this opinion is better." Each shall argue with the other with friendliness, self-control and reason, following at all times the road of commonsense. If there is something on which they hold a different opinion, let them try and decide first which viewpoint is best, which is clearest.

SVB:1:8 All the teachings in dispute will be settled in this manner, and where there can be no settlement between two, then let them both agree upon two others. If these cannot settle the matter, then they shall choose one other, whose opinion both agree to abide with.

SVB:1:9 These teachings are always right: Those, which teach the proper channelling of the desires and urges of the body, not those, which would pander to them or ignore them. Those, which place spiritual objectives above worldly things. Those, which uphold the virtues and principles of humanity and attack anything, which would bring them down.

SVB:1:10 Frugality is not meanness, and prudence is not fear. Wastefulness is not generosity, and weakness is not kindness. Happiness is not pleasure, and apathy is not peace. The defence of principles is not intolerance, and idealism is not prejudice. To compromise is not to surrender. To defer to the wishes of a loved one is not weakness of character. To avoid argument and discord within the family requires strength, while assertion displays inconsideration. They who stifle hasty or thoughtless words are better than they who speak according to their thoughts.

SVB:1:11 To stand up for your rights is not necessarily right, and to do all things for peace and harmony is often wrong. The way of goodness traverses a very narrow ledge. The man who says, "perhaps I am wrong" is always right; the man who says, "I am certainly right" is always wrong. To avoid a fight is not cowardice, and to fight with the certainty of victory is not courage. Weak men may often fight and strong men often run; motive is all that matters. To judge anyone by his actions alone is to judge unfairly.

SVB:1:12 Scriptures come in many tongues; they serve different purposes and vary in value, but each suits and serves a group of people in a particular stage of spiritual development. The lessons of an infant are as essential to its future as are the lessons of an older child. Each scripture gives a glimpse of the light, a spiritual revelation from a different viewpoint, but in each case, the light is the same, for there is only one light of Truth.

SVB:1:13 However, scriptures need interpretation, for they conceal more than they reveal. They are never just what they appear to be on the surface. If a particular scripture proclaimed that fire actually gives out cold instead of heat and that the sun really sheds darkness instead of light, the shallow-minded person would turn from it in scorn. But this irresponsible and thoughtless attitude cannot be applied to scripture, and it would be much wiser to assume that the scripture intended to convey a meaning and message quite different from the superficially apparent one. Scripture cannot be treated like entertaining and valueless literature; therefore, delve deeply and diligently.

SVB:1:14 The only conclusion an intelligent person can come to is that all great scriptures, read properly and really understood, originate at one source. All are divinely inspired, but the clarity of vision varies considerably, as does the purity of transmission. Each suits particular needs and varying stages of development. Each provides for certain requirements and satisfies specific spiritual capacities, but in all, the essence of Truth is watered down and the brilliance of the light is obscured. This is essential in all scriptures, for it is only when the divinity within is fully awakened that Truth and reality can be gazed on; then, the scriptures no longer serve their purpose.

SVB:1:15 More than most these scriptures reveal only a fraction of the whole on the surface. In worldly matters, in rules of life and code of conduct and morals, in all things governing life on Earth, they will be interpreted strictly according to their obvious meaning and intent. In all things pertaining to spiritual matters, the afterlife, the divinity, or not strictly concerned with earthly life and existence, they need not necessarily be interpreted literally, for no earthly medium is adequate to express such things concisely.

Chapter Two – Teachings of Elidor - 1

SVB:2:1 I am a prophet of the written word, a man with many books of wisdom, who comes to you in the name of The Supreme Spirit. I bear proof of my mission for all to see. I was a Sleeper in the Great Stone Chambers of Initiation; the voices of the Instructing Spirits spoke to me, and I answered with the words of power. I prepared myself by the Dread Rites and became worthy to be called an Inheritor of the Ancient Wisdom.

SVB:2:2 They who awaken the Sleepers charged me with the burden of a prophet, saying, "Go forth into the highways and byways of the land, bearing the scars of one seared by nearness to the flame of Truth. Be not a man of pleasure, a son of wickedness. Have no love of comfort and the flattery of fine clothes. Deceive no woman for fleeting satisfaction, nor be deceived by worldly shadows. Here, you have seen with the eyes of reality and know the true nature of earthly things; are they not shadowy forms without substance, in which no trust can be placed? All earthly things pass away, the loveliness of flowers withers and fades, the beauty of a woman's face slips away with the passing years."

SVB:2:3 The voice of an Instructing Spirit continued, "Go forth, Shaker of those who slumber in spirit. Go, stir up the minds of men, crying, "Awake, bestir yourselves within the prisons where you are doomed to decay, cast off the fetters of worldliness, and uncover the eyes of the soulspirit."

SVB:2:4 "Go, gather the sincere seekers, and reveal to them a little light; guide them through the bewitching fairyland of earthly illusion, so they leave it to enter the daylight of Truth and not the darkness of death. Deliver them from the delusions generated in dense bodies.""

SVB:2:5 Hearing these things, I said, "Who am I to be a prophet to men? My soulspirit, having bathed in the Lakes of Light, can never again be happy imprisoned within a daily decaying body." The voice of an Instructing Spirit came to me; "Be comforted, my son, by the knowledge of Truth. The world, as it is, we cannot change, for this is the task of men. Go, submit yourself to life, the harsh taskmaster and gentle saviour. Your own good works are not yet sufficient to pay the cost of entry into the Place of Light." I asked in sorrow, "Am I then a man of small righteous credit," and the voice of the Instructing Spirit replied, "Where is the righteous man who is blameless? All men are prone to error, for it is the father of courage and resolution. You have been found reliable in testing and fit for the covenant of prophesy."

SVB:2:6 I speak with the words of the Instructing Spirits, and I am their mouthpiece to men on Earth. They charged me with the burden of a prophet; he is one whose soulspirit is a communicating link with the Divine Inspirational Source; he is one to deliver a message to the world. He is the teacher allocated for the times to teach a particular religious truth. His courage must be tempered with gentleness, and whatever fate decrees he must always rise above it. He will become an attraction for tribulation, overwhelmed with troubles, rejected and mocked.

SVB:2:7 Then they said to me in the comfortless darkness illuminated only by the spiritglow, "You will be a physician dispensing a bitter draught. The message you bear will not strike men's ears like a charming lovesong; the words will not fall pleasantly like notes from a well-played harp. Pleasant things are fleeting and stir the hearts of men for only a brief moment; entertaining things are soon forgotten, and amusing things leave no mark. Your tongue will be a sting and your mouth a fiery furnace."

SVB:2:8 "Men will hear your words, but they will not penetrate to many hearts. Your hearers will say, "We are much moved and our hearts charged with godliness," but these are words of wind and their hearts will still follow the ungodly inclinations of their desires."

SVB:2:9 When a man enters the Great Stone Chambers of Initiation, he receives an infusion of the Divine Essence. His soulspirit is awakened to conscious awareness and passes out, to leave the mortal body still and silent within its tomb. He comes into the presence of Beings who know the will of The Supreme Spirit; he learns awful secrets; he knows whence he came and whither he goes. He is one reborn and awakens to rediscover himself.

SVB:2:10 When I heard my fate, I asked for a smooth path and success, and my plea was rejected. Yet from that day, I came to love life as never before; from that day, I was a lover of Truth. Now I no longer have any trust in the world; I am no longer deceived by its ways. I know the world and the works of men, and I know myself. I sought for my soulspirit, and I found myself. Ten thousand worlds and their mysteries are meaningless to me, I found Truth, and she stands higher than all the worlds.

SVB:2:11 In the Place of Terror, I saw other things. I learned the secret of the serpent with its tail in its mouth. I saw the workings of the spawn of evil and the fungus of corruption. I gazed upon the Dark Ones, and when they saw me, they became vicious; they sought to attach themselves to me, for burdens of wickedness are added to those who affiliate themselves with evil. But I was strengthened against them and came forth uncontaminated.

SVB:2:12 When the implications of my fate awoke knowledge in my heart, I wept, in the spirit-lit darkness, for my wife, for my children; for would they not become fatherless? Who would harness the oxen and scatter the seed over the soil? Who would tend the sheep and stand guard, who would protect from intruders?

SVB:2:13 The voice within the Tomb Chamber spoke of fate and destiny and the things, which were unalterable. It said, "The path of the prophet is beset with sorrow; your house is destined to become desolate, and no human hands could have deflected the blow of fate. Your lands shall be abandoned to wild creatures, and many years shall pass before they are resown."

SVB:2:14 Then I said, "Let my wife be spared and the children of my body, for they will be comforters to me along the way and strengthen my heart in service." The voice of the Instructing Spirit replied, "Were these things within my power to grant, gladly would it be done, but you have been chosen as a prophet, and the way is hard and lonely. In the years ahead, your family will be mankind and your companions the accompanying Spirits. The road is long, and its end rests in eternity. Fear lurks by the wayside, doubt haunts the forest to be traversed and worldly temptations will be like wolves at your heels. But you can look forward to the joy of reunion at the destination, and though the way is hard, the journey is not in vain.

Chapter Three – Teachings of Elidor - 2

SVB:3:1 I am the prophet of the day; now hear my voice. There is a law of compensation; good always leads to good and bad always to bad; whatever the demands made upon you, they are always within reason. To you who defraud the poor and oppress the weak and defenceless, I tell you, your day is coming.

SVB:3:2 You who make justice a bitter draught or two-pronged weapon, or who twist the laws of the land to suit selfish ends, you shall not escape the remorseless Divine Justice. You who hate those who expose your evil ways and drag dark deeds out into the light of day, you scorners of honest men, you bribers and acceptors of bribes, have a pleasant hour! For a grimmer day will dawn.

SVB:3:3 You who harvest in fields you have not ploughed, who snatch a few pennies from the poverty stricken; you who connive with the forces of ignorance, who are self-deceivers thinking yourselves learned; you who walk in the comforting security of God-bestowed riches, unheeding of your duty, enjoy your hour! The reckoning awaits.

SVB:3:4 You who are self-satisfied, priest-deluded, going about like blind men led by the blind; who dwell under a cloud of shamelessness, gaining riches and power by the ignorance and weakness of others; you who say, "By our own strength have we accomplished our own ends," rejoice while you may! The day will come when you will be severed from your possessions; what will you have then?

SVB:3:5 The inheritance of eternity is for the upright and frugal, but the wicked and wasters shall be shut out from the places of contentment and peace. Hear my voice; let every man deal justly with another, speak the truth, seek the path of true justice and never say, "We need seek no further." Walk in ways of modesty and simplicity, shunning all forms of deceit and hypocrisy. Seek earnestly and diligently, and surely you will find, but expect no results if you are half-hearted and lukewarm.

SVB:3:6 Hear my voice, for I am one who has tasted the waters of Truth at their source. I come to scatter the seeds of wisdom and enlightenment over the whole Earth. The edge of my words has been sharpened on the whetstone of inspiration, and the comforting companionship of spirits has stilled the tumult within my bowels. I am a smooth-polished arrow shaft of inspiration waiting in the quiver of my mission. My tongue is a sword stabbing at the cuirass of worldliness, to open a wound exposing the sensitive conscience beneath. Do not delude yourselves that because I am among you, I have chosen you above others; I come among the worst, not the best, and I am charged to go to all men.

SVB:3:7 Yet though I come as an eagle to strike the foxes who seek to wreck the fowlpen, I come also to salve the wounds of the broken-hearted and to lead those captive in ignorance to freedom. I come also to those whose hearts are fastened with the bolts of intolerance and prejudice and to replace misery with beauty and glory in place of degradation. I am a planter of acorns intended to rise up into oak trees of divinity.

SVB:3:8 I am not a prophet of new doctrines, neither do I declare Truth to be a new thing. Truth remains always the same, however she is clothed. I am not a foreteller of the future and do not claim the ability to know the end of any one of you, or even my own. What lies ahead for anyone of you is in your own hands. Some things are certainly revealed to me, and these I must reveal to you, for this is the obligation of a prophet. I come among you not as a miracle worker, but as one charged with the duty of warning you openly.

SVB:3:9 Among you are many who make secret mockery of their religion, or who conceal their true beliefs behind a false facade of righteousness. To those I say, beware; awake to Truth, for you are deceived by worldliness. They have failed the test of life; they are victims of its delusions. Hear my voice; every man is the maker of himself, this is Truth. No man can intercede for another, and, could any one sacrifice his soulspirit for another, such sacrifice would not be permitted by The Supreme Spirit, Who is the Essence of Justice. As a man makes himself, so will he be known.

SVB:3:10 Do not reject me because I differ not from you. Had the Powers Above chosen one of their number to be a messenger and sent him down among men, then surely, the appointed one would have taken the form of a man. He would have been clothed as men are clothed and eaten as men eat. He would not have been some freakish creature having wings or two heads. Man's body was made to serve man, and if a messenger from above comes to men, shall it not serve him also? Therefore, I speak in the words of men and act as men act. I make no claim to be more than man.

SVB:3:11 If you say to yourselves, "Why should we listen to this one who is no more than a man seeking to change our ways and undermine the teachings of our fathers," I say, have I come with guileful tongue and lips coated with honey? Do I wear garments of silk and linen and eat at tables of luxury? I do not come to speak pleasantries to you, but to declare the harsh and unavoidable Truth. What I bring is not a honeyed drink, but a bitter draught; are these the wares of a false prophet?

SVB:3:12 If I am in error, then all I endure is in vain; if I am wrong, then on me is the punishment, but I have the assurance of certainty. What I have can be any man's if he is prepared to suffer and endure as I did. I make no claim to having received illumination as a gift, or as a reward of righteousness. I received it because I toiled and suffered for it. I paid for it in anguish and austerity. I deprived myself of worldly pleasures and comforts for spiritual knowledge. Do you expect to obtain what I paid for so dearly, for nothing? To know Truth, you must accept my word or follow the road I trod. You have the choice.

SVB:3:13 If the things, of which I speak, be fabricated by myself, or be the fruits of my imagination, then I am like one who labours without wages, for I toil and suffer without gain. Even worse, I damned myself before the judgement seat of Truth. Therefore, if I am convinced of their truth, what cause have you to doubt my words?

SVB:3:14 I do not come before you declaring myself the confident of The Supreme Spirit, the knower of secrets unattainable by others. I do not lay claim to miraculous powers, neither do I pretend to have the ability to forgive sins; these things are beyond the ability of any man. This I do declare to you: I am no superior being, no angel descended from the Heavens above, I am a man, such as you. Will you not hear me as brother listens to brother, will you pay less attention because I am cast in the same mould as yourselves?

SVB:3:15 Hear my voice, for I have come to awaken those who sleep. I come to lead the blind, I am the eyes of those who do not see. I am not a beguiler promising soft beds or comfort. I come as a warner against those who promise an easy way, and I raise my voice against any who lull you into indolence by declaring the ability to intercede for you. There is no easy way, and no one can intercede for another, each man is the master of his own fate. As each man plants, so shall he garner and as he moulds himself, so shall he come forth. There is always a day of reckoning.

SVB:3:16 Long years I struggled and prepared myself, seeking to discover Truth and the purpose of life. Then, the day came when I entered into the sleep which awakens the soulspirit. Then, when the truth was revealed, I saw myself as one seeking for selfish ends, for the satisfaction and contentment of knowing. When first I was charged with the burden of a prophet, my heart cried out, "Is it for this greater affliction that I have suffered and toiled, where is my reward?" I who should be strong was weak.

SVB:3:17 The inner voice of my conscience came to my aid, and I obeyed its command. I devoted my full attention to the Instructing Voices. I tested them for reality and knew they were no delusion. I act only upon the knowledge and proofs I have been given. I am not a bearer of idle tales. Do you think me such a fool as to sacrifice all I held dear, to give up all I possessed, to come and preach a false doctrine to those who would repay me with nothing but scorn? Do you consider me so lacking in wit that I would commit such an act of folly?

SVB:3:18 Do not disregard what I have to say; the words I speak were dearly bought. Do you treat them contemptuously because it was not you who paid the price? Hear and heed. I come to proclaim the Way of Truth. I can neither save you from the effects of your own errors, nor remit even the slightest transgression. I can only point the way; I can only offer myself as a guide. I cannot drive you, I cannot carry you, neither can I assume responsibility for your fate.

SVB:3:19 If you are bent under a burden of sorrow, then I will lighten your load; if you are oppressed, I will come to your aid; if you are lonely, then I am your friend; my hand is ever ready to help. All things within my power to give I gladly offer, whether they be of this world or transcending it. False promises to gain popularity, fair words to make friends, appeasing words to turn away anger; those I cannot give. A day will come when we shall all stand naked before the glare of Truth. That day I do not fear; can the comforting prophets so readily acceptable speak likewise?

SVB:3:20 Sons of fools are fathers of fools. If you will not accept my words of Truth you deny them to your children. Revile me as you will; sheep bleat and asses bray, but the stalking wolf makes no reply. You clamour for signs and say, "Cause these trees to become uprooted and dance, this well to flow with wine, or he who died three days ago to rise up from the grave and live, and we will believe." You ask for childish things contrary to any law and therefore beyond my power. Even could I perform such miracles to gain your belief, I would refrain, for what would such belief be worth? Just one miracle could convert the whole of mankind, but even then the price is too high for such a worthless gain.

SVB:3:21 Go your own ways; follow your undisturbing beliefs. Had it been in accord with the Creating Intent, you could all have been born perfect in righteousness, but what would you have been then? Mere puppets dangling from the hand above. The Divine Intent was not to create puppets; what end could they serve? The Supreme Spirit wants men,

men with freewill capable of decision, free men reaching upwards to divinity, choosing it of their own accord.

SVB:3:22 I follow my belief; you follow yours, me to my end you to yours. You look upon me and say in your hearts, "Can we believe him?" Yes, look upon me, and see how I live; do I not live by my own words? Now look upon those who declare me to be a false prophet, who are they? Are they not those who trample others underfoot in a scramble for power? Do they not thrust the orphan aside and permit the poor to starve in the midst of plenty? Who is the less hypocritical, the man to follow and believe?

SVB:3:23 May the woes of the world descend upon those who pray with the lips while their hearts remain dead and unmoved. Likewise those who display devotion in public places, but turn a hungry man away from their back gate. Let them suffer no less who worship in the daylight, but in the darkness of night indulge in whispers of scandal and deceit.

Chapter Four – Teachings of Elidor - 3

SVB:4:1 Hear my voice, listen to my words, obey these rules of conduct: if any man names you a liar or treats you as one, have no further dealings with him. Keep away from the smooth-tongued man with oily ways, for he is unworthy of your friendship. Keep your face unsmiling in the presence of a man who uses vile language. What spews from his mouth is the overspill of the rottenness within; he is empty and weak and, if encouraged, will spread his disease far and wide.

SVB:4:2 All things which really benefit man, whether materially or spiritually, and do no harm, are good and should be encouraged; they are the particles of progress. If a man comes to you and says he has secret knowledge of benefit to man, then hear him fairly. Bear with him patiently, for if he is sincere, even though you derive no benefit and are told nothing new, his sincerity needs encouragement.

SVB:4:3 Though it is well to convert others to the Way of Truth, tread wearily. Many will seek to lay snares for you, or to find some hidden vice, but if you live as your conscience dictates, you will go free and they will become ensnared. Those who call your belief false are themselves blinded by the scales of gullibility and held fast in the meshes of their own net of ignorance. As the blind can never see, so are these inconvincible; did The Supreme Spirit Himself come down and manifest to them, they would declare it to be only an illusion. Men believe what they want to believe and see what they want to see.

SVB:4:4 Leave them to form themselves as they will. The day will come when they will see themselves as they actually are, and on that day fear will overcome them, they will not know where to run. All their cunning and trickery will not avail them then; their words of scorn and mockery will rise up within them as bitter bile rises into the mouth. Have compassion for them, for on the dread day, they will stand alone, their waiting companions, the uncomforting horrors, skulking just beyond their sight.

SVB:4:5 Those who have no desire for Truth will never be convinced of its existence. There are many who do not believe in the existence of The Supreme Spirit in their own mortality because they fear to do so, not because it conflicts with their reason or inclinations. Even if a door could be opened into Heaven, through which they could look, they would say, "It is all an illusion, we are under some kind of spell."

SVB:4:6 Hear my voice; listen to my words; I have books of ancient wisdom giving guidance towards the light. I teach from them, and if they remain hidden, it is to keep them from the hands of despoilers. You who remain with face set towards the darkness of disbelief, go your way. If your affairs appear to prosper better than the affairs of those who walk in the light, do not deceive yourselves. The Supreme Spirit is compassionate and they prosper because He pities you for your future fate. In His mercy, He is granting you an abundance of pleasure in this life; enjoy it while you may. To you who hear my voice, I say, let these things not bother you or appear unjust. It is proper that the just and upright should suffer, for they are the chosen ones to be tested for greater things. The weak horse is never heavy-laden.

SVB:4:7 You who withdraw, closing your ears to my words, who erect a barrier around your hearts so my teachings cannot penetrate, follow your way.

You take your road, and I will take mine. But when the gloom closes about you, do not say, "We have been treated unjustly." If any injustice is done, it will be by yourselves to yourselves. The wickedness you have done will then recoil upon you; the truth you derided will have caught up with you. Laugh if you will, but laugh well, for your laughter will come to an end. Beyond it lies an ocean of tears.

SVB:4:8 You mockers, who ask to be shown the man who has returned from beyond the grave so he can describe what it is like, you say, "Only by this will our doubts be stilled." Who am I to change the order of things and still your doubts? I have not come to bring assurances, but as a warner and awakener. Why do you talk like this? If my teachings do not stir your hearts to response, they will not be forced upon you.

SVB:4:9 Many times, I have been tempted to withhold part of my message, knowing you would hold it in scorn. I have been faint-hearted when others have mocked, saying, "Bring down a Spirit from Heaven or disclose the hiding place of treasure, and we will believe." Hard is the road of a prophet, and that is all I am, not a conjurer.

SVB:4:10 You turn from me, saying one to the other, "What does he want of us?" or "Where lies his gain?" I ask nothing from you except a receptive mind. I ask no riches; I seek no payment. My reward lies in the knowledge of a duty done, in a clear conscience, in having done my best. Were I seeking wealth, or even fame, this is the last way I would set about it.

SVB:4:11 I speak with a true voice, I am no deceiver with some subtle end in view. I make no claim to possessing sacred treasures of wisdom. I make no claim to the knowledge of hidden mysteries or great secrets. I am not an Angel, nor a Spirit sent direct from Heaven. I am one of your own kind. I am not a hypocrite seeking to curry favour by taking your side against those who ridicule your own views. I stand alone, asking favour of no man. I speak according to my heart; as my heart, so my lips. My words are true; if I did not utter them, I would be a coward and a betrayer of all I hold dear.

SVB:4:12 Wait and listen. Do not worship vainly and to no purpose. Serve The Supreme Spirit, for there is none greater to serve, If you think otherwise, you devise false things. Take my teachings into your hearts; I offer them gladly, asking no reward. Will you not open your hearts and incline towards the truth?

SVB:4:13 You demand proof of my prophesy, that I am what I declare myself to be. You say the darkness of the tomb has smitten me with madness and ask me to join you and become cured. May the Protecting Spirits bear witness that I do not join in ignorance and darkness. The proof of a true prophet is in his way of life. Have I ever lived otherwise than in accordance with my teachings? False prophets gain worldly things; true prophets suffer unrewarded, without complaint. Even then, what they suffer in the sight of men is only a small part of the whole burden.

SVB:4:14 You mock my teachings, declaring them to be false and foolish. You are suspicious of them; what do you fear? Be honest with yourselves; is it not because they disturb you, that inwardly, you know their truth? I have not come to bring you consolation; I come to cause you anxiety. I do not speak words of comfort, but words of urgency. Change your ways now, before it is too late. The road back is long and tiresome.

SVB:4:15 I speak with the voice of The Supreme Spirit; I serve Him, and to Him is my life dedicated. Were I to demand a sign from Him to bolster my own faith, would I not be unworthy of His trust and a failure as a prophet? Did I demand a sign to show you, would He not think me weak? It does not need a prophet to convert by signs and miracles; anyone could succeed by this means; the true prophet is needed when it is more difficult, when the opposition is really tough. A true prophet speaks harsh words; he is known by his unpopularity.

SVB:4:16 You may ask me whether it is my desire that you should abandon the worship of your fathers. This is not my desire; retain all that is good and beneficial; reject all that serves no purpose. You accuse me of being too solemn; you say I have lost the ability to laugh, that I set my face against merriment. In all this, you wrong me, for I never set myself against laughter and happiness. In all things, there must be balance; laughter and happiness have their place, but are not things of supreme importance.

SVB:4:17   You say, "Why should we not deal with our possessions and our lives as we wish? They are ours." I say, where the wishes and inclinations of a man's heart lead him along the most beneficial road, then follow them. But no man has sufficient wisdom within himself to know where his benefit lies; therefore, he must seek guidance if he be truly wise. Which is the wiser, to deal with your lives according to the prompting of inclinations and desires or to live them in a way most beneficial to yourselves?

SVB:4:18   Through my own efforts and sacrifices, through application and long years of patient endeavour, I have been granted an insight into the nature of things. I have been given a clear revelation and also been charged with making it known to men. What I have has been bought dearly; why then do you mock my teachings or doubt my sincerity? Have I asked anything from you except a change of heart?

SVB:4:19   You mock me, saying, "We cannot understand the import of your great teachings," or you deride me, saying, "Were it not that we have pity on your state of madness, we would drive you away from us." For your sakes I have given up all I once possessed; I have left all I hold dear; can you not spare me a few moments of your time? You ask, "Why did not The Supreme Spirit make all men conform to one creed, one belief?" This He could have done, but it would not serve His end. These are not superficial teachings; can you not spare time to consider them?

SVB:4:20   You say I am no more than a man like yourselves; this is true. You say I am powerless among you, that I remain only because of your benevolence and goodwill. If you think me powerless, you are mistaken. In the Stone Chambers, I learned secrets of power beyond your conception. Do not think me helpless because I come among you with humility and restraint. Had I so desired, my knowledge could have brought me riches and position; instead, I chose to live as I do and follow the road of a true prophet. Is this not proof enough of my sincerity?

SVB:4:21   The times are good. There are bountiful harvests, and the land is at peace. Men come and go without fear; pleasure and comfort are to be found on every side; it is a bad time for prophets. Turbulence and trouble are needed to stir the hearts of men, to lift up their eyes to greater things. When a man is beset with trouble, he turns to spiritual things for consolation and help, but no sooner has it passed than he reverts to his former ways. The man who pillows his head on a log is more likely to pray than one who lays on a pillow of down.

SVB:4:22   Many among you have come forward in a half-hearted manner and said, "We have heard and believe, we are followers of your teachings." The day came when they were called upon to make sacrifices for their beliefs; then, there was a speedy sorting out. Some regarded their afflictions as chastisements from above, being still unable to understand the nature of suffering. When misfortune came upon them, they said, "The Supreme Spirit is against us." When the sun of fortune shone they said, "The Supreme Spirit is with us." How little they knew of Him!

SVB:4:23   Heaven and Earth have been formed for a serious purpose, for a great and glorious end. Man is blind to them because of his small-mindedness. I speak of wonderful things, while you answer me referring to miserable matters. I am a plain man; I claim no extraordinary powers beyond acquisition by any other, I am not a conjurer or sorcerer. My mission is to choose those who wish to serve The Supreme Spirit. I come from the silence of solitude; I am not a man gifted with eloquence. Did I come performing miracles, all would follow me, even the hypocrite and evildoer would be among those who walked the road. Who then could separate the chaff from the grain, the weak from the strong, those worthy of Divinity from those who were not?

SVB:4:24   All creation is upheld by The Law, and the value of The Law is revealed in the fact that even The Supreme Spirit does not act against it. It would be less beneficial for men if miracles were performed by the prophets. If the Law is good, it must be strictly applied.

SVB:4:25   If men are insincere and shiftless, the performances of miracles will not strengthen their hearts. They are like voyagers at sea; a storm rises, and they are distressed; it abates, and they rejoice. When the winds roar and the waves mount up, they pray and proclaim their repentance; they profess their intention of living a new life, if saved. Yet when they come safe to land again, they forget all that passed; they return to their previous ways. They commit self-injuring excesses and deeds of selfishness; only further affliction brings these to an end; can you not understand?

SVB:4:26 Hear my voice, those who miserably bewail their misfortunes. When troubles beset you and new trials confront you every day, know you are being tested. Life itself is a necklace of tests. Accept with fortitude whatever test life presents, saying in your heart when meeting each one, "However this may appear now, it is for my ultimate good."

SVB:4:27 You, too, talk of miracles. You seek miraculous solutions for your problems. Do you not understand the nature of freewill, and that miracles are contrary to it as well as to The Law? Were they part of normal life, your fear of divine intervention, or reliance upon divine power, would sap your independence and stifle the expression of freewill. Your choice between good and evil would no longer be free, and you would become more of puppets and less of men.

SVB:4:28 Face up to every trial, for only the tests successfully undergone and the good deeds done have lasting value. To merely while away the time, to take the easy path through life, turning aside at every obstacle, has no value whatsoever.

SVB:4:29 No two persons have the same abilities and inclinations; therefore, let each man serve The Supreme Spirit according to his endowments. Do not try to imitate another in service, for such imitation accomplishes less. Follow the road of your own choosing; serve to the best of your ability; live a good life; little more can be required of any man.

SVB:4:30 However, do not close your eyes to Truth, thinking that service through earthly skill and ability is enough. What you think, and what you believe best, may all be wrong. You may not even know what is for your own good. You were born without being consulted; you cannot direct your lives according to your desires. You will die, whether you wish it or not. Such is earthly life, and likewise, your condition in the afterlife may not accord with your own designs and will.

SVB:4:31 You say, "Death is the end of all things; therefore, let us live as we will." Are you certain, that you can state this as a fact? What do you know of death? The only fact you do know beyond a doubt is that death is the universal lot of man. Therefore, exercise caution regarding something you know little about. Shed no tears for those who are already beyond the place of tears. Can weeping console them, or mourning assist them? What is life or what is death, that you should grieve for either? They come and go, they merge one into the other until neither is distinguishable.

SVB:4:32 Sorrow and joy, pain and pleasure, tumult and peace; they come and go. They play about man and are gone. They are like winds rustling a tree; they pass, and the tree remains unmoved, life is a lamplit room with two doors leading to the darkness of night.

Chapter Five – Teachings of Elidor - 4

SVB:5:1 Hear my voice. I condemn the slanderer, the talebearer, the hypocrite. They are the inheritors of darkness, the ones destined for the dismal abyss. I condemn those who amass riches and store possessions against the future, and those who delude themselves that wealth will shield them against the trials of life.

SVB:5:2 These are times of worldliness, when riches are the lure, the obsession of men. Only on the brink of the grave do they see the folly of their ways. Then when it is too late, they cry out in despair, saying, "Grant us just a little more time." Of what value would more time be to them? They have had sufficient.

SVB:5:3 Food which would sustain widows and orphans is thrown by the rich to their dogs, and they say, "This is the natural order of things." I condemn them, not for their riches, but for what they say. Here the widows and orphans cry, but who will cry beyond the grave? Who will inhabit the grim caverns? Ah, you indolent rich, fatten yourselves up, surely a lean time lies ahead! Do not shift the blame when your just desserts are meted out; you are the guardians of your future, the preparers of your future abode.

SVB:5:4 I condemn the self-deceivers. They say, with hypocritical lying heart, "This may be done, and this is forbidden." They split hairs; they have a conscience of convenience; they interpret the message from the formation of a letter. Hear my words; heed what I say. Do not twist the truth so that it becomes lies, and say, "These are rules for the conduct of others," at the same time masking your own deeds under a convenient veil of distortion. Never make laws for others, which you are unable to keep yourself. Are they better than you? If so, let them make the laws.

SVB:5:5 I raise my voice against mean-minded men. Would there be any justice, were they to share the same fate as the generous and self-sacrificing? I condemn cowards. When they are told, "Be men, this is your duty," their hearts quail inside them; their knees tremble; their feet shift; they know their true nature will be revealed and can find no words to avoid their obligations.

SVB:5:6 Those I do not seek as converts; let them go their own way. For if there is hardship or persecution, if the followers of Truth are to be tested for their worthiness to survive and bear the light, where will they stand? The smug, self-satisfied man is not called upon to follow. If good fortune smiles upon him, he will say, "See what I have been given, though I have done little. I must surely be a worthy man." Self-deceiver, he has been discarded as unworthy of any test; the good fortune has been granted in mercy and compassion; his future fate is awful.

SVB:5:7 I condemn the cowards and hypocrites who go about shouting indignantly against warmongers and injustice. They say, "Restrain yourselves, for we are men of peace." But when the enemy swoops down upon them, or a just war is proclaimed, they say, "Let your hand carry the sword and spear." Those who once shouted boldly now speak in whispers; their voices are no longer heard.

SVB:5:8 The weaver knows the design of the whole tapestry; the threads only the colour in their own part. This life must be viewed together with the life to come, if it is to be understood. Only The Great Designer can do this, and He metes out success and failure, joy and sorrow, all the tests of life accordingly.

SVB:5:9 I condemn the man who says, "I am pure; I am good." Who is he to judge? Does the polecat think its own smell bad? Does the adder throw away its venom? Only the deluded fool says, "I know what is good and what is bad and need no information on the matter." Heed these words; heed them well!

SVB:5:10 When good fortune comes, some men say, "I have led a good life, and this is my reward", or "This results from my own efforts." If misfortune befalls them, they say, "This is the fault of some other," or, "This is a chastisement from above." I say to you, all things flow from your own destiny; good and bad are sent alike to test you; both can be turned to your own benefit or your own undoing.

SVB:5:11 If some of you have done wrong and acted against your own future good, whatever it is, the harm is not irreparable. There is still time, how long is unknowable, but the uncertainty is essential. The damage must be repaired by a constant outpouring of good, and this alone is not enough; the roots of evil must be torn up within you; felling the tree is insufficient.

SVB:5:12 Those who heed my words and follow my teachings are Pilgrims on the Path. They must be resolute and resourceful, for the going is tough. Each victory a Pilgrim wins contains the promise of a harder one to follow. Every obstacle overcome brings another into view; from birth to death life is a continual overcoming.

SVB:5:13 The desires of the body and cravings of the flesh are divisible into two parts: those, which draw attention to the needs of the body (these can be satisfied in moderation) and those, which bring greater spiritual reward through suppression or re-channelling. The man of wisdom knows one from the other.

SVB:5:14 I do not speak of profound things; my words are for the ears of unlettered men. I try to speak within the understanding of every man and woman and according to their capacity, but because of this, the enlightenment given to the many may have no value to the few. Even so, there will be those who find it beyond their comprehension. My teachings are many-sided, and therefore, each must interpret them according to his own capacity for understanding.

My words are not for those whose minds are pools of stagnation; a pot filled with stagnant water cannot become a receptacle for the pure waters of wisdom. My words are not for the intolerant and prejudiced; fresh milk cannot be mingled with sour milk.

SVB:5:15 Hear my voice, for though I speak plainly, in unadorned sentences, I have been strengthened by an inflow of power. I have a shield to deflect the words of mockers and scorners. In a sea of hostility, I am not troubled or disturbed; my heart is like flint and my face confronts the unrighteous like a cliff withstanding the wind. Where are my wordy adversaries? Let them come forward and meet me in open discussion before you. Why do they keep away? Why do they seek refuge behind armed men?

SVB:5:16 It is time to separate the good from the bad, the serviceable from the worthless. The Earth is overloaded with useless things; progress is impeded in a welter of unnecessary things. It is deafened with the clacking of foolish tongues and overwhelmed in a spate of valueless words. Mankind wallows in the mudhole of a purposeless existence. It must pull itself out or be drawn under and perish.

SVB:5:17 Many desire fame or greatness, but these come only in accordance with destiny. If it be destined, they will come unbidden. Therefore, do not make these your aim in life. Obey the laws of life as recorded in the scriptures. Live in accord with your neighbours, for irrelevant quarrelling harms all and benefits none. Endure every trial with steadfastness, and between the tests, prepare for the next; never be caught unprepared.

SVB:5:18 Those who live a good life, maintaining themselves in uprightness and shunning the ways of wickedness, do this for their own good. They are wise, but would be unwise and hypocritical, were they to hold it was done for the sake of The Supreme Spirit alone, and not for their own sakes.

SVB:5:19 Some have been given riches in abundance; they lack none of the good things of life. Others have nothing, and their burdens are grievous and heavy. I have heard men say, "What kind of God makes this the order of things," but it is not God; it is man who establishes this as the order of things. The Supreme Spirit will not undertake the tasks of men, neither will He withdraw the tests of temptation when they are placed in the paths of men.

SVB:5:20 The Supreme Spirit has made a law covering the dealings between men. They are judged with a greater justice than Earth can ever know. It differentiates between the powerless slave who owns nothing and the man abundantly supplied with wealth and possessions. A kind word or drink of water from a man in bondage is of greater value than gold pieces from a man of wealth. A poor man who gives from compassion or comradeship does so in goodness, but the goodness of a rich man giving in consciousness of charity, or from pride in his possessions and position, lacks the same purity; it is tainted. Whose goodness has the highest quality, that of the poor man who shares all his food and clothing with a fellowman, or that of the rich man who gives two pieces of gold from the thousands in his treasury?

SVB:5:21 The same law differentiates between the maimed and afflicted and those who are whole and healthy, between the strong and weak, the dull-minded and the keen-minded man. The law is: from each man according to his ability and means. The feeling and intent behind an act give it value.

SVB:5:22 I speak again to the cowards, for in these pleasant times, who knows where they are; there has been no sorting out. Only their loud voices betray them, their love of comfort, their lack of hardihood, their appreciation of womanly things. They say, "Would that times were different and we had a call to action," but when a matter is placed at issue, when the opposition is aggressive and immovable, they melt like wax images before the heat of fire. Their hearts tumble, their bellies turn to water, they turn their eyes aside and mumble excuses. They say, "We have a sickness," or, "We have many responsibilities." Far better were they better men with enough courage to admit their own cowardice.

SVB:5:23 There are others, not cowards, who have a point of weakness in their family ties. Wives and children cause men to stray from the strict path of duty, but for this, the wives and children are to be forgiven.

SVB:5:24 Obligations have an order of precedence, which is to be strictly observed. Few men are so unbiased that they can decide such things for themselves. A wife and children are the sun of a man's life; they are almost indispensable to his full development. Yet they, like riches and power, are sources of trial, a means of testing, and every man should act in the light of this knowledge. By doing so, his life will be more harmonious and beneficial. He should also bear in mind that his relationship with all his family is judged according to a law similar to the one just mentioned. As he treats them, how he acts, so is he judged. The family living in a hovel of poverty is not expected to conform to such a high standard as the one in a place of plenty. That the former does is to its credit; that the latter fails and its standard falls below the other, is to its discredit; there will be a proper accounting.

SVB:5:25 Those who live contentedly, snug in the bosom of their family, safe at home, going placidly about their daily affairs, untroubled by the call of the cause or the demands of duty, shall not be treated or judged like those who sacrifice and serve. The placid and indolent are not judged the same as those who struggle resolutely and endure steadfastly. The constant and the inconstant are not treated alike; their merits are in no way similar. There is a greater recompense of merit for those who turn their back on home comforts than for those who remain content with peace and placidity.

SVB:5:26 These are times of peace and prosperity, but are they times of inner stability? Those born less fortunately, who have fought in bloody wars, who have been driven away homeless, who have endured famine, imprisonment or persecution, have learned that mutual suffering is the cement of humanity. The sweet flowers of friendship and understanding are found in the deserts of despair and distress, not in the pastures of pleasure and prosperity.

SVB:5:27 Peace and prosperity cannot remain with you forever; therefore when trouble and strife descend upon you, as they have in the past, remember that the pattern of life is one of light and shade. Happiness and sorrow, success and failure, contentment and strife, are sent alternatively among men, that the good may be known from the bad, the strong from the weak, the true from the false, the straight-forward man from the hypocrite and the selfish one from the unselfish.

SVB:5:28 Now, I will speak about deceitfulness, the evil rampant among you. Nay, do not seek to drown my words in an avalanche of mockery. Honest men do not fear Truth; words of Truth do not beat painfully against their ears. There is no deceit so profound as the deceit of the self-deceived. They are prisoners in a cell of their own building and have cast the key into the moat outside. They may hide their true selves from others in this life and think they have done well, but there will be no such deception in the life to come.

SVB:5:29 Some self-deceivers stand before me, half their thoughts proclaiming their goodness and the others preparing acts of deceit. Others say, "We are good; we are just" and twist the words of the scriptures with their own interpretations and misquote to comply with their own convenience. They cannot deceive one who sees the reflection of their inner image, but they may deceive you, for they put on the face of plausibility.

SVB:5:30 I see behind the mantle of goodness displayed to the eyes and discover the rottenness hidden underneath. The alms they give, the good deeds they perform are no more than palliatives to their consciences. They blow themselves up to appear great in the eyes of men, but there is nothing inside except wind. Beneath the mortal surface, there is a puny thing, weak and withered. Could these only see their future fate they would surely cry, "We are treated unjustly," maintaining their self-deceit. But who is unjust to them if it is not themselves?

SVB:5:31 To you who are healthy-minded, I say, keep well away from those self-deceivers, for if they do not corrupt you, they will surely lead you astray. Take no notice of what they say; their words are false; seek rather to discover the things hidden in the alcoves of their hearts. Some deceivers have come to me and said, "We believe your teachings and wish to follow your way." In their hearts, they do not believe, and they act from base motives. Because they are blind, they think I, too, cannot see. I may lack all worldly possessions and wealth, but I do have a treasure beyond price, granted me in the Great Stone Chambers, my eyes can see the inner likeness of men. I cannot be deceived by words,

SVB:5:32 Some of you who are Pilgrims on the Way will find many seeking to gain your confidence and appearing willing to repudiate their own kind. Have no dealings with them. A man who would betray his faith, his race, his nation, his convictions or his family, is a weak reed, from which no support can be expected, and upon which no reliance can be placed. If he plots your downfall, return cunning with cunning, it is not wrong to slay a snake with a snake's venom. If you disregard a man who schemes against you, you support his cause.

SVB:5:33 Those totally ignorant of Truth can do little harm, but those who know Truth and disguise her are dangerous. Those who alter the appearance or mask the face of Truth are servants of evil. Among them are those who turn the words of the scriptures to suit their own ends. They say, "This is the true meaning; it is more convenient, less harsh," or they say, "This we know is written, but we do not obey; it is too exacting; we accept part and discard part." Get rid of them, they confuse the genuine seeker for Truth and mutilate Truth with their knife of selectivity.

SVB:5:34 You ask, "Why do the good suffer as well as the bad, why are the innocent afflicted as well as the guilty?" It is because mankind is a single whole; if an arm is wounded the whole body suffers; men are not strictly divided into good and bad, guilty and innocent. Those who suffer or are afflicted through the faults and failings of others derive the greatest kind of benefit.

SVB:5:35 Just as the soulspirit experiences pleasure, so must it experience pain; were it otherwise, the pleasure would have no value. Can light be known without the contrasting darkness? If a man is prepared to accept pleasure and happiness from contact with others, should he not also be prepared to participate in their sorrow and suffering?

SVB:5:36 Pain is unpleasant; agony sometimes unendurable, but they can be accepted and borne by a realisation of their objective; the knowledge that they have a purpose and end. Suffering and strife have made man what he is; he suffers things unknown to lesser creatures, which do not know the pains of remorse, regret, shame and disgrace. It is suffering and sorrow, not pleasure and happiness, that have raised man to his present height.

SVB:5:37 You ask, "How can the troubles and tribulations of the good be reconciled with the statement that The Supreme Spirit is the fountainhead of Justice, Goodness and Mercy?" They can be. Man must tread the hard road of sorrow and suffering, because it is an inescapable route on the journey to claim his inheritance. Man has won the right to make the pilgrimage; he has passed the simple tests; should he baulk at the greater ones along the way?

SVB:5:38 My people, hear my voice; I am your prophet. Transmute the dark memories of your sorrows into light seeds of spirituality. The pearl of perfect peace lies in the dregs within the cup of suffering. The haven of happiness lies across the turbulent seas of strife.

Chapter Six – Teachings of Elidor - 5

SVB:6:1 Truth cannot be destroyed or changed; she cannot be stripped and displayed to the eyes of men. Wisdom and knowledge cannot be trampled underfoot by turning the sword against their upholders. I may not be powerful, I carry no weapons, my voice may be weak, but better men will come in days unborn, and they will sing glad songs of light. The night of ignorance will have its end.

SVB:6:2 I speak to the toilworn, to those heavy-burdened with labour. In the bondage of servitude, you are free, because you are not shackled with cravings begotten by idleness. The idle rich are not free; they are slaves to their possessions; they suffer under the lash of their thoughts.

SVB:6:3 Labour is not toil and nothing else; its rewards extend beyond worldly things; this is one of the tragedies of the rich who are denied them. Even the prophets of the past have not seen clearly the rewards of labour. I will teach you the truth, and it will make you free.

SVB:6:4 There is a right way to labour, and there is a wrong way. There is also a way of labour that is full of song and a way that is silent; both play their part. Men should choose their form of labour and not have it thrust upon them. In it, they should find contentment and self-expression, then it will not become wearisome.

SVB:6:5 The man who would be happy and contented must seek a form of labour free from anxious thoughts and fanciful desires. It must bring satisfaction and confer benefit. These things have been said before, but I say them again: do not pursue vain hopes or seek too high a reward. Ask only for a just return, and remain your own master.

SVB:6:6 It is unwise to seek a position too great for your abilities; by so doing, you burden yourself with a life of straining. Be satisfied with whatever fate decrees, and whatever problems perplex you, rise above them. Be without jealousy, never envious of another's position; meet success and failure with equal poise and your labour will not be burdensome.

SVB:6:7 Learn to see the hand of The Supreme Spirit in all things, and make your labour the sacrifice, your toil the offering, to Him. No others are asked than these. Care and diligence, honesty and skill being your form of worship, you worship well. Diligence in the task, a life of moderation, dedication of wealth, leisure hours filled with service or study, these are proper sacrifices, not poor dumb creatures.

SVB:6:8 Those who curtail pleasures and then do nothing useful with the time gained are fools. To abstain from enjoyment to serve beneficial ends is good; so also is dedication of worldly wealth beyond modest needs. Giving an honest days labour for wages, living modestly and frugally, without meanness or harsh austerity, these too are worthy and acceptable sacrifices. It is through sacrifices such as these that the soulspirit is truly glorified.

SVB:6:9 Neither contentment in this world, nor happiness in the world to come is for those who do not know the meaning of sacrifice. All good works, all honest labour, all charitable deeds, all payments of full and fair wages, not futile burnings, are worthy sacrifices. Another form of sacrifice is the time devoted to studying the scriptures.

SVB:6:10 Open your hearts to my words; I speak only for your benefit, my voice is not raised for my own amusement. There is much talk about the wickedness and arrogance of the rich. Have I said this? It is not only they who are wicked and arrogant, and no man can be called wicked just because he is rich. Wealth does not necessarily serve evil. What matters is how persons deal with the inheritance entrusted to them, not only riches, but also strength, beauty or talent. Search your own hearts before condemning others.

SVB:6:11 It is not only the rich who are idle. Each of you, ask yourself how you would fare under the test of riches, and answer honestly. Is it certain you are not reviling the rich through envy? Are you sure there is no hypocrisy in your hearts? Wealth is no light burden, and few, very few survive a severe test. But there are others, men of unusual ability, women of great beauty or talent, they, too, often fail. Look within before you look without.

SVB:6:12 Like those other things, labour is a challenge, the outcome can be a gain or a loss, victory or defeat. The slovenly man who labours only to supply his needs is one on whom life is wasted. The man who declines to utilise mind and limbs to the utmost is no better than the man whose riches permit him to live a life of uselessness. The fault lies with the man, not his money.

SVB:6:13 The enjoyments that flow from worldly things bear within themselves seeds of sorrow to come. Worldly pleasures are passing things, and peace and content are not to be found in them. The man on the right path is one who considers the earthly rewards of effort less valuable than the spiritual gain.

SVB:6:14 All men become Pilgrims on the Way when their labour and efforts are dedicated to serving mankind. They reach out for spirituality when they find pleasure in their task. The man who labours with zest and dedication, even though the result be small, is a better man than one who lacks these qualities.

SVB:6:15 Even as in all fire, there is smoke, so in all things created by men, there will be some imperfection, for perfection lies outside this world. The best man can do is strive towards perfection; whatever he turns his hand to; make it the goal.

SVB:6:16 You may think me a doleful prophet preaching the glory of the sorrowful path, but this I am not. The inclinations of men lure them from the road; to turn them back. I, too, must leave the road and take a stand where the inclinations have led them. I do not speak of things supporting them along the way, but of things leading them astray.

SVB:6:17 I say to you, seek happiness; enjoy yourselves; life is meant to be more light than shade. I also say, these things cannot be made the whole aim in life; see them in proper perspective. Happiness is not the goal of earthly life; it is a reward along the way. Everyday life is governed by duty and obligation, not happiness and pleasure. To be over-concerned with happiness and contentment is the surest way to unhappiness and restlessness.

SVB:6:18 Submission to the will of The Supreme Spirit is the surest means of avoiding too much suffering and frustration. Knowledge of His will comes from careful study of the scriptures. Joyfully accept whatever destiny bestows, be it joy or sorrow, good or ill. If you are blessed with many gifts, there is no better way to indicate your gratitude than just being quietly and contentedly happy, finding pleasure in even the smallest things.

SVB:6:19 A man's trust in the goodness of The Supreme Spirit must not depend upon the outward circumstances surrounding that man. This is a very important thing to remember. He should try and quell all expectations and preferences, accepting cheerfully whatever comes his way. The man who serves best rises above all desire attachments and sense allurements, his only earthly ties being those of love, duty and obligation.

SVB:6:20 To know the will of The Supreme Spirit and will what He wills, that is the supreme secret of spirituality. Labouring to fulfil that will is to worship with the daily task, a most profitable form of worship. I say, let the will of The Supreme Spirit be supreme, and subordinate all earthly labours to it. The path of life is on a mountainside; man can ascend or descend according to his inclinations; he can take the hard or the easy way. Upwards is the light, downwards the darkness; man has the choice; he goes where he pleases.

SVB:6:21 I speak to you as a warner, and I warn against the ways of evil men. They are selfish men unheedful of the good of others, the good, which includes them. Their thoughts do not extend beyond themselves and their own; they seek to isolate themselves from mankind when the good of mankind is an issue. They do not know what should be done and what should not be done; they do not understand the nature of good conduct and the path of Truth. They say, "Mankind has no need for goodness; it has no moral foundation. There is no way of knowing Truth. There is no Supreme Spirit, no Creating God. All creation is the result of chance, and lust is the only cause of birth. The only purpose of life is an earthly one, we begin and end in the dust."

SVB:6:22 Set in the ways of this belief, these unconscious soulspirits dutifully serve the cause of evil, working, though they know not, for the destruction of mankind. They taint their soulspirits with unrestricted desires and stain them with uncontrolled urges. Full of arrogance and deceit, they ride roughshod over the spiritual inclinations of others and hold fast to their own dark belief. Their destructive work is carried on in the name of progress.

SVB:6:23 Yet with all they have, they are unhappy and discontented. They are loaded with many unnecessary cares, and their restless thoughts never give them peace. They fruitlessly seek happiness in sensual enjoyments, in pleasure and gaiety, in the frivolities of life, in drinking and gambling, in luxury and ease, firmly believing they will find it there, that life can offer no more.

SVB:6:24 They are bound fast with fetters of worldliness; they are blind and insensitive to anything else. They seethe within; anger, spitefulness, indignation and malice are relieving outlets. They seek refuge in lies and deceit; they hope for relief in outbursts of temper, in lust and sensuality and in foul language. Their only aim is to amass wealth and possessions, or to live a life of idleness and ease; they cannot understand what drives them on.

SVB:6:25 They say, "What I have I have earned; it is my own; with it I will acquire whatever I need to satisfy my desires. I have amassed riches, I have come to a high position; men look up to me; I am praised and honoured. I can buy what I desire; I will enjoy life; I am a success; who else is like me? I give charity; I fulfil my religious obligations; I am sought after by those who need advice and help. I live comfortably; I eat well; I have all I need." This they say, but are they really happy and at peace, are they really successful having all they want? No, they speak from the darkness of delusion, though they know it not.

SVB:6:26   They have been deceived by the trap of earthly conditions; they have fallen prey to the alluring phantoms of the senses. They are entangled in a net of delusion; they wander in the deep fog of illusion. They are slaves to their urges, captives of their cravings; they are bound and helpless in a chariot drawn by runaway horses, carried swiftly towards the yawning abyss.

SVB:6:27   Weak men become drunk with the heady draughts of power and riches; they are carried away by their own arrogance and conceit. They try to turn earthly condition towards serving their own ends and struggle futilely against The Law. Willing slaves of arrogance and selfishness, helpless victims in the stormy seas of rage, lust and violence, these servants of evil hate the divinity within themselves. They hate and fear the small still voice inside. They stifle it; they smother it under the loud clamour of gaiety. They seek solace in strong wine, in sense-stimulating entertainment and in spirit-poisoning drugs. Stand aside; let them be carried swiftly to the place of sorrow and vain regret!

SVB:6:28   Hear my voice, and do not fall into the trap of worldliness; do not fall willing victims to the allurements of phantoms. Look for reality; be satisfied with nothing less than Truth. Do not reject the scriptures; study them carefully, and you will have a guide through life. They will reveal the right and the wrong; follow their light; do what has to be done; no more is expected of you. Heed what I say, for I am your friend.

Chapter Seven – Teachings of Elidor - 6

SVB:7:1   I will speak to you about the commonplace man. He is one in whom there is neither spirituality nor spiritual aspiration. He is not righteous, but neither is he really wicked, and he does not have any ingrained evil qualities. Because he knows neither vices nor virtues, such a man is untried and untested; he does not know what are the qualities needing development and what are the evils to avoid. He serves the cause of evil, though he is no more than a mere pawn. No man can stand aside from the conflict; men such as these are unwittingly drawn into the service of evil.

SVB:7:2   The commonplace man has an understanding of good conduct; he is genteel; he is cultured. People like him; he is at ease with them; they seek his company; he is useful to them, as they are to him. But though he is full of worldly knowledge, he has little knowledge or understanding of the scriptures, or of things transcending earthly existence. He cannot soar into the heights; his feet are planted solidly on the ground, but his wings are undeveloped. He cannot rise above the ordinary; his behaviour is that of the common crowd; he is a commonplace man. He has learnt from earthly experience and associations what conduct is right and what is wrong to serve worldly ends. This is not enough; to live fully and to good purpose, he must know more.

SVB:7:3   The commonplace woman is like the commonplace man; she moves easily in her earthly environment, but is incapable of raising her eyes above it. She has so much to stir the hearts of men; she can be so desirable; yet, she fails to inspire them. She can goad them on towards earthly goals, but not to anything greater. She can fan the flame of ambition in her children, but cannot inspire them to look beyond the world.

SVB:7:4   Commonplace people have commonplace traits and weaknesses. I will speak of one: revengefulness. An unjustifiable seeking for revenge springs from an inner weakness; the mean and servile person is most addicted to it. Malice, like revenge, is a trait of the weak, not of the strong.

SVB:7:5   If someone wrongs you without cause, do not let this disturb your tranquillity of mind. Do nothing else except scorn them. In this way, you will not be unnecessarily upset, but will also be revenged without any need for inflicting it. The tearing wind and flashing darts of lightning leave the sun and moon untroubled; their anger is vented on trees and plants below. So it is with wrongs done by mortals; the wrongs do not disturb the hearts of superior men, but cause turmoil in the fainter hearts of inferior men.

SVB:7:6 You laugh, you mock me and say, "We prefer life among the commonplace people, for they are easier to get along with; they do not criticise us." It is true, they will not; if they are unconcerned about their own future, how can they be considerate about yours? You ask why it is that the righteous people keep to themselves, while the wrongdoers are more companionable. The answer is simple, those who live good lives walk in the light and so do not fear to be alone; they have the companionship of the Spirit. The wrongdoers, however, walk in darkness and so have need of company, for they are secretly afraid.

SVB:7:7 Not long since, one came to me and said, "Prophet, I have offended against the law of the land, but not against the law of the scriptures; am I blameless?" I tell you this; the law of the land may extend out beyond the law of the scriptures, but should not conflict with it. The law outside the scriptures must also be obeyed. The law of the land is not perfect; it is made by men and cannot claim to be perfect. It should be what it is not, a pure marriage between justice and Truth, unadulterated by the deviousness of man. The child of the marriage should be loving kindness. It is not for me to tell you of these things. If men are content to suffer under bad laws, whose is the blame? The true nature of a nation is revealed in its laws.

SVB:7:8 This I do say: I condemn the lawmakers who issue unjust and devious decrees, who seek to hide their true intent under a mountain of words. I condemn the unjust laws armed with the sword of legality. I condemn the judges who spread a legal covering over cunningly laid traps and snare men in nets made with words. They deceive the ignorant and simple with false masks of legality. Truth and Justice weep outside the courthouse. I condemn also those who stir up strife under protection of the law, who cause legal mischief or deal in legal deception to rob the innocent and unwary. Wickedness has many faces, but the most hideous is that of those who twist the laws to serve selfish ends, or treat the downtrodden with harsh injustice.

SVB:7:9 I speak of these things, but I have not come to change the laws of the land or decide whether they be good or bad. I leave worldly things to worldly men. You say, "Tell us to which a man should owe greatest allegiance, to the leaders of his nation or the leader of his faith?" I say this, there is a scale of precedence, and man must serve whatever ranks highest. Spiritual things rank above worldly things, but the man who loves his nation and its customs, its mother tongue and its traditions, is a better man than one who decries them. The man who obeys his rulers, identifying himself with his people, with their progress, their welfare, their calamities, as though they were his, repenting for their wrongs and rejoicing in their triumphs, that man is a patriot, and patriotism has a proper place. He is above the commonplace man, but not above the man spiritually inclined, for spiritual things transcend earthly things. The good of all mankind transcends the good of any nation.

SVB:7:10 In keeping the laws of the scriptures, good intent is the main consideration. There must be a complete absence of hypocrisy and deviousness. I am a man with many books; I will tell you their teachings, but their words are for study by men of insight and learning. I speak in conformity with what is written, for if a prophet sets up a body of laws conflicting with established teachings, or laws claiming to replace them entirely, he is a false prophet.

SVB:7:11 Man reflects the powers, which are his heritage; he is the heir to divinity. He must, however, submit to the will of The Supreme Spirit who is much wiser than man, and this will is made known through the laws of the scriptures. Man must not submit abjectly, through fear of punishment or hope of reward, these things are unworthy of one aspiring to divinity. The will of The Supreme Spirit is revealed through those who have proved worthy of divine inspiration, who have spiritualised themselves sufficiently to communicate with the Powers Above. The prophet who has been fully tested, who has survived his trials, who knows the means for assuring himself that he speaks with divine authority, is a rarity even among prophets.

SVB:7:12 There is a spiritual value in submission to the Divine Will. Where the purpose is obscure and self-discipline required to conform, the value is even greater than where the reason is easily perceived. This discipline, too, has its value; it is the discipline of the heroic warrior, the man of courage and conviction.

SVB:7:13 The mind of man is like a water barrel placed against the house. On top floats a slimy scum of worldly lust and lewdness; beneath this grow weeds of ignorance, prejudice and selfishness. Below this is clear, clean water, unseen because of the scum above. I am one who clears away the scum; I am the revealer of the good underneath. My mission is to make the water fit for use, not to destroy the barrel.

SVB:7:14 I am not a man of fancy words. I have lived all my life among wise men and found nothing better for a man than silence. Study is not the most important thing; it is deeds. Contemplation and speech have their place, but actions shift mountains, while words blow around them. The knowledge that his soulspirit records every word makes a man careful in speech. It is the man whose inner self is wrapped in the mantle of ignorance, who keeps no rein on his tongue. If a man antagonises you, never answer him in haste; no reply at all is often an eloquent answer.

SVB:7:15 You ask me concerning marriage. Others more able than I have spoken about it; study their words. This I do say: It is not enough for husbands and wives to love each other; they must make their love known. A husband does this by showing his wife more respect than to any other woman; is she not the one he chose, or has she been chosen unwisely? If this is so, then it is wrong to make her suffer for it. A wife should be treated with delicacy and care, as the most precious of a man's possessions. As no man expects his wife to defile his home by adultery, he should commit no adultery either. A wise man leaves his wife to be mistress in his house and home; he provides for her needs to the utmost of his ability.

SVB:7:16 This is the way a wife shows her love for her husband: She is at all times affectionate and womanly, always considerate and gentle. She is careful in managing the household and supervises it diligently, being herself always neat and clean. She never does anything to cause her husband anxiety; she is never wasteful with his earnings. She pushes aside every thought of other men and never disgraces her house or shows her contempt for her husband by committing adultery.

SVB:7:17 I do not say that a wife should not think of other men, or husbands of other women; such thoughts come unbidden. It is not wrong or unnatural that they should do so, when the true nature of marriage is known. It is a state of trial; it is one of life's greatest tests; ignorance of this fact is the enemy of marriage, not human nature. However, I am not the prophet to declare such things.

SVB:7:18 Neither am I the prophet of peace; he is yet to come. I am the prophet to tell men of The Frightener, though many generations will pass before it appears. It will be a thing of monstrous greatness arising in the form of a crab; first its body will be red, then green, then blue. It will spread destruction across the Earth, running from sunrise to sunset. It will come in the Days of Decision, when men are inflicted with spiritual blindness, when one ignorance has been replaced with another, when men walk in darkness and call it light. In those days, men will yearn after pleasure and comfort; they will go down roads of ease, encouraged by women incapable of inspiring them towards the upward path.

SVB:7:19 There will be disbelief in spiritual things, but this will proceed from ignorance; it will be a thing of the lips, for disbelief is not in the heart and nature of man. No matter how much a man cries out his disbelief, in times of turmoil, in strange and unfamiliar surroundings, when frightened by the unknown, he turns to spiritual things for comfort and strength.

SVB:7:20 In the days of the great conflict, do not pray that The Supreme Spirit be on your side, this would be a futile waste of time. Pray rather that you be on the right side, the side of The Supreme Spirit.

SVB:7:21 Hear my voice, for I tell of things to come. There will be no great signs heralding the coming of The Frightener; it will come when men are least prepared. It will come when they seek only worldly things. In those days, men will be falling away from manliness and women from womanliness. It will be a time of confusion and chaos.

SVB:7:22 I have warned of The Frightener; I have done what I am charged to do. Now, one asks where he shall seek for Truth. I say this; They who set about it rightly will find Truth, no matter where their mortal bodies are located. It is never far from men. Truth is everlastingly unchangeable, Earth is false, because it changes and passes away. Truth and The Supreme Spirit are one, because they are eternal things.

SVB:7:23 Things as you see them and things as they really are, are in no way alike; illusion is the environment of Earth and it deludes the inner eyes with outward impressions. As a needle pricks a blister to let out the water, so does the sharp point of Truth pierce the veil of illusion and let out ignorance.

SVB:7:24 The mind of man is like a pool of water; while it is disturbed, only distorted pictures can be seen; but when it becomes calm and still, the light of spiritual Truth is reflected there in all its beauty. The inner being interprets things through a veil of emotion. The man who burns hotly within himself sees the world about him as a fierce fire seeking to consume him; but the man who is calm and quiet within sees all about him as tranquil and peaceful.

SVB:7:25 Everyone suffers from certain fears in one form or another; the feelings of anxiety, doubt, frustration and despair are only normal, but to be overwhelmed by them is a sign of weakness and immaturity. Therefore, to those who are fearful and anxious or have doubts, more will be sent, for this is meant to be experienced and overcome. Only by this means can man prepare himself for the greater tests ahead. Calmness, love, steadfastness and tenacity are the sentinels outside the first gate of spiritual development. Mere ceremonial, however uplifting, cannot of itself bring the soulspirit of man into contact with the Powers Above; something more is required.

SVB:7:26 You ask how much more sorrow one must suffer to win freedom from sorrow. There can be no such freedom on Earth; the waters of sorrow are drawn from a bottomless well. Only when the eye becomes incapable of some tears does it really see fully.

Chapter Eight –
Elidor Speaks to His Disciples

SVB:8:1 I have chosen you from the many because of your eagerness, your attentiveness, your serenity and your self-discipline. These are the basic qualities required. You must also prove yourselves loyal and adaptable, strong and trustworthy, intelligent and unselfish, free of all vices and bad traits, efficient, self-reliant and stable. When I was given my prophethood, I was told to initiate only the worthy persons who had proven their self-mastery and trustworthiness.

SVB:8:2 Each of you must snap the knot of the heart. You must study the scriptures constantly, and apart from these, read words, which are beautiful, inspiring and true. You must constantly strive for tranquillity of heart, for self-control, for self-harmony; be kind and considerate at all times, and always maintain purity of thought.

SVB:8:3 Live good lives; practise frugality, but false austerity for your own inner edification is impure. When self-control or self-discipline become self inflicted torture, or when their intent is to hurt another, then they are servants of evil. However, sacrifices such as I have taught, the kindly acts of everyday living, are not to be abandoned because you are disciples. Strive each day to achieve greater self-harmony, for this is the swiftest path upward.

SVB:8:4 The senses and body cravings must be disciplined, otherwise they would assume control. It is not sufficient to be spiritually developed, you must ensure that the body is completely controlled by the soulspirit within. Therefore, you must not succumb before the rigours of life. You must not pamper yourselves; you must obtain victory over heat and cold, over the craving for food and drink, over the weaknesses of the flesh and over the call of comfort. You must cultivate persistence and resolution, for determination is essential on the path.

SVB:8:5 The women must practise all womanly virtues, such as decorum, decency, pity, modesty, sincerity, devotion, purity in all things, cleanliness and love of love. They must be free of all sensuality, lewdness and crudeness. They must maintain an evenness of mind through all things, whether pleasant or unpleasant. They must aim for a single outpouring of pure love, a love never straying, never deceptive. They must have contentment of heart, so that they can enjoy solitude, avoiding vain enjoyments and the noisy multitude.

SVB:8:6   The men must seek contentment and calmness within and outwardly display a steadfast and unruffled front. They must be courageous, generous, truthful, strong in character and healthy in body. They must cheerfully accept austerity and have the ability to endure privation, solitude and a rigorous life. They will have a distaste for aggression, for bullying, for the arrogant and haughty, for the cruel and for the boasters.

SVB:8:7   In men and women, there will be a constant yearning to awaken the soulspirit; there is to be an ideal to be upheld and a vision to follow. You may practise all things and follow any way of life consistent with the spiritual aims set out in the scriptures.

SVB:8:8   Hating another unjustifiably is wrong, but hatred itself is not necessarily wrong. There is no wrong in hating cruelty, wickedness, arrogance and many other things of evil. The measure of all things is to be how they effect the sole aim and purpose of life, the upward flight of man.

SVB:8:9   In seeking contentment and peace, beware that you do not fall into the pits of complacency, passiveness and inertia. Apathy also sets its trap, and when caught in any of these, you will be doomed to a spiritual death. The purpose of earthly life is to experience. Therefore, be wise enough to understand that though contentment and peace may be desirable, they are no more than that, they are not prime objectives.

SVB:8:10   There are two kinds of people in the world. There are those who must chase enjoyment and pleasure because there is no happiness within them; they are empty and have to suck happiness from people with whom they associate, or from their environment, or have to obtain it by external stimulation. Those are the spiritually deficient. Then there are those who are inwardly happy; they shed joy and contentment; wherever they go, they are a lamp of happiness giving out a bright glow which all may enjoy. Those can enjoy external things and find happiness outside themselves, but are not dependent on them. They are the spiritually healthy.

SVB:8:11   Some people are like the uncomprehending butterflies fluttering aimlessly from flower to flower of sensation and pleasure. Then, there are the spiritually strong who are like hawk-eyed birds flying directly towards their objective, riding high above lower creatures. Those are the two kinds of people, but the spiritually deficient cannot recognise themselves.

SVB:8:12   Always seek the beautiful in life, and add to it. Turn aside from all forms of vulgarity and crudeness, but it would be better to replace them with graciousness and loveliness. However, do not forget that all too often, a man seeking the beautiful becomes soft, and it is well established that beauty can ruin a man. Be a man of few words; this does not mean become dumb, but make your words have value; it means avoid idle chatter.

SVB:8:13   A man can be judged by the company he keeps, so make sure you are always in good company. Avoid all persons of bad repute, for they follow a path of destruction. Be vigorous and alive, never fearing hard work; no living man can ever fully renounce work or effort, so avoid being numbered among the dead.

SVB:8:14   Be a Master of Life; this is one who has his body and emotions firmly in rein. Though hard pressed by tribulations and afflictions, he remains steadfast; his mind is never confused. He knows what has to be done, what is expected of him, and does it. He strikes swiftly when action is needed, or just keeps plodding along the path. His mind is clear regarding his duty, and he knows his obligations and does not shirk them. He is always a pillar of strength to his weaker brethren.

SVB:8:15   Who are the Masters of Life? When you can ride the stormy seas of sorrow, when you are not overcome by pleasure, when you can control the passions, master fear, discard anger, and whatever comes, maintain a quiet and steady manner, you will be a Master of Life.

SVB:8:16   When you can accept all your obligations cheerfully, do your duty at all times, accept whatever comes, be it good or ill, with steadfast heart, remain calm in the midst of confusion and upheaval, you will be a Master of Life.

SVB:8:17   When you can temper all your desires with prudence, resist temptations to weakness and bring all urges under control; when you can bring all senses into harmony, control all emotion, overcome the greed for possessions, smother unwholesome desires, you will be a Master of Life. When you can subdue anger, dispel dismay, never forget where your duty lies and be completely free from confusion of mind, you will be a Master of Life.

SVB:8:18 As the worldly work selfishly and in bondage to worldliness, so does the Master of Life work unselfishly for the good of mankind. He is inspired by the highest ideals of man. He knows that hatred and cruelty, lust and desire for possessions have their roots in the lower natures of men, in the beast within them. These things the Masters learned long ago. Searching their hearts with wisdom, they found a stirring response to something greater and discovered the bond of union between man and the spirit. When the Master of Life knows his true nature and understands the unity of contact, he is freed from all delusion and sorrow; he rises to something greater above.

SVB:8:19 Self-control and harmony form the first step towards becoming a Master of Life. Harmony meaning tranquillity within and harmonious relationships without. Self-control means self-control in all things. Even an artist must exercise self-control when creating; the tradesman must control his sharp tools, and the physician his knife. Everything man does requires self-control in one form or another.

SVB:8:20 The Master of Life has to do more than this; he has to transform his whole life into a creative act, self-control and creativity going hand in hand. Only self-control of itself is not enough; it must be subordinated to goodwill and loving kindness.

SVB:8:21 The Master of Life must be conscious of his true nature. He must develop the threefold power: self-control, creativity and effort within himself, and reach out for the threefold unattainables beyond: love, perfection, and Truth.

SVB:8:22 You, my disciples, must become Masters of Life, never regretting the past nor worrying about the future, but always applying yourselves to whatever is in hand at present. The Masters of Life know what are good thoughts and what are bad thoughts, the first being beneficial, the second not. They know what to tell and what not to tell; they know what to do and what not to do; they know what serves and what does not, what is good and what is bad.

SVB:8:23 If a house is seen to be on fire, this immediately suggests the getting of water or saving whatever may be within. The commonplace man does not know how to act; he acts foolishly or in haste. The Master of Life does not get excited; he keeps his head. He does not stand aside wringing his hands, he does not rush about or get in the way, impeding others; he does not raise his voice, he does not offer futile sympathy. He remains calm and quietly and efficiently does what needs doing; he takes charge or places himself at the disposal of those who are better fitted to assume control.

SVB:8:24 The Master of Life is not bound by fetters the ignorant wear; neither is he misguided into ways of darkness by the blind. Every thought and act is considered, for he knows the power of oft-repeated thoughts, desires and actions to cut deep grooves into the soulspirit. He is no longer a prisoner of the flesh, but the charioteer of his body.

SVB:8:25 I call upon each of you to take up your burden and travel the long road leading to mastership of life. The progress of all Pilgrims who have taken this road is indicated by their conduct. The instability has been left behind; the excesses are gone; the demanding desires are dropped; the spitefulness, greed and conceit have been discarded; wickedness and malice are thrown aside. One by one they have been sloughed off, as a snake sheds its skin.

SVB:8:26 As Masters of Life, you will call upon others to follow you in the pilgrimage. They will have to be resolute and strong, willing to devote their whole lives to serving the cause of Truth. They will have to study diligently the pages of the scriptures and search ever deeper into the inmost recesses of their being. Their first step will be in overcoming the greatest of all man's delusions: that of thinking the body comprises the whole being.

SVB:8:27 As Masters of Life, you will set an example far beyond reach of the commonplace man. You will be known from others by a profound serenity and resolute steadfastness, just as the commonplace man is distinguished by ignorance, by restlessness, the urge to hide himself in pleasure and by enslavement to prejudice and emotion.

SVB:8:28 Poise and confidence, the marks of real wisdom and knowledge, distinguish the Masters of Life. Unsteadiness, shiftiness, unreliability, ever changing opinions and fluctuating loyalties distinguish the commonplace man. Undue consideration for the outer body and the satisfaction of its desires marks the commonplace man, and his concern for material things is the prime cause of his delusion. In a Master of Life, the mind has escaped from worldly delusions, like a bird freed from its cage, and in the liberated mind every doubt is stilled by certainty.

SVB:8:29 My disciples, heed what I say. Be steadfast in heart and mind, dogged in pursuing the pilgrimage, cheerfully accepting the trials and tribulations, which will beset you. Always seek the companionship of congenial and thoughtful fellow wayfarers. If you must pray, then remember the prayers of quiet silence.

SVB:8:30 Develop your soulspirit by contemplation of life, meditation of the scriptures and visualisation of the soulspirit's form of beauty and glory. The following are things you must strive against and overcome, so that they are completely banished from your nature, you have heard them before, but they cannot be repeated too often: all forms of anger, recklessness, cruelty and boastfulness; all tendencies towards falsehood, deceit and dishonesty, or towards lewdness, obscenity or lust; fornication, seduction and the degradation of women are forbidden; cheating, insincerity, gossiping, slander and talebearing are unworthy of you; such things as an unforgiving nature, moral weakness, cowardice, instability, irresolution, fickleness and intemperance are to be eliminated; undue love of comfort, of worldly or sensual pleasures and all forms of uncleanliness in mind and body must be overcome; stomach gratification is not wrong, but is not to be overdone.

SVB:8:31 Never indulge in argument or discussion as to the form and nature of The Supreme Spirit, for this is folly. An understanding of these is beyond the unawakened finite mind, though the mind of a Master may grasp what they are; therefore, defer all argument and discussion until you are one.

SVB:8:32 There is much talk among you concerning the nature of worship. Understand this: true worship is seeking to unite the spirit below with the Spirit Above. To do this you must have a heart purged of all evil thoughts, a tongue undefiled by falsehood or tainted with deceit and hypocrisy, and a life free of all malice and hatred. Even this is not enough; you must have a life filled with love and good deeds. Only when in this state are you fit to worship. When you talk about the worthlessness of worship, are you condemning yourselves? Purifying worship of which you speak means all acts, which tend to burn up carnality and worldliness within the body.

SVB:8:33 As true disciples, you must spend your whole conscious life in purposeful and constructive thinking. You must be doers, not dreamers. When you withdraw into the silence to worship, remember the great jewels of prayer: serenity, purity and trust. The prophets who have gone before held that a kindly and pure heart is the only worship required to benefit man; this may be so, but surely tranquillity and trust are also needed.

SVB:8:34 You will learn that the true greatness and goodness of Pilgrims travelling the road with you are often hidden from the eyes of men, because of their unusual way of life. Commonplace men will often think them deluded or men who have lost their reason. How many of you have not hesitated because you feared the opinions of others, the entreaties of loved ones or the thoughts of possible suffering and discomfort?

SVB:8:35 I have spoken of discomfort; this I say again; too much comfort is not for you, neither should you sleep too much or too little. You must overcome all tendencies towards sloth and carelessness, for these will sap your spiritual stamina.

SVB:8:36 Do not be impatient for advancement; slow progress is often the best. If someone breaks a hatching egg before its time, no chick will emerge. When the time is ripe, the shell will be broken from within and a healthy chick will emerge to life. If the shell is broken before the chick is ready, that chick will be dead. So it is with the awakening soulspirit, let it emerge from within, of its own accord. Until you have purged your hearts of all impurities and washed away all the worldly filth, you cannot even set foot on the lower rung of the ladder leading to enlightenment and awakening.

SVB:8:37 When you speak of the mating of spirit and mortal, you are wrong. Under no circumstances can spirit mate with mortal, though it is certainly true that spirit can enter mortal. It is well to know what spirit can do and what it cannot do, for it has its limitations.

SVB:8:38 Should any man come, directly seeking Truth and knowledge of the True Way, let him first seek someone to introduce him into the body of the select who wait. Then in the course of time, as he is observed and his manner of talk and bearing is noted, so will one come to him and call him before the primary selector. Life is such that though it is easy enough to become an intimate of a moderately good or bad man, it is difficult indeed to meet a really good one.

SVB:8:39 You will choose candidates for discipleship who may become Masters of Life; no commonplace man may be accepted. They must be calm and wise, recognising what is real, desirable, important and true, and what is false, illusive, trivial and unworthy of attention. They must be ones who have overcome and are aware of true values, who have no inclinations towards anything not actively assisting them in the search. They must not be weak of character, neither must they be seeking a refuge. Three things must be brought together in combination: the sacred scriptures, the wise instructor and the eager and diligent pupil. The sacred scriptures are not to be swallowed as one does a medicinal compound, they are to be assimilated slowly and digested with reason and experience.

SVB:8:40 True enlightenment and the road to Truth are found only by way of intelligence rooted in truthfulness and reason. Some have said it is difficult to be both intelligent and absolutely sincere after examining true motives, but this shall not apply to the chosen candidates.

SVB:8:41 Never forget; it is the meaning, not the mere form of words in the sacred scriptures, which is of value. A silken mantle may look better than a coarse, woollen one, but which serves best in providing warmth? Also keeping mind that the scriptures are guides; they cannot undertake the hard work, nor assume the burden; these are things for the candidates alone. The purpose of the sacred scriptures is also to show men what life should be, how they should be governed, how they should conduct themselves, what they should keep and what they should discard.

Chapter Nine –
Elidor on the Sacred Scriptures

SVB:9:1 These are the sacred scriptures which are not like other scriptures, they are the scriptures of those who follow the Great Path of the True Way. They are not for the mocker, the unbeliever, the man of worldly affairs or the evildoer. They shall move forward with the ages, keeping abreast of man as he advances. They must evolve to keep pace with his growing intelligence, but he must also evolve spiritually. If he does not, then they must assume the burden and come forth to lead him.

SVB:9:2 There are men satiated with worldly learning, who have fallen into the pit dug by their own books. They are gorged and uncomfortable; their diversity of opinions and thought confuses them. The study of the sacred scriptures is not for the curious; it is useless unless the student knows where he is heading, his destination, unless he has an end in view. Though the truth within the sacred scriptures is unalterable, can never change, the revelation can always be interpreted according to man's progress. The hidden truths are to be made available to man whenever he is ready. The spiritual man who is truly awakened sees much more in the words than the commonplace man, who may see no more than the letters and words. Yet words are a forest, in which man can easily lose his way. Fine sentences and a grand manner of expression may just be a lure and a covering for the pit and stake.

SVB:9:3 There are those who talk about spiritual things, but do no more than weave a web of words to trap the unwary. To derive benefit from a bottle of physic, the contents must be taken, merely reading the inscriptions will effect no cure.

SVB:9:4 My disciples, read the sacred scriptures diligently, and never abandon your work and studies, for to do so when you are struggling to cross the stream of life shows lack of resolution, and it achieves nothing. You will sacrifice your own self-assurance; your inspiration will be lost. Never forget, these words are not fair weather friends; they are not things of feathers to blow away before a slight wind. They are stones in a solid causeway, firm and reliable under all conditions. Take these sacred scriptures as your daily guide, make them your advisor whenever a problem arises. Unless they are put into practice, they remain valueless, just things to be thought about in idle moments.

SVB:9:5   Pure reason, like bitter essence, is worthless alone. Even as the essence must be made palatable and drinkable by the addition of water, so must pure reason be diluted by faith.

SVB:9:6   The sacred scriptures are the midwife and nurse of the soulspirit. Some awaken the soulspirit by meditation; sometimes it is awakened through a vision; in some it awakens through good works, in others through labour. It can be awakened by creativity and love, there are many means to suit the numerous conditions of men. A few may not feel the stirrings of an awakening soulspirit; some may rely only on the words of others, but because they believe and act accordingly these, too, shall awaken to conscious survival.

SVB:9:7   So wonderful is the state of a newly awakened soulspirit, so delightful the experience of sudden realisation, that none who has known it will ever forget. None will ever find words adequate to describe it to others. There is no thought except a deep awareness of life, of being. There is a sense of deeper reality than that of ordinary consciousness. Faith in the reality of the soulspirit then gives way to certainty and assurance, for how can any man doubt the greatest experience of his life?

SVB:9:8   The glory of the stars shining in the nightskies is truly revealed once in the darkness. It is as children that men begin to sense the mystery of silence, the mystery, which reveals the universe. Silence is the secret of the soulspirit.

SVB:9:9   There are dark doctrines, which tell of soulspirits condemned to everlasting darkness and torment, but this is not so. They are not condemned to suffer forever, for after a long interval, they are taken out and recast. They are like mis-shapen casts of metal which are thrown back into the furnace to mingle and blend together, coming out purified and pliable, ready to be cast into new form. They come back to Earth completely unconscious of the past; it is lost to them in the purifying fires of the furnace, and so they start again. As a lump of salt dissolved in water, which can never regain its former shape, so are they.

LUC:1:6 Nothing, except The Supreme Spirit, can have a real, self-contained and independent existence. This does not mean that nothing else is real, and by 'illusion' is meant deception by the senses, which interpret falsely. Man is deluded by his senses and so cannot distinguish the real from the unreal.

Table of Chapters

LUC:1:1 – LUC:1:13	Chapter One – The Spheres of Existence	65
LUC:2:1 – LUC:2:16	Chapter Two – Vision of the Holy Spirit and Creation	66
LUC:3:1 – LUC:3:12	Chapter Three – The Making of Man	68
LUC:4:1 – LUC:4:17	Chapter Four – Man - Bond and Free	69
LUC:5:1 – LUC:5:11	Chapter Five – The Wandering Mission	72
LUC:6:1 – LUC:6:16	Chapter Six – The Forest Mission - 1	73
LUC:7:1 – LUC:7:16	Chapter Seven – The Forest Mission - 2	75
LUC:8:1 – LUC:8:18	Chapter Eight – The Forest Mission - 3	77
LUC:9:1 – LUC:9:12	Chapter Nine – The Forest Mission - 4	79
LUC:10:1 – LUC:10:4	Chapter Ten – The Mangod	80
LUC:11:1 – LUC:11:11	Chapter Eleven – The Vision of Evening	81
LUC:12:1 – LUC:12:24	Chapter Twelve – The Bodiless Body	82
LUC:13:1 – LUC:13:28	Chapter Thirteen – The Lifeforce	85
LUC:14:1 – LUC:14:21	Chapter Fourteen – The Last Forest Teachings	88

Book of Lucius

Chapter One – The Spheres of Existence

LUC:1:1 This is the whole law needful for man to direct his life: Know your nature, do your duty and live in harmony with others. To live in harmony means doing wrong to no man.

LUC:1:2 There is one Supreme Spirit, which men call God, because God means Allgood. But because men seek a closer relationship with The Supreme Spirit of Good, they refer to it as Father and as Him, and there is no wrong in this.

LUC:1:3 The Supreme Spirit contains the essences of all the perfections, and these flow out from Him in a form of vitality, which is called The Holy Spirit. The Sphere of The Holy Spirit surrounds the Sphere of The Supreme Spirit, and around this again, and below it, is the Sphere of Matter and Mortality.

LUC:1:4 In the sphere of Matter and Mortality, the Holy Spirit manifests imperfectly, for here it becomes mingled with the inert composition of this Sphere. Also, the penetrated offers resistance to the penetrator, and this, combined with the effects of intermingling, causes obscurity, illusion and ignorance. These are visualised in the form of a mist called 'agnosia.'

LUC:1:5 The activity of The Supreme Spirit in the Highest Sphere is unceasing, and this alone maintains the Universes of Matter. The basis of matter is an outflow of energy from The Supreme Spirit, which forms a kind of framework solidifying at its outer edge. The three Spheres comprise the whole, no part of which is devoid of the vitality originating within The Supreme Spirit. So the statement that The Supreme Spirit is in all and all is in The Supreme Spirit is true, though He does not manifest in the Sphere of obscurity, illusion and imperfection. This does not mean that The Supreme Spirit could not manifest here, or that the Sphere of Matter and Mortality is beyond His reach. These conditions serve a specific purpose.

LUC:1:6 Nothing, except The Supreme Spirit, can have a real, self-contained and independent existence. This does not mean that nothing else is real, and by 'illusion' is meant deception by the senses, which interpret falsely. Man is deluded by his senses and so cannot distinguish the real from the unreal.

LUC:1:7 All the Universes of Matter are contained within the Sphere of Matter and Mortality, which reaches out to touch the Sphere of the Holy Spirit.

LUC:1:8 Their greatness exceeds the bounds of man's most daring imagination, and even if man could penetrate through to their limits, he would still find The Supreme Spirit veiled and hidden.

LUC:1:9 The Holy Spirit flows from The Supreme Spirit, as heat and light flow from the sun, and, penetrating all things, holds them in form and solidity. The Supreme Spirit alone is unpenetrated by anything, He alone is whole and fully self-sufficient. He alone is the One Pure Essence.

LUC:1:10 The Sphere of The Holy Spirit is divided into Subspheres, and the Sphere of Matter and Mortality is likewise divided. The Supreme Ruler of the Sphere of The Holy Spirit is The Holy Spirit, and The Supreme Ruler of the Sphere of Matter and Mortality is Nature. So all the material universes are governed by one set of laws called The Law of Nature. Nature is the effect and manifestation of the activity of The Holy Spirit operating in matter, where reality is relative and not absolute.

LUC:1:11 The earthly body of man, his moral shell and spirit container, is moulded before birth by following a soul pattern drawn by destiny. Once born, many forces influence the life of man on Earth, but he is also given the responsibility of free choice. Notwithstanding this, the life of any man can only follow a course set by destiny, but while on that course, he can do as he wills.

LUC:1:12 Every single thought and act on Earth has its effect on the soulspirit projected into the Sphere of Matter and Mortality. Man himself is a threefold being comprising soul, spirit and matter, each having an affinity with one of the Spheres of Existence. Here on Earth the soulspirit is made ready for its life in the Higher Spheres, or it is neglected and ignored.

LUC:1:13 This is the outline of Truth, within which our master taught, and Pemantris, his devoted disciple, has recorded what follows. He taught to seven only, in a small hermitage beside the forest brook.

Chapter Two –
Vision of the Holy Spirit and Creation

LUC:2:1 My friends, the power of The Holy Spirit has led you here and directed your footsteps, so that you may be well guided in ascending the heights of divinity. No others shall be admitted to our circle, for so profound a subject as that dealt with here would be profaned by the presence of many.

LUC:2:2 To understand The Supreme Spirit is difficult, but enlightenment may be granted to those who diligently follow the Great Path towards spiritual development. To describe Him to others is impossible, for no man possesses the eloquence, and no tongue has adequate words. Then, too, it is difficult for the imperfect to grasp the meaning of perfection, or for the visible to comprehend the invisible beyond its range of vision. The Eternal is so distant from the Sphere of Mortal Man that the beauty there can only be glimpsed as a dim reflection. This is well, for if unshielded from the beauty beyond vision, mortal man would be consumed in its brilliance.

LUC:2:3 Without His creation, The Supreme Spirit would be uncontrasted and therefore not really supreme, so He created. No man has ever seen Him and lived, though many have been granted a sight of His reflection. So if any man says to you, "I have seen The Supreme Spirit and now understand His nature," be sure he has not seen Him, but only some distorted reflection. The Truth is that The Supreme Spirit is not understandable to us mortals. He is far beyond mortal conception, and hence, many say He is non-existent.

LUC:2:4 The Supreme Spirit is outside and beyond His creation, but His radiance is the basis of all things together. He is the Central Flame, and the souls of men are rushlights lit at the flame but enclosed behind thick horn, so that they scarcely shine. The task is to pare down the horn, so that the light within shines brightly.

LUC:2:5 Being without material restrictions, The Supreme Spirit is bodiless, and such a state is hard for the bodilocked man to conceive. But man does not contact Him through the body but only through the soulspirit, and certain places and conditions are designed to help man make contact.

LUC:2:6 Men may call The Supreme Spirit by any other name, which conveys a meaning of divine greatness. Provided the name is hallowed and held in reverence, there is no need to go into definitions, for this is an unworthy pursuit. Not any name or all names could adequately describe what is beyond description. The only way, in which man can come to fully know the nature of The Supreme Spirit is through The Holy Spirit, through whose Sphere passes the Godward Road. This is all I need say about The Great Name.

LUC:2:7   When I was young, I thought much about life here and above, and in times of sublime contemplation, my inner being appeared to penetrate into the very heart of things. Once, I became aware of a presence like that of some infinitely Good and Great Being who spoke to me, asking what I wished to learn and know. I answered, "I wish to learn the nature of things and my own relationships with them. I wish to know the purpose of life and why I was born." The Great Being seemed to speak again with a voice resounding in my whole being, "I know what you seek and what drives you to search. I carry the power of knowing all, and my vitality is a spring whose waters are available for the refreshment of every questing soulspirit. I am the manifestation of The Holy Spirit."

LUC:2:8   When the voice had finished speaking, a brilliant light seemed to glow all about me, and vast, radiant corridors appeared to open up in every direction. I became filled with an overwhelming feeling of love, and all about me shimmered soft lights, from out of which proceeded the most melodious sounds. Then, from one side came a dark and gloomy cloud, and I was filled with foreboding as it writhed and twisted like a heavy smoke. From out of it came the sound of wailing, and there was a low-murmuring moaning long-drawn-out.

LUC:2:9   Then I heard an exquisite sound, which rose and fell like the notes of a divine melody, and between the brightness and the dark cloud, a wall seemed to condense. It appeared to be of iridescent glass containing a living flame, not set in form, but with a flexible movement. From the wall came a kind of softly glowing vapour, which then rose above it.

LUC:2:10   I heard the voice again and it said, "Have you seen and understood?" I said, "I have seen, but understanding has not been granted." Then The Holy Spirit said, "I am the light and the light is mind. The darkness and the cloud are agnosia, which seeks to increase its sphere by the agency of man. But the wall prevents it, and the wall is the mind of the Spirit. It is the barrier, which agnosia cannot penetrate. The mind of man is a ray from The Holy Spirit pinpointed upon the spirit enclosed within a mortal body. Mortal existence is an echo, through the corridors of time, of the word spoken in the Chamber of Eternity. The Sphere of The Holy Spirit is where mind manifests freely, unhampered by mortal limitations."

LUC:2:11   I looked again, and the cloud and wall were gone, and then I saw the brilliance was divided by lights of many shades. Where the cloud had been, I saw a dullness amid brilliance, and then I seemed to be standing before it. I looked into the dullness as though down a corridor, and along its length, the darkness increased, so that at the end there was a deep-shaded gloom. In the dismal shadow I saw ugly, mis-shapen things moving sluggishly, as though the life within them was weak. They were creatures such as haunt the most horrid nightmare, and my eyes could not bear to rest upon them. I turned away, and the voice said, "In the place where garbage is disposed, life assumes unpleasant forms, and this is the spirit garbage of Earth."

LUC:2:12   Then I was drawn back into the light, and all about me was a joyousness and gaiety, which seemed to have no perceivable source, but to be a quality of the atmosphere.

LUC:2:13   As I stood joyfully, bewildered in the radiance, I saw beautiful shapes, which appeared to come and go like fishes swimming in and out of the water shadows. I sensed rather than heard laughter and the sounds of happiness, and my whole being seemed to be filled with joyful communications.

LUC:2:14   Again, I heard the voice and it said, "This is the beauty and glory so feebly glimpsed in earthly existence; this is the diadem of life. When mind first penetrated mind-created matter, it brought light and life into being in greater and lesser degrees of manifestation. While the heavier mortal elements of matter tended downwards, those, in which light and life manifested the most, tended upwards, towards eventual spiritualisation. When spiritualised, they were drawn, by natural affinity, into the Sphere of Beauty and Glory. Affinity directs the course of all things and governs the destinies of men. The thought that flows out through The Holy Spirit bears designs for structures of beauty to the boundary of the Sphere of Matter and Mortality, but the deeper it penetrates, the more these are distorted and dispersed. So it is that things unbeautiful and unsightly are produced in the depths of matter under the rulership of Nature. In the reasonless density of the lower subspheres of matter, the influence of creative mind is less manifest. Elsewhere in the same sphere can be seen the effects of evil mind energy, which floats up like fumes from the disposal pit of spiritual garbage."

LUC:2:15 Then I said, "But what caused all this to come into being," and the voice of The Holy Spirit answered, "All things began with the intoning of the first creative sound. This rushed outward like a great wind-borne roar, and creation marked its passage. Then, like a great tidal wave falling back towards the sea, it drew back on itself, leaving the least of its substance at the farthest point of penetration. The waters of creation are deepest in the Sphere of The Holy Spirit and shallower at the spiritual edge of the Sphere of Matter and Mortality. Outward from there, they lessen to nothing."

LUC:2:16 "Now", said I, "understanding is mine, but what of man; what of myself? How was man created?" The voice of the Good and Great Being which I knew to be a personalised manifestation of The Holy Spirit, answered me.

Chapter Three – The Making of Man

LUC:3:1 "The image and nature of The Supreme Spirit reside in the soulseed of man, just as the image and nature of an oak tree reside in an acorn. The pattern for the mortal body of man was formed in the Sphere of The Holy Spirit and projected to the Sphere of Matter and Mortality where Nature built upon it. When the time was ripe, the body prepared by Nature was implanted with the soulseed of divinity, and the creature of Earth became a man. From that day, man, unlike all other living things on Earth, became a twofold being in his own right, mortal in body but immortal in soulspirit. He is immortal only because he has been made the heir of divinity, and as such, all things are within his grasp. He is mortal because he lives within a mortal shell and is subject to a destiny in mortality."

LUC:3:2 I said to the Being who seemed so near, "Whatever man was when given divine life, it is said that he suffered a downfall or disinheritance." I heard the voice say in reply, "Man will not be disinherited, but he can make what he will of his birthright. The downfall of man was a fall from the sunlit heights of spirituality into the dark valley of agnosia. It was also a fall from a position of responsibility and trust, and man has yet to regain that position."

LUC:3:3 "Man fell because he declined to undergo the necessary preparation and discipline needed by one who aspires to climb the heights. Also, he possessed the powers of creation, and being free could express them as he pleased. Man used them to satisfy his lower desires and so brought about his own downfall. Since then, he has no longer enjoyed them to the full. Given freewill and the ability, it was intended that man should direct his own evolution, but he proved unequal to the task."

LUC:3:4 "Man was intended to be the redeemer of reasonless matter and the controller of Nature; for that reason, he was first called Lord of Creation. But it was Nature herself, who dominated the will of man and tempted him to betray his trust. She lured him into entanglement with the senses, so that instead of being free, he became the slave of desire. The sweetness of the bait disguised the poison it contained, and the spirit of man was dragged into forgetfulness and mindlessness."

LUC:3:5 "Instead of being the master of a noble steed galloping along the road to immortality, man was now a blind creature bound upon a runaway horse. Notwithstanding this, he found the sensation enjoyable, believing that in being freed from the responsibility of control, he had found true freedom. Man made little effort to assume control, for this meant struggle, effort and responsibility, and so he remained in the state of spiritual inertia called the Mire of Matter. The soulspirit had entered the body, only to be caught in the toils of the flesh. Man was heading in the wrong direction, and the way was all uphill."

LUC:3:6 "So now you see," the voice continued, "that man was made a twofold being. Within, though this is a misleading description, is the soulspirit, but to all outward appearances, man is a mortal shell subject to decay. Though born to a heritage of divinity, man himself has freely chosen to suffer as the slave of his desires and the vassal of his weakness. He has bartered his spiritual birthright for a handful of fragile material baubles. Man, becoming enamoured of the glitter from the first bauble offered, has lost his sense of values and has closed his eyes to things of real value. He has drunk the material waters of spiritual oblivion and now lies asleep beside the stagnant pool. He slumbers, awaiting the Day of The Awakener."

LUC:3:7 There were things I understood and things I could not understand, and I said to the Good and Great Being, "If The Supreme Spirit is indeed the essence of love and kindness, could He not have created man in conditions, which gave him complete contentment and happiness, absolutely free from pain, sorrow and restraint? Is all this suffering and distress really necessary?" The reply came as though radiating from a Being full of compassion and understanding, "He could have created a perfect being and placed him in a condition of absolute contentment and happiness, but what purpose would this serve? Could such a being respond to love? Where could he learn its full meaning except in a state of lovelessness? Such things as love, pity, gratitude, mercy, unselfishness and all the other virtues are uncreatable qualities which can come into existence only through experience. Nothing can realise itself through a state of purity and perfection. Only by contrast can it become conscious of its existence."

LUC:3:8 "Pain checks man in the midst of senseless enjoyment and makes him ponder his fate. It causes him to turn his thoughts towards greater things and to reflect on the approach of death. Suffering, sorrow and trouble are tests, which, if passed successfully, qualify the soulspirit for entry into the greater sphere of existence. They create in him the qualities, which are needed there. To those who realise that these tests and trials have a purpose, they do not appear too harsh. But to those who cannot rise above them or who blame The Supreme Spirit or their fellowmen for what befalls them, the tests and trials appear as unnecessary hardships barely endurable."

LUC:3:9 "Regarding restraint, ask yourself what it teaches and what qualities it creates, and then you will know whether it is necessary. Does not restraint also lead to greater enjoyment and appreciation? No man can say that the ordinances of The Law really detract from the joys of life. Neither can it be said they are obstacles to the gratification of normal desires and the natural craving for pleasure. Read and examine them carefully; to what normal desire do they deny gratification? What natural impulse do they attempt to destroy? What reasonable pleasure do they prohibit, and what beneficial outlet do they seek to suppress?"

LUC:3:10 "On the contrary, the ordinances of The Law seek only to elevate and purify the lower impulses and bodily desires by controlling them with wise limitations, seeking only to subordinate them when it serves a greater good. Mortal cravings are made subject to higher aims, while lust and carnal passions are transmuted into useful material for constructing the glorious palace of love."

LUC:3:11 "The ordinances of The Law are a means of guiding the evolving man towards beneficial and necessary ends. They unyieldingly oppose the bestial urges and the craving for harmful pleasures. They oppose the tendency towards mortal inertia, which expresses itself in apathy and indifference, in the search for comfort and ease. There are things, which, though harmful, they do not absolutely forbid and seek instead to utilise towards a good end."

LUC:3:12 I said, "This I understand; if the world was created to serve man, then its fate depends upon his conduct."

Chapter Four – Man - Bond and Free

LUC:4:1 These things were revealed to me in the days of my youth, while I was still pure-minded and unsullied by the world. For I, like primal man, was tempted and fell, but though my descent took no more than a few days, the way back took twice as many years. Yet the things I learned when elevated in spirit to the Sphere above have always remained clear in my mind. If then you ask, why did I who had been granted this vision fall from grace, let me say that the pitfall was well and artfully covered. It was not baited by things that usually tempt, but by imitations and representations of things which usually inspire the best in men. Man is a crafty fish not easily caught, and the hook must be carefully concealed and the bait well chosen.

LUC:4:2 My friends, it would serve no purpose for me to tell the tale of my own fall, for never are two birds brought down by the same arrow. It serves better to tell what I learned in the Sphere of The Holy Spirit, and this is what I discovered about man fallen into bondage, or into slumber.

LUC:4:3 "The Supreme Spirit communicated with man through The Holy Spirit, and the message was that he should multiply and cover the Earth. Man was told to never forget that he was the custodian of his race and the designer of his earthly dominion. He was also told that submission to carnal desires meant spiritual death and that love is a lady worthy of the greatest respect, and not a menial serving maid attending to the demands of a master. Those were the things man was told, but he gave heed only to the first."

LUC:4:4 "The man who has recognised his true nature has already stepped into the domain of spirituality. The man who has craved only for things pleasing to the mortal body and been led astray by carnal urges is lost and wanders aimlessly in the darkness of moral wastes. His doom is to be devoured by damnation, the predator of these wastes."

LUC:4:5 The stern manner of speech appalled me and I asked, "Why must the ignorant suffer dire consequences, and why is man not more fully warned?" The voice of The Holy Spirit answered me, "The ignorant do not suffer because they are ignorant, for that is the state, into which they were born. They suffer because they are content to remain in that state and have chosen to take the easy road of effortlessness. The consequences of ignorance alone are not so dire; it is wickedness, chosen either deliberately or unthinkingly, that damns a man. What he suffers is not a punishment but the natural consequence of his actions. If a man places his hand upon a hot iron and is burnt, the pain is not a punishment but the consequence of his actions. If a man cuts himself, he must expect to bleed, and if he walks through mud, he cannot expect to remain unsoiled.

LUC:4:6 "Those who seek refuge in the darkness do so not because they are condemned to suffer in this manner, but because it is the only place in which such as they can live. The worm does not seek the sunlight, or the leech find refuge in anything except slime. All things are drawn into conditions, with which they have an affinity; that is a law of Nature, as well as a Greater Law. Man is sufficiently warned, for the light has never been denied those who seek it earnestly, and everything about him proclaims the law of affinity."

LUC:4:7 I understood the words of The Holy Spirit, and I was told other things which I may tell you, but you must not record them in writing. One instruction I was given, I now hand on to you. "This is the choice: Too much regard for the mortal body and craven submission to its demands and desires, a craving for sensual pleasure and surrender to the lures of ease and luxury, enslave man in the Sphere of Matter and Mortality. He is held captive, exiled by his own choice from his true homeland. Such men are the slaves of mortality. Or man can free his own true self waiting to greet him. The humiliating fetters of mortal bondage are then exchanged for the dignity of divine vestments. Man has the choice; he can be bond or free."

LUC:4:8 "Bondage means abject submission to something more powerful than yourself, while freedom entails the acceptance of responsibility and the expenditure of unenforced effort. The choice is before every man. Each has perfect freedom of choice and may accept the challenge of his nature or decline to do so. But upon his choice will follow happiness or misery, survival or destruction. As you have read, man is capable of righteousness and is called upon to be righteous."

LUC:4:9 I thought of these things and saw the working of a natural law where each cause was followed by its own effect and consequence. I thought, too, of these things written in the Good Books, and said, "I have read, 'let the man who has a soulspirit awaken it;' have not all men soul and spirit?" The voice of the Holy Spirit said, "All men are souls within a spirit, for the spirit and soul are not one and the same. To the souls who earnestly struggle towards spiritual unfolding, The Holy Spirit comes to reinforce the powers of the spirit. The presence of The Holy Spirit supports them and, because of this, is called The Comforter, though more often, this is used to describe an earthly comforter."

LUC:4:10 "Even before the soulspirit departs from its earthly habitation, The Holy Spirit is there to comfort, for it is the Guardian at the Gates. But The Holy Spirit does not come near to the servants of evil and the wicked ones, for it has no affinity with them. Those who spent their earthly lives in bondage to the senses and bowed to mortal allurements, those who accepted their state with servility and paid homage to ease and luxury, have no affinity with the light in the Sphere of The Holy Spirit."

LUC:4:11 I spoke to the Good and Great Being who personalised The Holy Spirit, and said, "Tell me the manner in which I shall enter the Sphere of The Holy Spirit." The answer came, not in a voice that beat against the ears but as a melodious note struck on the chords of responsive understanding within. "When the mortal material body is abandoned to dissolution at death, the form you once had no longer exists. The vital breath goes out in one gasp and devitalised, returns to mingle with the air. All mortal things return to their own sphere. What passes over and enters the Sphere of The Holy Spirit is the soulspirit with all its energies and containing an intangible design of etheric framework, upon which the new being will be moulded. Just as the acorn contains the design of the oak and the seed of man the design for his body, so does the soulspirit contain within itself the design for its own unfolding."

LUC:4:12 "Entering the Higher Sphere, all mortal remnants will be discarded, and, looking upward, the soulspirit, freed into eternity, will see the glory above. All the spiritual powers will be gathered about it and may be possessed. The song of the Newcomer will greet the newly arrived soulspirit, 'Welcome into our company, for we are your compatible companions and all one with you.'"

LUC:4:13 I spoke again to The Holy Spirit and said, "It seems there are many degrees in the Higher Sphere, where beings are separated into groups; how then can loved ones be found? Are all groups cut off from each other?" The Holy Spirit replied, "The divisions may resemble groups, but they are not parted by tangible or impassable barriers, for the thing keeping them apart is the law of affinity. The same law operates on the Lower Sphere, where some forms of material expression are so unlike others that one may be completely unknown and unmanifested to another. The grouping is no more rigid on the Higher Sphere than on Earth. The law of affinity draws compatible soulspirits together, just as creatures on Earth seek compatible surrounding and the company of their own kind. In both spheres, there is affinity and antipathy; understand the laws governing these, and you understand the nature of the divisions in the Higher Sphere."

LUC:4:14 I thought awhile and said, "I understand, there are creatures of the light and creatures of the darkness on Earth, and they are kept apart by their different affinities. A gentle lady is revolted by filth and sordidness because she has an antipathy towards them, while the besotten drunkard or unclean bawd is not repelled."

LUC:4:15 The voice of The Holy Spirit was still with me, and I heard it say, "This, then, is the end of the first stage, and here the tired wayfarer may rest and refresh himself. The first flight towards divinity has been accomplished. This is the end of material mortality, and the mists of agnosia swirl far below. Now, the conscious soulspirit can rejoice in the sunlight above."

LUC:4:16 There, in the Sphere of The Holy Spirit, surrounded by a form of glory, which words cannot describe, and immersed in beauty as a swimmer is immersed in water, I was lost in rapture. I could think of no more to say, and having gazed on the face of reality, I would never more be a victim of doubt. The joyousness I knew can be known only through experience, to tell of it is as futile as describing colours to a man born blind, who cannot know one from the other by mentioning their names. Having glimpsed this glory and knowing what is planned for each and every soulspirit, I was filled with zeal and overcome with the desire to awaken my brothers who lay wrapped in the sleep of indifference. I wished to stir them out of their lethargy and make them aware of the effort needed to attain glory. But in my enthusiasm, I rushed forward too hastily and instead of achieving my objective fell into the pit, which always awaits the hasty and unwary. Perhaps it is well, for in my callow youth, I lacked the experience and knowledge of the ways of men, to have been a proper teacher.

LUC:4:17 Having told me these things and granted me the vision of glory, The Holy Spirit withdrew, and I sensed, rather than saw, the departure of the Good and Great Being. Gradually, I descended from the Higher Sphere and awoke on Earth with an abounding feeling of wellbeing. The sleep of the body had freed the soulspirit, and the closing of earthly eyes had marked the opening of spiritual ones. From that day onward, I was a new being.

Chapter Five – The Wandering Mission

LUC:5:1 I fell and struggled upward. My feet hardened on the stony road of experience. I drank heavily of the bitter waters of regret, and the purging fruit of remorse was gall in my mouth. Then, when I had purged and purified myself and once more become a proper receptacle for the light, illumination was granted me. I was in communication with The Holy Spirit, and since that day, grace has never gone from me.

LUC:5:2 Having been filled with power and inspiration I was sent out to teach the doctrine of the Supreme Vision. I proclaimed The Supreme Spirit to men and tried to direct their steps into the paths of beauty and Truth. I was received with mockery and taunts, and many were the blows directed my way. I did not seek alms or beg, and wherever I went earned my bread by working as a cobbler.

LUC:5:3 My friends, this is how I spoke to any who would listen: "Awaken, you sleepers who have abandoned life for slumber, who have scorned the effort of living. You have given yourselves over to the wineshop of mortality and quaffed too deeply of the wines of sensuality and lust. Now you lie in a drunken sleep, ignorant of your spiritual existence and nature. You have sipped long from the cup of ignorance and drunk deeply from the flagons of thoughtlessness. Awake, open your eyes to a sober awareness of the beauty and love about you. Wake up, and look into the light of soulspirit recognition. It hurts your, eyes but that is because they are accustomed to darkness."

LUC:5:4 My friends, I led a life of frustration, for I was like a child who finds a loved parent, too heavy to move, lying drunk in a burning house. I tried to awaken people from their stupor and to draw them out of the darkness of ignorance, but they were bewitched by spells of vain ritual and held captive by irrational but beguiling teachings.

LUC:5:5 When I said, "The Law is that man must struggle and strive, or starve and perish, and this applies not only to the mortal body of man, but equally to his soulspirit", their answering voices came to me from the darkness of ignorance and from the depths of matter, into which they has sunk. I heard them from the thick mists of agnosia and they all said, "We have our saviours and those who plead for us; we make acceptable offerings and pay due homage. Our priests stand between us and destruction, and we are content to leave our spiritual wellbeing in their hands. Leave us in peace, for your voice disturbs us, and with our hands full of mortal affairs we have no time to give for the contemplation of these things."

LUC:5:6 My friends, my heart was sore within me, for I was a lone voice crying against the tempest. I said, "Open your hearts just a little, and raise your spiritual gaze above the sordid drabness, which surrounds your daily existence, Do not ignore the hopeful, helping hand I extend to you, for this ignorance which serves as the servant of evil, floods the whole Earth. Its currents sweep along all the aimless, drifting soulspirits shut up within unguided bodies, which are carried away, to be sunk and lost in the depths."

LUC:5:7 My voice appeared to call in vain, and my heart sank in despair, for with each failure and setback, my confidence drained away. Still I was not left abandoned, for The Comforter came to me in my darkest hours, and I was not left friendless. Refreshed by a surge of spiritual vitality, I continued my pleas, "Men of Isolia, do not let yourselves be carried off by the strong currents of carnal desires. Do not ride the rafts of wickedness, which must go with the wind and waves without direction. Row back against the tide of apathy and indifference; bend your backs, and pull with vigour. Seek the harbour where your soulspirit can step ashore in its homeland. Why have you abandoned yourselves to drifting aimlessly on the sea of mortality, where, unless you awake from the stupor of apathy, you will be destroyed upon the dark lee shore. Awake, awake, pull for the harbour to windward."

LUC:5:8 My body was seized and confined in a dungeon deep, and cruel keepers tormented me. I longed for the fresh air of the free highways, and when at last I was freed, I hastened to another place. Again, I raised my voice to any who would stand and listen and said, "Why do you share your homes with error and make ignorance your guest? Why do you welcome the misguiders and turn away those who bear the gifts of Truth?" Come out of your comfortable cottages, where you sit quaffing the sleep-inducing draughts of agnosia. Get out into the fresh, bracing air of fully conscious life. Be a whole being, wholly awake, instead of a half being half asleep. Come, lay your hand to the plow, and till the fields of immortality. Turn under the weeds of your past mistakes as green manure, and trim your share to turn them deep."

LUC:5:9 "Come out from the stiflingly sleep-inducing air contaminated with fumes from the fire of complacency. Come out into the reviving cold, and fill your lungs with the bracing air of reality. Arise from the comfortable drowsiness of apathy, and step out into the stimulating winds of challenge and care."

LUC:5:10 Again few heeded my message and most went away mocking, calling after me, "Where is your temple? Seek no offerings from us." Still, here and there, a few remained, and I gave them the knowledge of The True Way, of how and by what means they could tread the road to divinity. In them I could sow the seeds, which, in order to grow had to be harrowed in by worldly effort and watered by rain from the Sphere above. For these few, I was duly grateful, and in them comforted by the thought that I had not laboured to dig a well in vain.

LUC:5:11 My friends, I did not wait to see the harvest grow where I had planted, for fresh fields always lay ahead, I spoke as I walked, and I taught as I laboured at my task. I protected the feet of men stoutly with good workmanship, and the spiritual wares I vended freely were no less serviceable.

Chapter Six – The Forest Mission - 1

LUC:6:1 The tests each man must endure have an affinity with him and with no other, so no two persons are tested alike. I who have shod the feet of others, making walking more comfortable, was fated to suffer the trials of a cripple; and the day came when I no longer enjoyed freedom of movement. It was then I came to this place, and my stay here has been blessed in many ways.

LUC:6:2 My friends, I will tell you now about The Supreme Spirit and His properties, and although The Supreme Spirit is neither male nor female, by convention men say 'Him,' and I will do likewise. Just as the eye cannot see The Supreme Spirit, or the finite mind understand Him, so can they neither see nor understand the perfect, the beautiful and the good. These are properties having their source in The Supreme Spirit, and they are things with which He is in love and therefore responds to. They are the things having an affinity with the soul.

LUC:6:3 So if a man strives after perfection, beauty and goodness, even though he lacks knowledge of the soulspirit, he will attain such knowledge. If he has no knowledge of the existence of The Supreme Spirit, this, too, will be given him. For if a man takes the road to York, even though he has never heard of York, he will certainly get there if he continues along the road.

LUC:6:4 Therefore, my friends, if your desire is the attainment of the ultimate in perfection, beauty and goodness, the knowledge of the ultimate in Truth and Reality, then it would be pointless to deny The Supreme Spirit. It would be no more than foolish for one determined to follow the road to York to its end to deny the existence of York. In any case, whether or not he believes it to be there does not influence its ultimate appearance.

LUC:6:5 Because this is so, perhaps too much has been said about the destination and not enough about the road. The man who travels the road to York is better served by information about the road, its turnoffs and landmarks, than about his destination. Ford the rivers and cross the hills before you concern yourself with the hostelry fare.

LUC:6:6 The best way to know and understand anything is to study its properties, and this applies no less to The Supreme Spirit. So, therefore, consider: What is beauty, what is goodness and what is perfection? Is it not true that they can be known here only by their contrasts and reflection? If this is so, then where are they existing? Can a non-existent thing have a reflection, and what contrasts with nothing?

LUC:6:7 The Supreme Spirit is the sun of The Sphere of The Spirit, as The Holy Spirit is the light of that Sphere. The worm raising itself up at daybreak sees the light but departs before the sun rises, for it is too lowly to withstand the rays that have no affinity with slime. It has never seen the splendour, which reigns above, though it knows of it through the light. The swallow soars and swoops in the sunlight and revels in the warmth, with which it has an affinity, but it cannot rise above its established limits. It can see the splendour it cannot attain as a bird.

LUC:6:8 When the land is covered in mist the worm remains above ground with safety, while the swallow defers its flight. So it is with the mists of agnosia, for when they cover the mortal sphere, the blind, creeping things move more freely, while the winged creatures are restricted.

LUC:6:9 Men who are dissatisfied with an unsubstantial reflection seek the reality, which gives it existence, and these are they who gaze in the direction of The Supreme Spirit and divinity. One who, seeing the reflection, says to himself, "Behind this, there must be something greater, which I must seek", is a religious man. One who says, "The reflection is pleasant and satisfies me, for to seek for its cause is too tiresome", is a non-religious man.

LUC:6:10 Reflections are illusive, and those cast on the dark mists of agnosia the most deceptive. Many mistake the ugly for the beautiful, the imperfect for the perfect and evil for good, and so are trapped by their desire for worthless and unprofitable things. To seek for perfection is to seek The Supreme Spirit. To seek for goodness is to seek divinity. To seek for beauty is to reach up for both.

LUC:6:11 Seekers after enjoyment and pleasure gain little benefit, but to seek true happiness is a worthy aim, for it points in the right direction. Unhappiness, despair and remorse are the products of ignorance, folly and apathy. Evil effects flow from evil causes. Enjoyment and pleasure are unprofitable trees whose fruit may be tasteless or bitter. Ignorance is the darkness of the soulspirit, the smothering fog in, which it becomes lost. It beguiles the spirit of man into a kind of drugged dullness, man is no longer spiritually alert, keen and energetic. He becomes inert, caught in the mire of matter.

LUC:6:12 My friends, if any of you see imperfection in The Supreme Spirit, be sure that the apparent imperfection results only from your mortal limitations. It is like looking at the sun through coarse, soiled glass and thinking the spots and distortions you see belong to the sun itself. It is not the sun that is spotted or distorted; the defect is in the glass or even in the eye of the viewer, but the effect is as though the defect lies in the sun. However imperfect the reflected image may appear, the reality behind it, The Supreme Spirit, is perfect.

LUC:6:13 The Supreme Spirit has always remained unmoved in the centre of the wheel of eternity, which rolls its out rim through the universes of the Lower Sphere. He alone is the central, unchangeable reality, the hub, around which all things revolve. Time begins in eternity and ends there, though it may itself appear eternal because expressed in revolving cycles modified only by change.

LUC:6:14 For me to speak of a beginning is a concession to mortal limitations and, in any case, it is pointless. The resolute wayfarer does not look back along the road. Suffice to say that there was The One Sole Consciousness containing the essence of perfection and reality, which words cannot describe. When the potential power was stirred by thought, it flowed out in rhythm, and this was the beginning. Do not concern yourselves with these things or talk to others too much about the nature of The Supreme Spirit. To seek Him without first becoming aware of the soul spirit is like looking for darkness while carrying a lighted lamp.

LUC:6:15 The Supreme Spirit is the source of all spirit, and this is the power, which flowed out and brought all else into being. The power flowed outward in the same order, in which it returns.

LUC:6:16 My friends, these are things difficult to understand, and it is pointless going into waters beyond your depth. Man has more pressing problems to solve within himself, so before delving into the nature of The Supreme Spirit, he should first seek to unravel the secrets of his own nature. Still more important, he should deal with the flaws and defects in his own make-up before seeking to probe further. When a man has to travel a long road, his first care should be the soles of his feet.

Chapter Seven – The Forest Mission - 2

LUC:7:1 From the Sphere Above, a Spirit Force descended, penetrating into the Sphere of Matter and Mortality, and this is called Nature. Using the laws of cause and effect, necessity and the conservation of life, Nature cherished and nurtured the descending lifeforce and, with earthly moulds, modelled it to spiritual patterns.

LUC:7:2 Life comes from The Supreme Spirit and reaches the Sphere of Matter and Mortality through the Sphere Above, and Nature works with clay. Man is the receptacle of life in both parts of his twofold being, though he should learn to concentrate it in his higher self. The lifeforce becomes strong in the spiritual man but is weak in the worldly man, just as it is strong in the eagle and weak in the grub.

LUC:7:3 There are forces in Nature beyond the knowledge of man, but whatever they are, man must harmonise himself with them. It is unwise to contend with the unknown, or challenge powers incapable of assessment. To live harmoniously, man must revere all forms of life and treat his fellowmen with consideration and courtesy. All that is beautiful and beneficial is to be preserved, and man must never tire of adding to these. Nothing having life, beauty or uniqueness must be wantonly destroyed, unless it is known to be harmful.

LUC:7:4 Thought is mind working through matter, and feeling is life manifesting in matter. Thought and feeling are not separable in man, for feeling unrecorded and unconditioned by thought would serve no higher purpose than a mortal one, and man is more than that. Therefore, all feeling has to be conveyed to something that experiences and reacts to it. Thought and feeling are not absent from the Sphere of The Holy Spirit and are even greatly intensified there. That is one reason why man has to learn to control them here, for the Earth is a place where he is schooled to handle great forces and powers now beyond conception.

LUC:7:5 My friends, the things I wish to teach form so high a doctrine that it is difficult to convey them to the clouded minds of men. Some will never grasp the meaning and message, others will laugh them to scorn. Those who try to help man along the steep, upward road and who extend the hand of friendship are more often mocked than heeded. Man prefers to sleep on the soft bed of agnosia rather than be awakened to harsh reality. Those who disturb complacent slumbers are usually reviled. To think is to understand and believe, but to be unthinking and unbelieving is less disturbing and follows the wide way of ease and apathy. All most men seek spiritually is to be left alone, undisturbed.

LUC:7:6 Most things spoken here in the hermitage are not for the uninitiated and must not be recorded, for an infant cannot be entrusted with the firebrand. Initiation is a meaningful rite, the purpose of which is to awaken the sleeper and open his spiritual eyes. Little purpose is served by talking to a sleeping man, still less to a deaf man and even less to one who has no desire to hear. So it is that men walk as though in a fog and see things hazily or with distortion. You, my friends, must go out among them and take their hands and be their guides. If they will not follow, they alone suffer, for if you do your best, you can do no more.

LUC:7:7 Dealing with mind. This comes from The Supreme Spirit by way of The Holy Spirit and is, to The Supreme Spirit, like sunlight is to the sun. It is often likened to light. Though previously explained to men in this manner, their sons, in their delusion, began to worship the sun, for man has always misunderstood the teachings and sought to bring them down from a high to a lower level.

LUC:7:8 Those who seek the truth about their nature are men becoming more than men; they tread the road to godhood. Those who close their minds to Truth are actually closing the doors of the cage, in which they remain as little more than animals. The apathetic man becomes deluded under the influence of his own ideas and imagination; he readily accepts teachings requiring no thought or effort. If ever a teacher comes along who says, "Surrender your will and reason to me and I will assure you of life everlasting," he will be unable to count his followers.

LUC:7:9 Knowing the truth, you now realise the futility and foolishness of repeating thoughtlessly the feeble formula, "I am a helpless, miserable wrongdoer bound by the misdeeds of my fathers. I am one naturally inclined towards evil and cannot save myself. Save me, have mercy and forgive me, meek and miserable as I am." Those, my friends, are actual words spoken, and doubtless, you will let them speak for themselves. Such an outlook is not only degrading, but it condemns man to disinheritance. It blinds him to his true nature and, binding him with knots of ignorance, hands him captive to enslavement in matter.

LUC:7:10 Without doubt, it is difficult to understand The Supreme Spirit and His Great Plan and all too easy to sneer and dismiss the disturbing thoughts and shun the effort. It is only after long and careful consideration has been given to the matter that a man comes to believe in spiritual things and his own immortality, and that is only the first step. Time has established that disbelief and lack of faith spring either from an inability to think deeply or from apathy. In either case, the mind falls prey to agnosia and, being weakened by ignorance and prejudice, slides wearily down the precipice into hasty and false conclusions.

LUC:7:11 True spiritual enlightenment cannot be found through the written words of man alone or through reason and logic, but those are important signposts along the way. They point in the right direction, and the Good Books are reliable guides along the road, but there comes a point where, to find spiritual enlightenment, man has to commit himself to a spiritual vehicle and be conveyed beyond the bounds of matter. The ability of any man to attain spirituality and know the truth is limited only by his steadfastness in the search and fortitude in the struggle.

LUC:7:12 Can any man think long on the wonder of creation and the complexity of created things and declare truthfully that he believes they came into being of their own accord? Can he look at the awesome beauty of the spinning universe, now so old and yet so full of vitality, with never a sign of declining powers, and say there is no motivator behind it? Can he look at the life-giving light of day and the growth-controlling light of the night, at the teeming Earth and burning stars, and honestly believe that all this is a matter of pure chance? Could all this vast and splendidly run universe have created itself? It could, if a tapestry can weave itself, or a statue chisel itself out from the rock.

LUC:7:13 Everything throughout the whole of creation conforms to certain basic laws, and where there are laws, there must be a Lawmaker. There is only one set of unchangeable laws and so there can be only one Lawmaker. Were it otherwise, there would have been a clash of laws, with resultant chaos and confusion instead of order and stability.

LUC:7:14 Men have often asked me concerning evil and sought to lay traps with their questions. Evil is a kind of mildew, corrosion or rust, which forms on the pure creative impulses of good, when they penetrate the lower Sphere of Matter and Mortality. These impulses can be purified from the adulterating evil through change and regeneration. Everything descending from the Higher Sphere finds itself contrasted or reflected here, for this is the quality of matter. This contrast or reflection may be so different as to appear to manifest as evil.

LUC:7:15 Everything on Earth is evolving either upwards or downwards, becoming more like the pure pattern, which left The Divine Designer or more grossly material and earthly. Evil does not come from above and results only from existence in an elementary sphere of change and decay. Here on Earth, change is fundamental and, like everything else, can be made to serve a good or bad end. When a thing becomes too good, it is removed by change, and anything, which becomes too bad is likewise removed. The unbounded wisdom of The Creator is beyond criticism, and only the ignorant and apathetic would criticise anyway.

LUC:7:16 Unless there is direction and control, everything tends naturally towards chaos and confusion. Undirected change can lead to nothing except disorder. Therefore, wherever there is orderly movement, there must be direction, and where there is direction, there must be a Director. No sensible person who thinks deeply enough could possibly conclude that the great universe and the whole of creation are undirected. Who, then, could The Creator and Director be but The Supreme Spirit?

Chapter Eight – The Forest Mission - 3

LUC:8:1 Each soulseed is implanted into the whole being according to a preset destiny, and from this grow the two branches of the whole being, the soulspirit and the mortal body. Though not of mortal elements, the soulspirit, by law of affinity, draws to itself particular elements when entering matter, and so all soulspirits manifest differently on the Sphere of Matter and Mortality.

LUC:8:2 Within the seed of man, there is the life potential, which has an affinity with the life breath impregnating the Lower Sphere. And this, when two complementary life impulses unite, causes generation of life. The new being grows within the womb by dividing within itself into particles too small for the eye to see, and these arrange themselves so as to form a copy of the model contained in the soulseed.

LUC:8:3 Nature composes the body in the likeness contained in the soulseed, according to the law of affinity, and each new being attracts or repels certain elements and conditions according to its destiny. Affinity and destiny act in such a way that no two persons are compounded and blended alike. Everyone is different, down to the smallest particle of his being.

LUC:8:4 The soulseed is not drawn into the Sphere of Matter and Mortality by the desire for existence in matter, but simply by the law of affinity. Success or failure, fame or life as a non-entity, do not depend on a preset destiny, though this may make them easy or difficult to achieve. A man's destiny may cause him to be born rich or poor, frail or sturdy, civilised or savage, but it cannot make him accept or remain in this state.

LUC:8:5 The power of pro-creation exists in both man and woman, though the power manifests differently in each. It is one power with two aspects, the nature of which is not easily described. The Ancients called it the 'twofold ray' and referred to an active and a passive side; one, they said, was lighter than the other. The reaction of the two aspects to each other expresses itself in the interplay of love. The compelling force is also twofold, expressing itself in a lower and higher form.

LUC:8:6 My friends, I am often asked about death, which seems to frighten most people who consider it the greatest evil, which can befall them. This is a wrong attitude caused by ignorance and spiritual apathy. Death comes when the body has served its earthly purpose, or should have done so, and is now worn out and ready to break up. The vital forces, which have hitherto held it together, withdraw and concentrate within the soulspirit. It is not the end but only a separation, the severance into two parts, each returning to the place, with which it has an affinity. It is not dissolution but renewal. The immortal is absorbed back into its own element without dissolution, while the mortal part obeys its own law of decay and renewal. Death destroys nothing, except the link between the soul spirit and the perishable body.

LUC:8:7 There is something you should know and consider most earnestly, for it bears directly upon the afterlife condition. It concerns two kinds of wrongdoing: that done openly, and perhaps I may say courageously, if such a word can be permitted to describe an evil deed, and that done secretly and slyly. Punishment for the former is often meted out by man, and this can in many cases cause spiritual readjustment. In the latter, however, the furtive deed is close hugged and so becomes accentuated within the sensitivity of the soulspirit. Because their evil deeds were hidden and not uncovered, the sly ones will suffer far more than those whose evildoing was exposed.

LUC:8:8 Because of this, hypocrisy is to be condemned as a most detestable vice. Those who go through life practising evil undetected, particularly if done under a cloud of virtue, will surely suffer much more grievously than the condemned murderer and thief. This is why the Good Books condemn hypocrisy and deceit more than murder and theft, for spiritually, the former are more potentially evil. It is a thing little understood. Just as little understood is the nature of sorrow and suffering. Of these there are two kinds, that which follows as the result of a foolish, wicked or ignorant act, and that which destiny prescribed to test the soulspirit. Consider these things well, for it will lead to a better understanding of life.

LUC:8:9 The soulspirit gives out a kind of glow called the 'spiritlight,' which can be seen by many of those who are spiritually awakened. It envelops the earthly body and forms something like a radiant ring above the head. In good men, it appears bright and shining, but in the unrighteous it looks dull and drab. This is why it is said, "The faces of those who have abstained from wrongdoing shall shine like the sun." It also indicates the different death conditions of people. However, it would be well for you to remember that abstaining from wrongdoing is not enough; you must act positively in the service of good.

LUC:8:10 It is not pleasant, my friends, to dwell too long on the fate of the evil-minded ones, whose afterdeath condition is a nightmare of unending strife and unrelieved ugliness. These are the wretched, undying dead who long for oblivion and the supremacy of death. This is not a pleasant teaching, but it is unwise to shun reality because it is painful to dwell upon. This is the escapism of weakness. Suffice to say that there is a place to which the evil-minded ones are drawn by affinity, where remorse and regret are more pressingly painful than any cancerous growth. The suffering falls heavier for its postponement beyond death. The undeserved honours, the unwarranted good name, the unearned credits and benefits, are not overlooked either. No man can escape the judgement of his regenerated conscience, which measures and judges according to what is revealed against a contrasting standard of absolute purity.

LUC:8:11 Now, there is one thing often asked touching the teaching concerning the unclean place, the ultimate disposal of the spiritual garbage. My friends, the doctrine of eternal condemnation is false. This cannot be, for it asserts a downward finality, which not only is against the whole creative intent, but also questions the goodness of The Supreme Spirit. The misery suffered by the unclean beings in their self-selected, filthy abode of shadowy horror, is in fact a purging and purifying cure. Though it lasts many ages of time, and the road upward through the density of matter is long and arduous, there is an end, be it in glory or oblivion.

LUC:8:12 After so-called death, which word in former times meant no more than removal, each soulspirit goes to the habitat to which it is drawn by affinity. There, all its latent powers and qualities built up and hoarded during earthly life are released and revealed. These should suffice for complete spiritual happiness and freedom, and this is what the Ancients meant when they said, "His qualities will provide his food." Man, having learned to live harmoniously on Earth, continues in a state of harmony above. The Ancients also referred to this when they said, "He who sows the seeds of discord reaps the wild wind harvest."

LUC:8:13 My forest friends, the soulspirits of grown men and women are often enclosed within a hard-set cement of materialism. Compare this state with the innocence of a child whose soulspirit, unstained by evil, still retains affinity with the source of its being. But as the mortal body develops, so it closes in upon the being inside, encasing it in ever thickening layers of grossness. Soon, the light no longer penetrates and the recollection of the beauty beyond is stifled. The vision departs, and the soulspirit, shut off from contact with its homeland, sinks into forgetful slumber. The fleshy prison walls hold it fast, and communication with the freedom light outside becomes more and more difficult. The beauty fades away in the enveloping darkness.

LUC:8:14 I, my friends, do not wish to dwell unnecessarily on these aspects of the higher teachings, they are ably enough presented in the Good Books of the Ancients and may be studied there. I would rather speak of the divine qualities. The greatest of these is love, for it is through love that man can best learn about immortality. True love brings all other virtues in its wake, and with them must come spiritual awakening. With spiritual awakening comes the influx of calming power, which makes men tranquil and quiet. It stills the rowdy haste, which saps vitality and calms the unproductive bustle. Dispute and argument upon spiritual matters become futile, for the awakened soulspirit is no longer dependant on unsubstantiated outward beliefs, but upon inward spiritual realities and assurances. Others have said that here, on the Sphere of Matter and Mortality, man cannot have assurance, but from my own experience, it would appear that assurance can be gained. There is a road to certainty, albeit a long and weary one.

LUC:8:15 However, too much is said of spirituality in a world where it is an infrequent manifestation. Only a few are in sight of the destination, while by far the most are still well back along the road. To these, the conditions to be met along the way and the location of refreshing wells and sources of sustenance are the most important things and the most serviceable information. So unless you are one who has the end in sight do not aim to immerse yourself too soon in the waters of spiritual rapture and devotion. There is a proper time and place for everything.

LUC:8:16 First, gain complete mastery over the body, and control every urge and desire arising from it. This is the first step only, and the way and means are contained in the precepts of the moral law. Study these diligently, but remember that study and understanding without practice and performance is absolutely futile. First, learn to live as you should, and only then seek to advance further.

LUC:8:17 Vice is the cancer, and depravity the plague, of the soulspirit. Mean and petty acts of spitefulness and malice are the pockmarkers. Such things are like spiritual diseases, which strike during spiritual weakness and debility. They flourish where there is avoidance of obligation and shunning of responsibility; where there is an inability to withstand pain with patience and fortitude and a selfish seeking for diverting pleasure and unrewarding frivolity. These are the things condemned through the ages, and who, looking back, would dare say such condemnation was wrong?

LUC:8:18 The greatest gift of spirituality, by which the soulspirit becomes conscious of its own existence, is not a state of easeful bliss. On the contrary, it is a driving force spurring the soulspirit ever onward along the road to godhood, to the tackling of greater obstacles. The first struggle is towards self-conquest, mastery over the mortal.

Chapter Nine – The Forest Mission - 4

LUC:9:1 Man is prone to error because of his mortality and because his earthly habitat is compounded of matter apt to lead him into evil ways. He is directed by destiny and subject to laws he cannot break, so the freedom he enjoys is largely a delusion. Escape lies in only one direction, which is upward, and this upwardising is called the road to spirituality or the True Way. Mortal man is enslaved to the demands of necessity, but this is an essential quality of earthly life, which prepares for the enjoyment of the greater freedom beyond.

LUC:9:2 Like a sleeping man in hostile terrain, the slumbering soul spirit is defenceless and exposed to attack. Good and evil spirits exert influence upon it and, unless stirred to wakefulness, it cannot discern one from the other. From the moment of its conception into mortality, the soulspirit is subject to influences operating under the law of affinity, which either attract or repel. These move to the irrational soulspirit centre of sensitivity where they set up throbbing impulses, which move like ripples circling outward, seeking compatible responses. These movements are under the administration of destiny.

LUC:9:3 Just as the body has rational and irrational centres, so with the soulspirit. The rational part of the soulspirit cannot be dominated by spirits, either good or evil, without its own free choice. This is the part not naturally inclined to evil and more receptive to the ray-like impulses from the Sphere of The Holy Spirit.

LUC:9:4 The lives of all are ruled by a preset destiny. But whatever this entails, each must rise above it, for destiny is the challenger, the handicapper and the test selector. The soulspirit alone can be freed from the domination of destiny; the mortal clay cannot. Therefore, the designs of destiny should be left to work themselves out solely in the mortal flesh.

LUC:9:5 My friends, I am asked, "What is the soulseed, and whence does it come?" Above all is The Supreme Spirit surrounded by the soulsea, below which is spirit and, lower still, matter. The soulseed is a drop from the soulsea, which has been separated out and become encased in a shell of spirit. It descends through spirit and returns there, and may do this many times. What flesh is to the soulspirit, so is spirit to the soulseed.

LUC:9:6 The laws of The Supreme Spirit cannot be evaded, but man has within himself the ability to rise above them to greater freedom. He can, of course, choose the downward path and surrender instead of struggling, but as he descends so does he become more subject to restriction; more the plaything of forces beyond his control, more like a windblown leaf. Freedom lies at the end of the upward road, not in the depths of matter.

LUC:9:7 The true evils in the world are all man-made; even disease and sickness originate in the evil tendencies of men. Evil can reach out even from the midden in the Sphere of The Holy Spirit and strike at men. But did this not originate in their own wickedness? Here are generated unseen evil things, which become parasites in the susceptible mortal flesh. They are indescribable in words, and there is no way of making them known to you. Yet, they exist even as the soulspirit exists, unseen and mortally unknowable.

LUC:9:8 My friends, the world need not be a place overrun with evil. If men could only cleanse the unclean garments of their minds, it could be a place of unceasing joy. Men bear the burden of their body with unintended sadness. They are like a man living in an empty tomb, who shrinks from the bright sunlight outside. The longer he hesitates, the whiter and weaker his body becomes. Men still choose to ignore the message handed down through the ages.

LUC:9:9 So, my friends, we make little progress. Man looks around him hopefully, seeking inspiration from distant places, when all the time, everything needed lies to his hand. The Ancients spoke wisely when they said, "That, which lies nearest is hardest to see." The ancient wisdom is as fresh today as it ever was; it is just as applicable now as it was then and will never grow stale. Man places too much faith in things he can see and grasp, while unseen things give rise to disbelief and doubt. Yet, his whole life is dominated by unseen things and forces beyond his knowledge.

LUC:9:10 The only rock, to which man can cling with faith and assurance, is the unshakable ancient wisdom contained in the Good Books. The only thing man can strive for with certainty of benefit is goodness. Man can travel the road to perfection, but it is endless and discouraging. The road to Truth is wearisome and full of pitfalls. If you asked for one rule to guide you safely, I would say, "Ignore the authoritative voice of the body, and listen to the quiet whispers of conscience."

LUC:9:11 Now, you ask whether the unclean soulspirit, degraded in darkness and humiliated by remaining in the substance, with which it has an affinity, ever resumes life in worldly form. It may indeed extend out into the brutish body of a man, or into one more graceful though heavily fettered by destiny. To say that any soulspirit is completely reborn in a new body is not strictly true, though it may manifest again on Earth. Rebirth is accepted by those who worship the great goddesses and by some others, but it is a much more complex matter than they believe. Their assertions are clouded by ignorance of the true nature of the Higher Sphere and the laws governing birth. There is, however, some truth in the doctrine, which is much deeper than they suspect.

LUC:9:12 Nature models the earthly containers, into which the soulspirit descends. She moulds them according to a prescribed pattern and adheres to the Spiritplan drawn by destiny. She likewise moulds the bodies of animals and birds; though here, the pattern is general and not differentiated by destiny, as it is with man.

Chapter Ten – The Mangod

LUC:10:1 The reaches of the Sphere of The Holy Spirit and the Sphere of Matter and Mortality are not without limitations, though within each, there is everlasting change. The godlike divinities worshipped by man have their abode in the Sphere Above, and unless formed only in the imaginations of men, are no more than superior soul spirits. Least among these, though greatest among men, is the godlike man called Mangod, the ideal towards which we all should strive.

LUC:10:2 The Mangod is candidate for a godhood within the reach of everyman and has special godlike qualities of goodness and spiritual strength, which set him apart from ordinary men. He is the strong runner in the race of life and one who never withholds a helping hand from the laggard. Such men are rarities indeed; yet, they are destined rulers of the world, the vanguard in the march towards godhood.

Their day will come as surely as the sun rises above the treetops.

LUC:10:3 The virtue of the Mangod lies in his strong tendency towards goodness and his keen sense of judgement and justice. He knows when to stand firm and when to give way, and when to say, "This is enough." Not with-standing this, he always inclines towards peace and reconciliation, even in the face of accusations of weakness. He knows it is the weak man who accuses another of weakness, and the man unsure of himself who has to be reassured by a spate of his own words.

LUC:10:4 The Mangod treads with soft footfalls, but he steps from mountaintop to mountaintop. He prevails by reason and example and not by force, for he is a natural leader of men. Though I abide by the teachings, I cannot see that it is wrong to honour the names of great men who inspire loyalty and obedience, and who restore peace and justice. I would let the very names of the Mangods ring out to fill the wicked with dread and the righteous with contentment. However, while the true Mangod is not recognised among the world leaders and not even sought for high positions, perhaps it is best. The day of the Mangod will come, and the nation, which honours him will be raised above all others. But it is for the nation to bring forth the Mangod, and not for the Mangod to bring the nation.

Chapter Eleven – The Vision of Evening

LUC:11:1 This land, which was once the school of spiritual enlightenment, is still the sanctuary of spiritual civilisation, though we are cut off from our brothers over the water. Even now, terrible foreigners press about the pure land held in trust, as divine estates and religious rites are neglected. But my friends, this is just a beginning, and the time is not far distant when there will be laws prohibiting us from the practice of worship, and heavy penalties will be laid upon the righteous. Yet I still lay the charge upon you; go forth and teach.

LUC:11:2 The matron of the coming days will bear strange children, aliens blind to the light of beauty and nobility. The chants of weird forms of worship will be heard, and meaningless hymns will echo through the land. The devotional places will be wreathed in agnosia, and the purity of white enlightenment will be exchanged for the drab blackness of ignorance. Men will cease to seek their soulspirit sustenance in the light and will feed on agnosia. Unknowingly, darkness will be preferred to the light. The theme of life will be death, and death will even be idolised in the form of a man.

LUC:11:3 The righteous man will be held up to scorn, and the irreligious will be deemed wise. Those with twisted minds will be held intelligent, and those who declare that good can only serve a worldly end will be considered righteous. All this will result from spiritual poverty and lack of enlightenment, yet they will declare themselves rich and enlightened. The impoverished cannot surround themselves with grandeur, and this applies both to the flesh and to the spirit. Consideration for the soulspirit will be non-existent, and belief in its immortality will be treated as a jest. The mind of man will either be set on worldly things or be clouded by a fog of spiritual darkness. There will be no respect for spirituality.

LUC:11:4 There will be persecutions and wars, riots and looting, all manner of deceit and oppression will be practised in the name of angry and revengeful gods. Worse still, all this will be practised in the name of good, and men will blindly accept what they are told and execute orders running contrary to their natures.

LUC:11:5 When spirituality has reached its lowest ebb and religion has decayed, the wheel will turn again. Man will either rise up with an influx of spiritual regeneration or go down and utterly perish in the dark depths of moral degeneracy. The world cannot be permitted to remain a spiritually festering sore failing to serve any purpose.

LUC:11:6 There are things buried in the future, with which it is unprofitable to deal, so what is said must suffice. Better by far to deal with the problems of today, though even these are less important than learning the secrets of the True Way.

LUC:11:7 The awakened soul spirit of man becomes filled with a yearning not there before, an overwhelming desire for constant communication or unity with the Sphere of The Holy Spirit. As this manifests more strongly and desires and inclinations tend to disappear, the soulspirit grows from strength to strength.

LUC:11:8 Since the Earth is the work of The Supreme Spirit, he who cherishes and improves it, or adds to its beauty and goodness, becomes an assistant to The Creator. This is a position all should aspire to, for the Earth must not be uncouth or unadorned. Those who benefit most from life are those who serve it best.

LUC:11:9 I have spoken of the Mangod, of the very few who are gifted with purity of mind and high intellect. These are the ones who should marshal the forces of mankind to serve The Creator, but all too often, good men are not great men, or great men good. As things are, the man who is both good and great is a rarity.

LUC:11:10 To be spiritual means living life to the fullest, in its widest sense; making conscious contact not only with the Sphere of Matter and Mortality, but also with the Sphere of The Holy Spirit. As this means that the spiritual man differs from ordinary men, the crowd is not able to understand him, and often, he is treated with scorn. This does not deter the spiritual man who knows the mockery and scorn of the crowd are usually directed against someone superior to it. When I was held up to ridicule, scorned and even believed mad, I felt flattered.

LUC:11:11 Reality and Truth are not to be found on Earth, though man, being more than mortal, can conceive their existence, and some may even be granted a divine vision of them. How can such qualities exist in this sphere where good is adulterated with evil? Where there is no stability, where pain, sorrow, decay and change press in on every side? How can any unstable, changeable thing be real? How can it be true to itself? Everything that is unstable changes and is therefore false to itself, and the false is unreal. The real is something unchanging. When a man can conceive what Truth and Reality actually are, he stands on the threshold of comprehending The Supreme Spirit.

Chapter Twelve – The Bodiless Body

LUC:12:1 My friends, I see myself as one who has been granted a divine vision, a gift of insight beyond that of most men, these things coming to me through the grace of The Holy Spirit. This I know beyond any doubt; I have broken through the closed ring of mortality about me and taken possession of a deathless body. I am now an awakened soul clothed in spirit and, having drunk the waters of life in the Sphere Above, am more than mortal. Would that I could explain this better to your understanding. But the things, which can be easily taught are of this world only, and higher things can be learned only by direct experience of the Sphere of The Holy Spirit.

LUC:12:2 The soulspirit is like a bodiless eye, seeing as men see visions or recall scenes from the past without the sight of the eyes. Yet, this is no more than a poor representation of Truth, for there are no means known to men, whereby these things can be explained. To understand fully, each man must go out from the body to the Sphere Above where only the soulspirit can go, and only then can the vision of beauty and reality be seen. It seems to me that this is not achieved even by the powers of the soulspirit, great as they are, but rather that, in such cases, man is uplifted by the very arms of The Supreme Spirit. There appears to be two subspheres co-joined: one, the lower where form and colour still manifest, and above this, another where these have their origin, and this is a place of quiet, restful serenity. It is a place of unchanging stability.

LUC:12:3 You ask me about the higher vision. Again it is difficult to express myself in words. It comes as a brilliant light, but not like the blazing glare of the sun, before which men are forced to close their eyes. It is a spiritual form of light, shining only to an extent within the ability of the one granted the vision to receive it. Those who, like my own master, can drink deeply at the well of visions, are lulled into a sound spiritual sleep outside the mortal body, and can remain long in the place where visions reflect reality more clearly.

LUC:12:4 Such men are true Illuminated Ones, and they are not many. By far, the greater number are deceived by the upward reflections of illusion, but because these appear as glorious visions, they accept them as reflections of Truth. This is always the great danger, but there are tests to guard against deception.

LUC:12:5 Sometimes, when an illuminated One speaks of the Sphere of The Holy Spirit, its power will flow down into him to such an extent that his mortal senses will become blocked out. He will then appear to lose the trend of his own speech and, instead, his mouth will become an outlet for the flooding channel of inspiration. Sometimes, in such cases, it is difficult for the listener to grasp what the illuminated One is saying, unless he, too, is in equal harmony with the Sphere Above. The words race ahead of his understanding. If sitting in darkness or gloom, it will be noticed that, at such times, a light or radiance surrounds the Illuminated One, and it is this, which establishes the reality of his spiritual elevation.

LUC:12:6 Spiritual things are far more difficult to understand than earthly things, and their study requires much greater effort and self-discipline. That is why there are so few spiritual people. The lower mortal mind can gain only a faint insight into them through spoken words, and then only by a supreme effort of understanding. This proves too much for most people, and so spirituality goes into a decline. If the effort directed towards destructive or purposeless worldly things had been directed towards spiritual ends, the race of man would now be a race of Mangods.

LUC:12:7 There are some among you who do not understand the mystery of rebirth. It means rebirth into spiritual consciousness, and this is the central secret of all time, the knowledge of which will change men into Mangods. The reborn man can bid his soulspirit go into any place he chooses, and it will be there quick as a thought. It will pass over the seas or penetrate through the denseness of the forests, not as a thing moving swiftly, but as a thing already there. The soulspirit, once freed, can rise above all denser material things, though it cannot penetrate into the upper subspheres of creation in the Sphere of The Holy Spirit.

LUC:12:8 Now, those of you who have experienced the power and speed of the soulspirit and examined, by careful study, the reality of the experience, can surely understand the nature of the Supreme Spirit. If you can do these things, how much more capable will He be of doing them. Therefore, expand yourself to the utmost limit; break out of your confinement, slip away from the mortal body, and escape the shackles of space and time. Behind and beyond this, you will see the gateway at the path leading to the door of The Supreme Spirit.

LUC:12:9 If, however, you prefer to imprison the soulspirit within the body and to treat it with contempt, saying, I know nothing and fear to reach out into the unknown. I fear the limitless spaces, the unfathomable depths and the boundless heights. I am afraid to seek too deeply in order to discover what I am or what I can do, or what I will become," if you are numbered among those who tremble and fear, then you are not fully alive; you are already more than half dead. You can understand nothing of the truly beautiful; you cannot perceive glory and if you love the mere mortal body so much, then you cannot really know good and are easily inclined towards the bad.

LUC:12:10 Even the slumbering soulspirit can know, through its dreams, the joy originating from its affinity with the Sphere Above. It is experienced when the restlessness of the thinking mind is stilled, in the joyous lilt of the heart filled with melody, in the glory of a sunset. In the warm smile of love, in the confidence of a child, in the sweet scents of a garden, or in the cool caress of the wind. The cumbersome words of Earth cannot describe its glory or reveal to mortal mind the majestic picture of Truth. These words of mine do no more than reflect a pale shadow of the splendours of reality. Once again I repeat; the true knowledge of the Higher Sphere can be gained only from personal experience, through self-awakening.

LUC:12:11 The soul spirit is potentially beyond spatial limitations and exists outside earthly time. It knows that everything is everlasting; yesterday remains where it was; it is man who has moved on and left it behind, out of sight. Life is a steady advance, it flows on like the waters of this stream and cannot turn back on itself. The same stream passed this way a hundred years ago. It remains the same, though moment by moment every drop passing by is new. So it is that we cannot return upstream, through the waters of life, to yesterday. However, when cast upon the bank by death, no longer swept onward by the flowing stream, yesterday becomes approachable.

LUC:12:12 These are vital truths known to all Illuminated Ones. The childish mind of the worldly man sees things in unreality. The partially awakened, while in trance or ecstasy, see reality as though through a veil. They realise that the mortal eyes see only the unreal and deceptive, but they are between two spheres, seeing neither clearly, and so do not see reality either. The illuminated One alone sees clearly and so knows for certainty that he is an immortal being.

LUC:12:13 The discipline of the moral teachings, when fully practised and lived, is the first essential step towards illumination. It is only by completely eliminating his own self-centredness that man can become aware of the communicating point within himself, whereby he can contact the reality above. By this means alone, he escapes from a world of shadows and illusions. When the greater self awakens within, the peace and joy of spiritual consciousness fills life with splendour, but first the childish struggle for worthless, unreliable things must cease. The spirit of man is like a caged beast, ever restless, ever seeking to escape to a greater sphere, but too often the restlessness is stilled by drugs of worldliness.

LUC:12:14 The unenlightened man is unaware of anything beyond his limiting mortal wall, or outside the scope of his own ideas and interpretations. Yet, his ideas are clouds of preconceived prejudices and his interpretations deceptive illusions. He is dead to reality, entombed within himself.

LUC:12:15 The man who sees a treestump in the night and mistakes it for a man is deluded. Yet the treestump is real enough; it is the misinterpretation by the man that makes it what it is not. Likewise with the Earth and material things; they too have a reality of their own, but man misinterprets, making them something they are not. His mortal body is also real, but this, too, he has misinterpreted, to make it something different. The Earth, material things and his body are not what man mistakes them to be; he is deluded in the nightmists of agnosia.

LUC:12:16 The soulspirit is truly awakened when it has a personal experience proving the reality of the Sphere of The Holy Spirit, and this is a far from easy accomplishment. There may be brief glimpses in a half wakened state, but these are not enough, nor are they satisfactory. The Higher Sphere can be known and experienced; it is not something completely cut off from the knowledge of man. There, the answer is to be found; there, the secret of the opposites is revealed; there, Truth shines with greater clarity. There you will discover that the soulspirit is a fragment of The Supreme Spirit containing the essence of His creative power.

LUC:12:17 Thought, combined with the power of The Holy Spirit, can create whatever it desires, whatever it wills to come into being will do so. The originating creative thought has been modified on Earth by the thought activities of many soulspirits, and so there is much that cannot be directly attributed to The Supreme Spirit. Meditate on this, for it explains much. Man remains generally completely unaware of his own powers, his limitations being in fact no more than the result of his own lack of knowledge and awareness, his lack of insight and preference for walking in the comforting calm of agnosia.

LUC:12:18 The soulspirit can be whatever it wills itself to be; it is the fashioner of its own form and destiny. It can, if it wishes, see all things as they are in reality by sweeping aside the clouds of illusion and removing the veils of deception. Do not misunderstand me when I talk of the real and the unreal. Earth, earthly experience and material things are not unreal, for the unreal would have no existence. The things so often called unreal do exist and have a reality of their own, it is man's interpretation of that reality that is wrong. The things are not what man thinks them to be; they are false, deceptive, illusive. Even the words 'real' and 'unreal' are themselves deceptive and lead into error.

LUC:12:19 This higher knowledge has been gained by those who have built up their spiritual powers, so that they could enter into direct communication with the Sphere Above. By their sacrifices and self-disciplines, they so refined and strengthened their soulspirits that they could penetrate to the place where the light of Truth shone clearly. That they were not misled is easily provable.

LUC:12:20 The means of freeing the soulspirit are available to all men who first seek to discover their true nature. This is the beginning of the only direct road; the others lead to illusionary Heavens. Each man is his own ruler and the director of his own destiny; whatever advance he makes, even though it come through the teachings of others, will result from his own individual effort.

LUC:12:21 The road to spirituality lies within himself, but too often, it is blocked by barriers erected through his own ignorance and mortal weaknesses. The pain and suffering, against which he so often protests, are only attempts at goading him into clearing away the barriers. Study of the Good Books provides directions for traversing the road, but such study is worthless unless the teachings are put into practice. That is the secret, not knowledge but practice.

LUC:12:22 There are teachings, which declare that man will become lost in a sea of oblivion, but this is incorrect. It comes from a misunderstanding of the All. Man will not become lost in the Eternal All, but this will become a part of man, of each individual soulspirit. Were this not so, there would be no need for the continual conflict, the continual testing by affliction and the continual presentation of new problems to overcome.

LUC:12:23 However, it is useless speculating on the truth of other teachings until the truth of your own is established. One thing you now know for certain is that man is more than he thinks himself to be, far more than the mortal expanse of unawakened potential. This you know, for you have experienced the rapture of the Illuminated. What you have done, others can do, for it is within the scope of anyone prepared to accept the necessary austerities and self-discipline. Not many will reach the goal of complete illumination, but all can obtain a momentary glimpse through the veil separating this sphere from the one above. All can awaken their soulspirit to consciousness, and only those who have done so can realise its glorious wonder. They become completely freed from every material limitation. They know themselves to be truly immortal, and to them, birth and death are now no more than milestones along the road. They lose their significance in the great inpouring of consciousness, the invigorating surge of new life.

LUC:12:24 All the awareness most persons encompass at any moment in time is just a minute part of the whole being. Some portions just on the fringe of the mortal are tapped from time to time, and these, such as memory, play a large part in life. However, out in the vast expanse beyond, comprising the undeveloped part of man, lie the latent powers, which he is incapable of utilising. Within the reach of each man is an infinite spiritual treasure, if only he would expend the necessary effort to grasp it!

Chapter Thirteen – The Lifeforce

LUC:13:1 When the child grows up, becoming a youth or maiden, it enters into a struggle with existence, with worldliness. It becomes like a swimmer setting out to cross a turbulent river. Individuals try to mould the world to their own way of thinking, but the world fights back, and in so doing shapes each one into an image differing from his own conception. To each person Earth takes on a different aspect, according to individual thoughts and inclinations.

LUC:13:2 The lifeforce centred in man is not something unique in nature, and the vast ocean of life seeks to draw it back into itself. Therefore, if the lifeforce is to remain separate within the individual, the individual must be prepared to face conflict and opposition. The struggle to retain life cannot be renounced; no one can cut himself off from the difficulties of worldly existence, or discard the burden of manhood or womanhood.

LUC:13:3 While strength and vitality throb within the mortal container, worldly problems and difficulties must be steadfastly faced and overcome. But at the onset of middle age, each one should prepare for the downhill run, and by this time, the soulspirit should be aroused to consciousness and be well and harmoniously formed. Each person should, by this time, be strong enough to face the inevitability of old age, decay and death, with equanimity. At this, the turning point of life, there should be an inward turning, a greater effort expended in seeking to understand the purpose and meaning of life. There should be a seeking after spirituality, after fulfillment.

LUC:13:4 The sole purpose of earthly life is to realise and develop the latent powers in man. All the problems and struggles, all the spiritual difficulties and obscurities, all the paradoxes, the experiences of joy and sorrow, pleasure and pain, simply serve to awaken the soulspirit. Life is all-embracing, it includes both birth and death, growth and decline, the contrasts, the opposites, the active and the passive, male and female.

LUC:13:5 It is the knowledge of his individuality, his seperateness, his consciousness of self that raises man above the level of the dumb creatures, but this position cannot be maintained without effort; it will always be easier to fall than to rise, to go back instead of forward. The child knows little of the burdens imposed by life, but as it grows older, its light-heartedness becomes overshadowed by the knowledge of duties and obligations, which must be assumed. The hearts of our weaker brethren are so often filled with a longing to return to the state of protected childhood, that they are easily beguiled by parental faiths, which treat them as children. They find it easy to cast their spiritual burdens at the feet of comforting priests, but such action is not only childishly irresponsible; it is also morally cowardly.

LUC:13:6 The spiritually irresponsible, who seek a comforting creed, are generally apathetic or selfish persons careless of their spiritual life and its needs. My friends, the ultimate, the final thing we must depend upon is the soulspirit. Only that accompanies the individual into the life eternal, but it is too late to come to this realisation upon the deathbed. Those who have confidence in their future existence are the only truly contented ones on Earth.

LUC:13:7 Man should never forget that his most important aspect is the soulspirit, and he should not be neglectful of its needs and demands. He should not confuse it with the frail mortal body whose needs and demands, if given full rein, will override those of his greater self. Man must understand life; he must understand its forces, which play about him. To understand it fully is to know one's own destiny, one's own heritage of struggle and one's own trials. Man must resolve on the inner search and follow its trail diligently.

LUC:13:8 When a man's life becomes a pattern of perfection reflecting the perfection above, he is a container for the lifeforce and a channel for the down pouring power which serves to uplift the whole of mankind. Becoming this is in fact the only real service man can render The Supreme Spirit.

LUC:13:9 Man's prime duty is to himself, and even when he serves others he is serving his own ends; therefore, he should not be hypocritical about his goodness. The good deeds of men are the soulspirit moulders, as also are spirituality, freedom from agnosia, forbearance, love of Truth and justice, tranquillity of heart, simplicity, austerity, generosity and integrity.

LUC:13:10 Only in a well-balanced being can the lifeforce manifest harmoniously. Therefore, all excesses of joy and sadness, pleasure and melancholy, despair and exhilaration, are to be avoided. The rule must be oft repeated: Moderation in all things and complete control over the self.

LUC:13:11 My friends, I have revealed to you the nature of the inner being who controls all things from within, now it is up to you to use this knowledge to good effect. I have shown you the chords, by which the spheres are held together and the same chords bind all things.

LUC:13:12 You ask me, "What is a good man?." He is one in whom goodness triumphs over evil, whose qualities grow stronger daily, while his evil qualities weaken. In him, conceit, avariciousness, selfishness, anger, rashness and agnosia are diminishing each day, and he governs his life in accordance with the Good Books.

LUC:13:13 Self-mastery is freedom, not restraint, for it is bondage to the body which makes life a misery to the man who aspires to goodness and the spiritually inclined. This bondage is caused by ignorance of the true nature of man and his destiny, and can best be overcome by a steady advance towards self-knowledge, spirituality and soulspirit awakening. The essential qualities for such advancement are tranquillity of heart (which means serenity), self-mastery, fortitude and resolution under the afflictions of life, kindness and consideration for others, a life led in accordance with the Good Books. The man who is truly good understands the troubles of another and stands ever ready to help the weak and oppressed. He never boasts of his achievements and treats every woman with respect, the same respect he has for his mother. He does not sully his lips with falsehood and is free from the fetters of greed and envy.

LUC:13:14 The lifeforce diversifies into many expressions, the greatest of which is love. This is a prime quality essential to soulspirit awakening, but it may take on many forms. Reverence is a form of love, so is the appreciation of melody and beauty. Uprightness is love manifesting in self-control; wisdom and desire for Truth is another form of love. Duty and obligation call forth an expression of love in a different aspect, though no less strong and beneficial.

LUC:13:15 My friends, there are those who teach that spirituality comes from turning away from the world, but this is a wrong teaching, for life is meant to be lived fully, and to live means to experience. A man who shuts himself away from the world can love no one except himself. To say he does it for love of The Supreme Spirit is empty talk.

LUC:13:16 No step is lost on the path of experience, though sometimes what appears to be a gain will be a loss, but so may a loss be a gain. The wayfarer must keep one objective ever before his eyes, and that is the ultimate end. He must strive towards this with all his resolution and allow nothing to divert him. The alluring sideroads are many-branched and lead to dead ends, and along them, worldliness beckons bewitchingly. Along the road, there are strugglers and stragglers, seekers and non-starters.

LUC:13:17 Therefore, if you would travel the road, firmly rid yourselves of the burden imposed by worldly and selfish desires. This does not mean that worldly things are to be completely shunned, for worldly success is not to be despised if sought with moderation and without prejudice to greater things. In all things there is a proper balance and state of harmony. However, whatever comes your way do not become too elated with success or too downcast by failure, both are tests and serve the same end.

LUC:13:18 Labour in the cause of earthly gain is of less value than labour, which benefits mankind or glorifies Earth. Therefore, if a creed brings men together only for worship, it serves little purpose; but if it is also a creed where men labour to learn, to beautify life and to advance mankind then its value is beyond estimation.

LUC:13:19 The lifeforce must be conserved and guarded, it must not be dissipated in the uncontrolled tempests of passion and emotion. These carry away the lifeforce, as the winds carry away the autumn leaves.

LUC:13:20 My friends, one of you says my words confuse him because they contain contradictions indicating two paths, and asks which is best for the attainment of the supreme goal. Let me say, and heed it well, that the most profound truths can be explained, in the limited expressions of men, only by seeming contradictions and paradoxes. Man may travel two paths to the perfection lying beyond Earth, one is the path of wisdom lit by the lamp of vision, and the other the path of action lit by the lamp of determination. There are men of wisdom and counsel, and men of deeds and action. All are equally necessary to maintain the balance and harmony of life, and an existence with one and not the other becomes chaotic.

LUC:13:21 Two things man cannot do, he cannot refrain from learning and he cannot refrain from action. He must not turn his back on life or renounce the worldly struggle. However, there is learning that is beneficial and learning which is not, there are actions which are good and others which are bad. It is the choice that counts.

LUC:13:22 Man is like a cornered bear, and life is like the hunters who surround it, goading it into action, forcing it to strike. So are all men driven to action by the nature of things, and any who seek to avoid it while permitting their thoughts to wander idly towards life's pleasures, do inestimable damage to their soulspirit. The true man is one in whom wisdom and action are balanced, whose mind, controlling his inner forces with harmony, governs his resolute steps along the path of action, and the mortal body could not exist here were it not continually active.

LUC:13:23 The lifeforce in man turns the wheel of progress, aim to be good, and carry out your allotted tasks in life, and progress in the right direction will follow. Though it is folly to sit irresolutely at the crossroads, it is no wiser to press forward along the wrong road.

LUC:13:24 Have faith in these teachings and follow the indicated path with cheerfulness, goodwill and resolution, and your soulspirit will safely reach the high pass where it can look out over the good country spread before it. Ignore the inner urges which rise from the depths of mortal flesh and drive a man, often even unwillingly, to act wrongfully.

LUC:13:25 Have faith in the reality of the soulspirit, for it is the only permanent thing in the ever changing waters of life. It may be hidden deep in agnosia, it may be clouded by mortal desires, as fire is clouded by smoke, by petty unfruitful pursuits, as a mirror is darkened by dust, or by the denseness of matter, as a kernel is hidden by its shell, but the reality lies underneath.

LUC:13:26 The lifeforce must never be consumed by flames of desires generating in the flesh. Unhealthy or abnormal desires, like wood ants, burrow into the minds of men and breed there, eating away their reasoning powers and wisdom. From such desires arises a noxious cloud of vapour which, having overcome reason and wisdom, smothers the soulspirit in darkness. Therefore, be masters and directors of your desires.

LUC:13:27 Great are the powers of the senses and the worldly desires to which they pander, to bind and blind. But the resources of the soulspirit are infinitely greater, if you will only call them forth. So stretch out and grasp the sword beyond the limits of mortality, and slay the enemies of the soulspirit. Even though you lack the resolution to fight for any cause, however great, fight for yourself, for your own preservation into eternity.

LUC:13:28 Those who lack faith in the existence of Truth, who cannot summon the strength to struggle, who have not the fortitude to stand the long weary years of preparation, will never penetrate the veil to see the wonder and glory beyond. There is a glorious, eternal beauty shining over the universal vastness, and in rare moments of illumination, man may glimpse the everlasting in things which pass away. This is the message handed down through the ages; this is the message of all true spiritual teachers.

All poets, musicians and artists, all who beautify and glorify life, convey only the same message in infinite variety of expression.

Chapter Fourteen – The Last Forest Teachings

LUC:14:1 My friends, the purpose and meaning of life are no longer hidden from you, and you know why men should follow the way of good rather than the way of evil. Every restraint and restriction, every responsibility, every duty and obligation, however obscure the purpose, are imposed with only one end in view, your own ultimate benefit and good. Everything unnecessary or purposeless has been winnowed away and only the sustaining grains remain, nothing not worthwhile has been kept.

LUC:14:2 Yet there is another reason for following this path, for, by refining and strengthening the soulspirit and awakening all its latent powers, each man is potentially a Mangod. He is no longer restricted to this sphere and can even contact Greater Beings beyond the mountain, and from them learn the truth.

LUC:14:3 Life itself is real, but as expressed in the Sphere of Matter and Mortality, it is little more than an illusion. The true being lives elsewhere, and where it lives man awakes to eternity, the illusion vanishes and he is confronted with the real. In this sphere man dwells in bondage to a belief in the reality of the illusion, he is attached to passing shadows, he seeks to grasp something of substance in a place where nothing is true, substantial and unchanging. Grind a stone to powder, and the powder to a powder of powder, and in the end, you will have something tangible. Such is the basis of this unsubstantial place.

LUC:14:4 My friends, you know too well how few soulspirits are awakened from their slumber on the soft couches of agnosia. Of those who do wake to consciousness are some who did so quickly and lovingly embrace the Great Light. They seek diligently and carefully for the tree of love and eagerly eat its nourishing fruit; those are the noble soulspirits, the truly illuminated among men. A ray of light from the Sphere of The Holy Spirit pours the vigour of renewed spiritual life into them, and they become more than men.

LUC:14:5 You wonder why there are so few awakened, but is it not man himself, by his own folly and blindness, his own spiritual apathy, who has slammed shut the gate leading to the road of enlightenment? Perhaps the truth is that man declines the necessary spiritual effort. It is your task to sound the awakening call, to rouse man from his spiritual drowsiness and stir him into action.

LUC:14:6 Do not concern yourselves overmuch regarding the nature of The Supreme Spirit. He is a Being incomprehensible to those with only the limited faculties of the Lower Spheres. He exists within a divine principle, upon which speculation is impossible, since it lies beyond the limits of mortal conception. Only the truly Illuminated Ones, the noble soulspirits, can approach the border of understanding, for they can see from afar. The treasures of His sanctuary are the ultimates of Love, Beauty, Perfection, Truth. Justice, Compassion and Goodness.

LUC:14:7 I am asked how this Far Away Formless One, awesome in changelessness, whose Spirit fills the whole universe, can be worshipped. My friends, how can He be influenced from the lower depths of His creation? Can rain wet the sky or rivers fill the ocean? Concerning the form of worship which is praise and prayer. Do you think that doleful chants, mournful music and mumbled prayer add to His glory or fill His heart with joy? These are gifts gathered from the woodland. Far more acceptable would be a freely dedicated heart purged of evil, the offering of a body wherein lust and unhealthy desires have been uprooted, the display of a mouth untainted by lewdness and falsehood, and the showing of integrity, honesty and purity.

LUC:14:8 True worship is the purification and elevation of the soulspirit, no more, all that purifies and elevates is worship. The purpose of worship is to arouse the soulspirit to wakefulness, it is the companionable unity of those serving a common cause. It is an act of mutual experience. It is not the servile humiliation of a slave before his master, but the linking of spirit with spirit.

LUC:14:9 These are the only sacrifices to bring: Bodily lusts and passions, evil thoughts, lies, deceit, slander and all forms of wickedness. To offer the blood of harmless creatures is easy and cowardly, and an insult to He who created them. These are the offerings to dedicate to His service: Diligent study of the Good Books, wisdom, courage, moral purity and steadfastness, together with all things serving the purpose of good. The only vestment needed for worship is a loyal, kind and pure heart.

LUC:14:10 To act as men do when worshipping is to belittle The Supreme Spirit. How can One so great be worshipped and served by fires and candles, by mumbled words falling thoughtlessly on unhearing ears, by sacrificial blood and by ornaments and incense? These things may serve a purpose in aiding man's awakening, but it is hypocritical to say they are necessary to The Supreme Spirit, and blasphemy to say He requires them from man. The Supreme Spirit rises above the thinking of men and says, "If such things please man, then let the offerer become the recipient."

LUC:14:11 The truly enlightened worship by a compliment, in trying to match their purity and goodness with the reflection of these qualities coming down from on high. The ennobling of the lesser self, goodness in thought, word and deed, the subjection of material urges, a constant disciplining of the body, an unwavering devotion to the cause of mankind, which is the cause of The Supreme Spirit, this is true worship, providing they are not clouded with hypocrisy.

LUC:14:12 Worship serves the soulspirit and therefore is beneficial, if sincere. Many have felt its first restless stirring in worship. My friends, how sad that the greatest treasure there is, the jewel beyond price, the soulspirit, still remains so often buried out of sight, unheeded, unsought, unwanted!

LUC:14:13 Nothing is more impressionable than the soulspirit, and every act forms a guide to its future appearance. Thus it is that every experience tends towards a repetition; and so a habit, good or bad, once formed is hard to break. It is like water which cuts a channel all other water follows.

LUC:14:14 Man has a material sounding board called the brain, which means a drumskin, and this is very apt. However, if it is battered with impure desires or taken over by worldliness it thickens and becomes a barrier against the spiritual forces. The brain, made dense with insensitivity and calloused by wickedness, forms a door which closes out all things of the spirit and becomes the servant of the senses. It no longer admits the light, and what light does penetrate becomes disguised and distorted into gloom. The door to the soulspirit becomes overgrown with weeds and brambles, the material and spiritual are separated by an immovable barrier and the soulspirit slumbers while the body decays.

LUC:14:15 Lacking the light, ensnared in sorrow and smothered in agnosia, degraded and sunk in the depths of matter, the soulspirit languishes and pines. Mercifully unconscious, it is pounded, twisted and torn, uncared for and unheeded, its infant cries falling upon deaf and deadened ears. Slowly it is smothered under the great overburden of wickedness and worldliness. Little need you wonder why the Dark Spirits are so often called 'abortions!'

LUC:14:16 Man, having chosen to spurn spirituality and thus lost the union in consciousness, which is his birthright, now seeks to console himself with worthless worldly baubles. With the arrogance of ignorance and blindness he claims the reality of his environment and endeavours to possess something outside himself, something to which he is half alien. This striving for worldly things still further buries the inner divinity, which becomes so encased in materialism that it can no longer be roused from its deadly slumber.

LUC:14:17 While man turns his soulspirit outwards, towards the illusive and deceptive world of matter and mortality, seeking fulfilment there, so long will he be unaware of his greater being. Here he will never find true contentment, and cut off from companionable communication with his true self, he will remain restless and dissatisfied. He will be always seeking for something, though he knows not what.

LUC:14:18 The greatness of the soulspirit, with all its potential powers, a true spark from the fire of divinity, is now smothered under layers of worldliness formed by pandering to the body experiences of the senses. The true being becomes a prisoner within a material prison of man's own creation.

LUC:14:19 Life is like a wide river containing the waters of manifestation deeply clouded by the silt of illusion, wherein the soulspirits of men swim back and forth. The Supreme Spirit is reflected in the waters through His rays of Holy Spirit, just as a mirror reflects the face of the looker while itself remaining untouched. The image in the waters is the soulspirit.

LUC:14:20 Those who say they can find The Supreme Spirit through means outside of themselves will seek in vain; what they will find will be worthless pebbles, the real jewel lies within. Only when the unreal is revealed for what it is and penetrated in consciousness, can the real come into sight. This can be proved beyond any dispute by personal experience, but few care to pay the price of such knowledge. The waters of illumination cannot be gathered on the heights of arrogant self-assurance, or on the hilltop of prejudice. Neither can they be drawn from the valley of apathy or the dale of agnosia.

LUC:14:21 I am asked concerning the people about us. They are not altogether ignorant in their teachings and it is not amiss to understand what they declare about the nature of man. They say he is a divine thought caught up in heaviness and wrapped about with clay. The thought, imprisoned in darkness, desired to see the light and the effort generated by the desire caused two holes to appear in the clay, and these became eyes. One of them looked to the right of things and the other to the left, and so directed straightly. No eyes appeared behind, as the divine thought never intended man to retreat, only to go forward. The eyes, being fixed on the path ahead, wished to know what was going on beside them, and so the effort generated by this desire brought forth two holes, which became ears. Because the clay desired to remain moist, a mouth was formed to provide water and then arms were formed, to push aside whatever got in the way. Then, so that it might know more of what was happening about it, the clay became sensitive and felt. So they say man is a divine thought trapped in a body and seeking to escape. They say the body is no more than clay reddened by sunlight, and can anyone say this is not a good description?

WSD:1:2 When a conscious, awakened spirit occupies a material body in conscious unity, the whole being is united with The Divine. It expands out beyond the limitations of space and time. Mindfulness controls the thoughts and feelings and clears an inner place, so that in silence and peace it is ready to receive an influx of the Divine Mindfulness, and meditation opens a way of communication, whereby the spirit of man may communicate with the spirit surrounding The Divine. It is a higher form of prayer, a controlled concentration of thought.

Book of Wisdom

Table of Chapters

WSD:1:1 – WSD:1:38	Chapter One – Meditation and Morals	95
WSD:2:1 – WSD:2:11	Chapter Two – The Dispensations of Life	99
WSD:3:1 – WSD:3:22	Chapter Three – The Harmonious Life	100
WSD:4:1 – WSD:4:18	Chapter Four – Defects of Character	103
WSD:5:1 – WSD:5:8	Chapter Five – Within Your Home	105
WSD:6:1 – WSD:6:8	Chapter Six – The Treatment of Women	105
WSD:7:1 – WSD:7:9	Chapter Seven – Duties, Obligations and Service to Life	106
WSD:8:1 – WSD:8:8	Chapter Eight – Respect for the Rights of Others	107

BOOK OF WISDOM
Table of Chapters (Continued)

WSD:9:1 – WSD:9:8	Chapter Nine – People and Places to Avoid	108
WSD:10:1 – WSD:10:8	Chapter Ten – Neighbourly Living	109
WSD:11:1 – WSD:11:11	Chapter Eleven – The Cause and its Champions	110
WSD:12:1 – WSD:12:18	Chapter Twelve – The Good Life	111
WSD:13:1 – WSD:13:19	Chapter Thirteen – The Religious Life	112
WSD:14:1 – WSD:14:11	Chapter Fourteen – Personal Conduct	115
WSD:15:1 – WSD:15:8	Chapter Fifteen – The Spiritual Realm	115
WSD:16:1 – WSD:16:9	Chapter Sixteen – The Meaning of Marriage	117
WSD:17:1 – WSD:17:9	Chapter Seventeen – The Upbringing of Children	118
WSD:18:1 – WSD:18:9	Chapter Eighteen – Friends and Enemies	118
WSD:19:1 – WSD:19:10	Chapter Nineteen – The Tendency Towards Evil	119
WSD:20:1 – WSD:20:15	Chapter Twenty – Teaching, Study and Learning	120
WSD:21:1 – WSD:21:39	Chapter Twenty-One – A Word to Prophets and Preachers	121
WSD:22:1 – WSD:22:17	Chapter Twenty-Two – The Good Religion	125

Book of Wisdom

Chapter One – Meditation and Morals

WSD:1:1 The only way a man can become fully awakened spiritually is to know his true nature and to strive for communication with the Spiritual Realm. This can best be achieved by meditation, or perhaps 'mindfulness' expresses it better. This is a state of conscious awareness of all the potentialities within man; the ability to cut off all material disturbances and to bring the spirit into harmonious relationship with a higher, more compatible realm. It means gaining complete mastery over all material impulses, urges and desires.

WSD:1:2 When a conscious, awakened spirit occupies a material body in conscious unity, the whole being is united with The Divine. It expands out beyond the limitations of space and time. Mindfulness controls the thoughts and feelings and clears an inner place, so that in silence and peace it is ready to receive an influx of the Divine Mindfulness, and meditation opens a way of communication, whereby the spirit of man may communicate with the spirit surrounding The Divine. It is a higher form of prayer, a controlled concentration of thought.

WSD:1:3 Clearing an inner place to form the Shrine of the Heart does not mean that it serves no purpose. The usefulness of a cave is in its empty space; the usefulness of a basket or a pot is in its emptiness. All wisdom and all knowledge, the answer to every question, are not to be found outside of man, but within him. He need not seek outside himself for the solution to the riddle of his nature. He need not traverse the Earth to find the answer; it can be reached from within himself. There, too, he will find all that supplies the needs of his spirit.

WSD:1:4 In his daily life and in all he does, each man should conduct himself as though intending to be a living example to others. He should act as though proclaiming his dedication to service in the greatest cause any man can serve, and as though inviting others to join him. He should be a leader showing the way and a guide indicating the path others should follow, the path each must travel alone.

WSD:1:5 Every thinking man must surely realise now that there is something more to life than a search for happiness, wealth or luxury. That life must be more than an idle drifting, the only efforts being bent towards seeking the still waters of contentment and the shallows of pleasure. There must be more than walking around seeking enjoyment. There is indeed something more to it than that; there is a purpose to life, and that purpose is living.

WSD:1:6 Living is meant in its fullest sense and does not refer to mortal life alone. Mortal life is the servant, the threshold of a greater life and should be regarded only in this light. The duty of all is to awaken their own spirit to consciousness. If, however, this has not been achieved, then the best thing to do is to follow the precepts and advice contained in the writings of those who have themselves awakened their spirits to consciousness.

WSD:1:7 For the first step it is sufficient to be self-controlled and self-disciplined, the efforts of every man being bent towards learning more about himself. He must cultivate mindfulness, to discover his own motives and to know what lies behind every thought, every word and action. He must discover every cause and understand its effect. He must know why he does a certain thing and by what means he achieves it. He must decide upon a plan of life, upon certain objectives and carry them through to a successful conclusion. He must choose a path and follow it through to the end, not looking too far ahead that he ignores what lies before his feet. He must firmly ignore the cries of diverting desires and disregard the bypaths of foolish fancies.

WSD:1:8 As yet, no mortal man knows the true laws of justice, and no mortal man has ever seen the face of Truth unveiled. No man has yet risen sufficiently in greatness to proclaim his ability to live free from all restraint imposed by others. Some may proclaim their ability or right to do so, but these do it not from strength but from moral weakness. Their affirmation of their own freedom is in fact a declaration of war upon the liberties of others. They are no more than spineless creatures who decry the laws of morality and high principles only because these seek to restrain their baser instincts and restrain their unhealthy carnal outlets.

WSD:1:9 While disparaging the existing codes, whereby men live, they have neither the ability nor the strength to replace them with anything equally good and worthy. Certainly, whatever they did produce would never tend towards the spiritual elevation of mankind. Such as these must not be pandered to and, if they refuse to bear their fair share of the burdens of mankind, they should not be humoured. Those who seek to assert their individuality at the expense of others are a menace not to be tolerated. The rule shall be that everyone is to be granted the greatest possible freedom up to, but not beyond, the point where it infringes upon the freedom, rights or contentment of others. It is impossible to give complete freedom to any man, and no man is worthy of it. Any freedom attained at the expense of another man is an unworthy freedom.

WSD:1:10 No man has the right to condemn a moral code or standard of principles until he himself has risen above them. No laws, no principles and no code should be discarded until they have been replaced by something proven to be better. The replacement of those already established anywhere is no easy task and one certainly far beyond the experience and ability of any one person. Therefore, in the present condition and development of mankind, goodness and righteousness are expressed by the disciplined acceptance of the moral law and courageous submission to the written law. These must, however, evolve with man, to meet his changing and greater needs.

WSD:1:11 An evil custom or law is to be cast aside, even though it be established and accepted by many generations. A good custom or law should be taken over and followed, even if it be observed by your enemies and followed by them. The decision as to what is good and what is bad cannot lie within the province of any one man.

WSD:1:12 Laws are made, and laws are changed, but no man truly knows what is right and what is wrong. This can be discovered only in the inspired books compiled by the hands of illuminated men. The time is not far distant when men should no longer think in terms of being good or wicked, rich or poor, sick or healthy, but in terms of being spiritual or material.

WSD:1:13 The basic motive behind a righteous and good life is not the quest for happiness. Righteousness, goodness and morality are other words meaning self-discipline, duty, obligation and service. These form a foundation, upon which a proper way of life can be built, and within the framework of this foundation, the quest for happiness is certainly not restricted. Indeed, not only is it encouraged but also earnestly urged.

WSD:1:14 Nearly everyone has principles of some sort, but all have a tendency to push back the frontiers of these principles to suit themselves. Their idea of morality is subordinated to their material interests. Men should not be hypocrites with themselves and should freely admit to this tendency to subordinate their principles to their own selfish interests. A standard of morality or code of principles which is not absolute and unshakable is worthless as a support and no standard at all. Only the very wisest of men can set their own standards, and the wisest of men are too wise to do so.

WSD:1:15 As far as man is concerned, the purpose of life is development and preparation for something greater. This cannot be undertaken in a half-hearted manner or at specific times; it is a process continuing every minute of the day. Every test confronting man here is purposeful and necessary, even though its reason and end may be obscure.

WSD:1:16 The measure of the duties, obligations and service demanded from any man is dependent upon the strength, talents and possessions, which have been bestowed upon him. The more a man has, the stronger he is, so must the returns be in proportion, for he is that much better able to serve. Every man has been given according to the extent of the service expected from him.

WSD:1:17 One of the less easy tasks for the enlightened man is to develop the ability to genuinely assess the service to be rendered in return for the things, with which he has been endowed, and to serve without selfish hesitation. Each man has his particular place in the ranks of those who serve, and his own talents and possessions should be regarded only as a means of enlarging the pool of common good and the advancement of mankind. Those who deny their obligations inflict a lonely, awful doom upon themselves.

WSD:1:18 As the weakness and faltering of any one man lessen the total of service rendered and retard the advance, it becomes the obligation of the strong to protect the weak, not in order that they should be shielded from things leading to their ultimate good, or to carry a burden they decline, but to help them towards the attainment of strength. The aim should always be towards increasing the total amount of strength and ability at the disposal of the whole.

WSD:1:19 Suffering and affliction are unavoidable if man is to develop into the godlike being intended. He must grow spiritually strong, possessing both courage and compassion, and, to do this, he cannot be protected from suffering and affliction. Can the over-sheltered plant kept indoors withstand either the sun's heat or the windy blast? Compassion was awakened in the heart of man only through suffering, and the noble qualities of courage and dedication were roused only through affliction. Those who, in the past, bore their suffering with fortitude became uplifting examples to their fellowmen.

WSD:1:20 However, it must be remembered that pain and suffering do not, of themselves, develop spirituality. They are not so important, but what is important is the manner, in which they are endured, the spirited rising to the challenge and the courageous conquest. The suffering of each man should be an offering dedicated to the uplifting of mankind.

WSD:1:21 What any man has to face and overcome is unimportant. What really matters is how he faces it and by what means he overcomes it. Where a man stands is also unimportant, the important thing is the direction, in which he is moving. Life on Earth was never meant to be spent in rest and tranquillity. Its very tribulations and problems give it an added zest for those brave spirits who face up to them with courage and cheerfulness. Each man must discover for himself his own weaknesses and frailty.

WSD:1:22 The Creating Divinity could have brought a painless world into being, but it would also have been one without purpose. It could have been peopled with perfect beings, but these could not have understood the meaning of suffering and tribulation. They would have been devoid of pity, tenderness and sympathetic understanding.

WSD:1:23 It is not through the Divine Will that man suffers. The Divine Will is that man fulfil the Divine Plan through learning to overcome the restrictions and illusions of a material existence by rising above them. The troubles and trials are there to goad man on, to stimulate him, to rouse him out of material lethargy and urge him towards the development of spirituality and wisdom. If man suffers unduly, it is because of his own heedlessness and waywardness, his ignorance of the true meaning and purpose of life.

WSD:1:24 The Earth is imperfect because its imperfections are essential. The social imperfections, as distinct from the natural imperfections, are the result of man's lack of understanding and his dedication to material ends rather than spiritual ones. The trials and tests resulting from the natural imperfections of Earth do not oppress man nearly as much as the afflictions man has brought upon himself, through seeking to establish a life wholly within the material. It is necessary to know the difference between the two and to separate one from the other.

WSD:1:25 The reason that there is so little divine intervention is not that The Divine remains indifferent, but that man has been given all the powers and wisdom necessary to deal with the affairs of Earth. If he fails to make use of them, who then is to blame? The duty and obligation placed upon man relate to his reaching upward towards spirituality and outward towards perfection. If man declines to do this, he must accept the consequences and can blame none but himself.

WSD:1:26 Were there no pain and suffering, man would be like a jellyfish drifting aimlessly with the currents in a sea of matter. Suffering, pain and sorrow result from an existence within a material body and are not a part of man's spiritual heritage. The bonds of humanity are forged in the furnaces of life and not in its tranquil breezes.

WSD:1:27 These are the directions for those who follow the Great Path of the True Way, the never failing guides and sustainers: Be grateful for the good things of life. Be patient under suffering and steadfast in adversity. Be diligent in the performance of your duty, and never shirk your obligations. Bear the blows of affliction with cheerfulness and courage. Do not be quick to anger, hasty to argue or rash in judgement, for this reveals your lack of self-control. Avoid the weaknesses of unjust hate and envy, for they rebound upon yourself. Do not engage in undue frivolity, lest people come to think you petty-minded. Keep your temper under control, for an angry person is a confused one. Let your deportment be serene and confident. Keep your mind above earthly things, and look towards the Kingdom of the Spirit and Mansions of the Soul. Never pay homage to evil men, and never commend what is wrong.

WSD:1:28 Do not use lewd expressions or foul language, for this advertises your inferiority to others. Do not laugh at sly or dirty humour, for this displays an unclean and unhealthy mind. Do not raise money or possessions to the status of a god. Fit yourself to earn an honest and useful livelihood. Skill and knowledge are jewels in times of prosperity, a sword and shield in times of adversity, and sure guides through times of uncertainty.

WSD:1:29 In the midst of material illusion, do not add to the confusion by acting falsely in word or deed. Be diligent and consistent in studying the wisdom contained within these books. Never forget the benefits that accrue from a life well led, and remember that whatever befalls is intended for your own good. If a man, establish yourself by your manliness and, if a woman, by your femininity.

WSD:1:30 Be modest in manner and calm in bearing, for men avoid the excitable man who is a weak reed to lean upon in times of stress and a hazard in danger. The boastful man falls far short of the image he intends to create, so weigh your words carefully, for the spoken word cannot be recalled. A man careless with words is also unreliable in other ways. Never make a confident of one who babbles.

WSD:1:31 Forget what has been done and cannot be altered, and do not be concerned about things, which may never happen. If you have anything of value, keep it away from an envious man. Arise early in the morning, and greet the day eagerly, for the sluggard and lieabed are already partially dead. Eat and drink in moderation, taking sufficient for the wellbeing of the body without overloading it. Seek the company of those who are your superiors in wisdom, skill and spirituality, so that you will be raised up to prosper. Always be ready to heed advice and to accept instruction, bearing in mind that it is more profitable to listen than to talk.

WSD:1:32 The man who cannot restrain his tongue rides a wild stallion. Keep it in check, and avoid returning a hasty answer to those who say unkind things, which may stem only from their own weakness. Be patient and forbearing under provocation, and restrain your arm when tempted to raise it in anger. The man who remains unmoved under provocation is a better man than he who strikes. Always speak calmly and with few words. Speak softly and clearly, for only fools shout to cover their own ignorance. The ox bellows, while the bull snorts.

WSD:1:33 One of the great failures of life is to lose a friend. If this misfortune befall a man, he should search his heart carefully and sincerely, lest it happen again. Never seek to maintain a friendship through hypocrisy or flattery, for this is no friendship, and it displays the double heart of a deceiver.

WSD:1:34 Be proud but not haughty, straight-talking but not insulting. Bold but not aggressive, patient but not servile. Bear in mind that it is better for a man to be numbered among the insulted than among the insulters, among the slandered and not among the slanderers.

WSD:1:35 Keep your feet firmly upon the Great Path of the True Way, using moderation in all things as your guiding light. Never be effusive of speech or too friendly towards those who are no more than acquaintances. Keep all at arms length until they have established themselves for what they are and their true natures are revealed. Never allow the secrets of your heart to be handed around as common property.

WSD:1:36 Do not be over-sensitive and ever ready to take offence, for this will only turn people against you. Never trespass upon the privacy of others, and let all follow the paths of their inclinations. Attend to your own affairs, and keep your thoughts from the affairs of others.

WSD:1:37 Of thoughts, words and deeds, only deeds have any established value on Earth. Thoughts are intangible things in a world of matter, while words have no meaning unless translated into action.

WSD:1:38 Goodness and wisdom should not be secreted, for when their possessor cuts himself off from others, what purpose do they serve and how can they be measured and tested? The good man who fears contamination by the world has no confidence in his goodness and renders no service. If a man is found sinking into a morass of mud, he who tries to rescue him cannot be rescued by anyone standing off. The man who attempts to clean up the morals of the people is like the dusting cloth which cleans only by becoming soiled itself.

Chapter Two – The Dispensations of Life

WSD:2:1 If visited by affliction or sorrow a man should not bewail his loss, for these should be the means of drawing him closer into the embrace of Divinity. They are meant to strengthen his spirit and develop his spirituality. No man has any right to expect an untroubled life, and one who has passed half a year without trouble or affliction has already received ample reward for living and should not ask for more. Sorrow is the purging agent of the spirit and suffering the flux merging man with Divinity. They also help to distinguish purelove from mocklove, for purelove is the unquenchable fire, which the waters of tribulation cannot put out.

WSD:2:2 A man should always be prepared for testing and never be caught off guard, for calamity may well strike in the midst of prosperity and peace. He should also bear in mind while undergoing his test, that at any time it may be eased by a stroke of good fortune.

WSD:2:3 After every calamity, a man should review the words he has spoken and the things he has done, for perhaps what has befallen him is only the result of incautious words or the outcome of foolish deeds. Chastisement is a necessity of earthly life. If it did not follow a wrongdoing, how could a child ever learn the difference between right and wrong? The chastisements of men spring from Divine Love alone, for through suffering comes sympathy and through tribulation comes understanding. The man who can cheerfully accept affliction, knowing its true purpose, is one who has learned one of the deepest secrets of life. No man is afflicted beyond his endurance, for the cold blasts of calamity are always tempered to his weakness. Only the strong and chosen are called upon to carry the heavy burdens, for the strong runner does not care if the wind is against him.

WSD:2:4 If trials and tribulations descend upon a man, he should meet them with quiet resolution and courage. It is useless to rage against them or seek to rise in revolt against his lot. Only the faint-hearted and ignorant are turned from the Path because they think their endurance may be in vain. The righteousness and goodness of a man will not protect him from suffering and may even add to it. The fruits of his labour are not plucked along the road, which lies this side of the border. How often is a man seen bewailing his misfortune and so sorry for himself that he fails to gain any benefit from it? All too often, men take their misfortunes as a sign that they are abandoned.

WSD:2:5 Men set their hearts on certain things and make plans for their attainment, but unless the plans they make complement the Divine Plan, they will come to nothing. Earth has a mission, and everything upon it is there to play its part in the fulfilment of that mission. Material ends have little importance beside spiritual ends, and creation is only intended to satisfy spiritual needs and develop spiritual abilities.

WSD:2:6 The good and the wicked are tested, and no one is exempt. The difference is that the righteous man uses the tests to benefit himself, while the unrighteous turns them against himself to destroy his own soul. No man should be overwhelmed by the troubles and tribulations, which come upon him. They are intended to be utilised for the benefit of his soul and the strengthening of his spirit, and, bearing this in mind, he should be better able to endure them.

WSD:2:7 Every man is born to be tested and tried. Sorrow and suffering, problems and tribulations, are meant to be the lot of men. Yet, they are never his continued lot, and the brighter moments of life far outweigh the darker. Man was not given life for the sole purpose of enjoying Earth and its pleasures. Earth is a place man must cultivate and prepare for harvest, and what he produces will be his sustenance when the season is ended. Tribulation is his plough, and trouble his spade. Sorrow and suffering are his seeds, and the joys of life the fertilising waters.

WSD:2:8 Be grateful for the good things of life, for they far exceed your needs. Offer a prayer of thanks in the morning and another in the evening, and if you can find no reason for doing so, be certain the fault lies within yourself. Even to know that the worst possible thing has happened, and the cup of misfortune been drained to its last drop, brings a strange compensation, for there is a deep peace of mind known only to those who have lost all and cannot lose more.

WSD:2:9 If a man is favoured with prosperity, he should be vigilant, lest it permit his desires to lead him astray and his spiritual diligence be diminished. In the greater scheme of things, the times of affliction and adversity are not to be feared so much, for then, men incline towards spiritual things. It is in times of prosperity, when they acquire wealth and become conceited and self-centred, that the danger lies, for then they twist the commanding words and austere meanings of the sacred books and pervert them to console their own consciences. Therefore, in times of prosperity and contentment, a man must be more careful in the interpretation of the Sacred Books than he would be when he only turned to them for strength and consolation.

WSD:2:10 The intelligent man observes the ways of Nature and the forces she utilises. He learns how they operate, so that he does not become the slave of blind forces beyond his control. Those who do not understand the workings of natural forces, or are overawed by them, become their slaves. This is a place where nothing is seen clearly, and even Truth can be distinguished only against a background of contrasting falsity.

WSD:2:11 The dispensations of life are not entirely beyond the understanding of man, and indeed he has a duty to strive for understanding. Everything serves a purpose, even things, which seem the most hurtful. Every ungainly rock has, within itself, a potential statue, and potential beauty lies in every block of wood or lump of clay, but what is there cannot come out of its own volition. The image and the beauty are brought out only after the untouched materials have been subjected to the discipline of thought and the forming action of chisel, knife or fire. According to the good things done by a man, so will he be rewarded, and by the nature of the evil he does, so will he be punished. A man is paid according to his labour, and idle hands make a hungry mouth.

Chapter Three – The Harmonious Life

WSD:3:1 Whatever is wrong on Earth is wrong with man. The discord among men comes from within themselves and not from their environment, and it is in his relationship with others that man displays his deficiencies and weaknesses most clearly. Hypocrisy is one of the most deep-rooted evils in the natures of men, for they hate in others the things they fear in themselves. The man who is the most voluble against a particular form of vice is the man who practises it in secret. Men wrap themselves in a mantle of hypocrisy and never uncover their real selves. They declare themselves for or against; they say they believe one thing or the other; they like this or that, but rarely do they declare themselves truthfully or reveal their true thoughts and feelings to others. To overcome this evil, this weakness in men, is one of mankind's greatest battles. To this, the Good Religion must dedicate itself.

WSD:3:2 Those who follow the Good Religion should seek their friends among others of similar belief and inclination, and they should not try to walk a double road. No man can hide a thing within his breast forever, and if he is a secret hypocrite, some day it will be made known. Nothing done, known or experienced during earthly life is lost forever.

WSD:3:3 If your neighbour offend you, then restrain your anger so that your spirit may be benefited. Burdens borne patiently and with courage, and insults ignored, are better for the spirit than any form of penance. Always restrain your anger for the sake of neighbourly harmony, but for your own good, remember that the words of an angry man are like glowing embers in his mouth. Anger alone does no great harm to the spirit, but anger with malice or hatred certainly blemishes the purity of a soul.

WSD:3:4 Never try to appease a man in the hour of his anger, but leave him to be consumed in his own fire. Before you vent your anger on a man who has offended you, pause and try to discover some goodness in him, which you lack. It is not required that a person never get angry or become stirred up inside, for sometimes circumstances demand the response of righteous anger. Therefore, be one slow to anger and with complete mastery over the temper, rather than one without the ability to be stirred to anger. Do not be too sweet unless you want to be eaten. When two persons quarrel in anger, both are always in the wrong.

WSD:3:5 The most burdensome person in any community is the one who will not do what he is capable of doing because he cannot do the things he wants to do. Every man must learn the difference between the little things he can do alone and the greater things, which can be done with the co-operation of others, for unity bestows strength.

WSD:3:6 Always be generous in your dealings with a neighbour and bear in mind that as water quenches fire, so does cheerful restitution atone for a wrong. When a neighbour greets you cheerfully, answer him in the same manner, for a surly face or a frown frightens away the hand of friendship. Generosity and kind-heartedness are excellent qualities, but those who possess them should be vigilant, for it is not inconceivable that the goodness they do may sometimes result in more evil than good.

WSD:3:7 Always treat the property of your neighbour or his friends as you would wish your own property and friends to be treated. Never speak without thought, for words cannot be recalled and things said may remain beyond recall forever. A lightly spoken word may ruin a life or destroy the contentment of a family. The guiding rule is not only to say the right thing in the right place, but also to leave unsaid the wrong thing at the moment when it is most tempting to utter it. This is the rule of conversation: Is it true, is it instructive, is it kind, is it necessary?

WSD:3:8 Do not be crude in speech or rough in manner, for these reveal a hidden weakness. Courtesy, consideration and good manners are necessary ingredients in the cement of neighbourliness. The cement of friendship is mutual suffering.

WSD:3:9 A man should never talk to a woman in a manner, which would outrage her modesty, but common women have sacrificed their modesty and cannot be outraged. Therefore, the manner of a man's speech in the presence of a woman indicates his opinion of her and her reputation. Always be vigilant when in the company of women, for no greater insult can be offered to a man than to imply that his wife, mother, daughter or sister is a common woman. A strong man can afford to be gentle and quiet wherever he is, but a weak man must be rough and boastful to boost himself. The man who is always boosting himself is certainly one who needs boosting.

WSD:3:10 If some misfortune has befallen a neighbour, or he is out of favour with the rulers, he will be suffering the miseries of shame, and therefore to visit him under these circumstances might add to it. It is a matter of discretion and tact as to when he should be visited. Whatever he has done, treat him with kindness and consideration. The fruits of kindness are sweet, but the fruits of hatred and malice lie heavily on the stomach. As surely as night follows day, as a man deals with others, so will he be dealt with.

WSD:3:11 If a man does not wish his own possessions to be touched, he should show the same respect for the possessions of another man. Likewise, if he respects his own reputation and expects others to respect it also, he should hold the reputation of others in the same high regard. If he does not wish to become the subject of gossip, he should not gossip about anyone else.

WSD:3:12 As a man expects his own home and family to be treated, so should he treat the home and family of another. As he cherishes the good name of his wife and the welfare of his children, so should he cherish the good name of another's wife and the welfare of his children.

WSD:3:13 Deal charitably with your neighbours, and wherever the opportunity to do good arises, do not hesitate to do it. However, a single act of charity means that the heart has been stirred only once. It may be just a sudden urge that passes, and charity is a continuing process.

WSD:3:14 A man can find peace and happiness in his home only when his wife and family have it, and these things cannot be portioned out. The man with strife at home has a lot more misery than that of a hungry dog. When a guest, bear in mind that the ways of a host are always right in the eyes of his guest.

WSD:3:15 Always live according to your beliefs, for to do otherwise is hypocrisy. One of the tasks of the Good Religion is to teach men that they have to bridge the great gap between what they believe to be right and the way they live. Also, though many men know how they should live very few do in fact live that way.

WSD:3:16 Though it is proper for a man to marry early, it is not right to marry with undue haste. For a man to take a wife before he can support her, or before he can understand her, is foolishness. The man who takes a wife in unwise haste ties a millstone around his own neck and can blame none but himself for the consequences. A man should never take a wife until he has read through the Sacred Books many times.

WSD:3:17 Stand firm in your belief as to what is right and what is wrong. Never surrender your principles or betray your ideals. Yet, do not let your mind become bigoted or prejudiced, for the man of unchanging mind is as water, which, standing still, becomes stagnant and filled with slime. His thoughts are like water imprisoned within a vase until it becomes foul.

WSD:3:18 Tact and self-control, the exercise of moderation in all things and a disciplined ambition with attainable aim, a kind heart and truthful tongue, these are the things, which smooth the way along the path of life. The maggots that eat away the body of peace and contentment are: undue haste, thoughtlessness, indifference and malice.

WSD:3:19 Do not be unduly afraid of being poor. It is better to have only a few possessions with just sufficient to maintain the health of the body, than to have vitality-sapping and spiritual-enervating abundance of the rich. Happiness cannot be bought, and a joyful heart makes a healthy body. Pure love, not wealth, is the most desirable of treasures, for it hallows the brief days of life and fills them to overflowing with spiritual wealth of everlasting value.

WSD:3:20 Along the high road of life, man and woman must walk together hand in hand. The two together are meant to make their joint love a harmonious whole, and the life of one without the other is incomplete. Yet in these times, true matrimonial harmony appears to be one of the most difficult things to achieve, because of the spiritual immaturity resulting from the inadequacy of existing religious doctrines. This, too, must be remedied.

WSD:3:21 Do not be too hasty in judging a wrongdoer, for it may well be that though he has been found in some wickedness, the good in him is greater than the good in you. Perhaps in the Divine View, he is a better man than you are. Disobedience to the laws of men with the sincere and considered intention of doing good, is better than abject submission to them without any such motive.

WSD:3:22 The golden rule of harmonious living is that a man must master his desires, control his will and serve his conscience.

Chapter Four – Defects of Character

WSD:4:1 The man who talks much does so to cover his own weakness. Words, of themselves, are worthless things and where there is much talk there is little action. Words alone are lifeless things having no value until they are quickened within the heart and demonstrated in deeds. Therefore, the rule is never to engage in idle chatter and always to avoid the company of those who babble.

WSD:4:2 Those who find pleasure in chattering and gossip display the outward signs of a small and irresponsible mind. Those who sow mischief with their tongue can be assured that they will reap the harvest of scorn. Speech is one of the qualities, which set men apart from the animals, but it is also a drug to be handled with care. Therefore, treat all words as an apothecary does the drugs of a prescription. They must be carefully measured out and weighed, with every precaution taken against an overdose.

WSD:4:3 Over-indulgence in talk displays a defect of character. Therefore, even when praising another or lauding his virtue, excessive talk should be avoided, lest the speaker be accused of hypocrisy or patronage. Effusive speech is the babbling water flowing over a shallow mind. Nothing is more becoming for the intelligent man than silence, and how much more so for one who is not!

WSD:4:4 The motto for those who follow the Good Religion should be: 'Say little, and do much. Replace words with deeds.' The good will find this no hardship, but the wicked will prefer talk to action. The mouth of a man is like a horse; it must be restrained by firm control and bridled before it can serve him. If allowed out of control it will carry him off to calamity. Therefore, guard your tongue as you would your wealth, bearing in mind that the less the words spoken the less the errors made.

WSD:4:5 Though all the wisdom of the past condemns overindulgence in chatter, this still grows in volume, while the ills of the world do not lessen, though they may change in nature. Therefore, if you would serve the Good Religion well, hold your tongue in check. Do not overlook it in youth, then in maturity, it may pour out wisdom, which will advance the greater cause of mankind.

WSD:4:6 Words are the weapons, which give power to falsehood and equip the liar. Lying and deceit are the defects of character, which most reveal its underlying weakness. The earthly punishment of a liar is in the fact that nobody believes him when he eventually speaks the truth, but he condemns himself to greater punishment in the realm of the spirit.

WSD:4:7 Lack of hospitality displays the defects of meanness. Therefore, always be hospitable to the wayfarer and stranger, treating them fairly and with consideration. Do not cheat them or betray their trust and confidence in you, for this is the action of a mean nature. Those who are mean or who lead others into meanness cannot avoid a blemished soul.

WSD:4:8 Few are those who recognise their own defects and fewer still those who honestly acknowledge them. Even less in number are those who earnestly strive to overcome them, though this is an essential part of life's purpose. Most are hypocrites and self-deceivers whose regeneration commences only when they honestly search their hearts and discover what they actually are within themselves.

WSD:4:9 One of the greatest defects of character is sheer indifference and lack of interest in anything beneficial and useful. A man can gain wisdom and enlightenment only when he has laboured at reading and diligently studied the Sacred Books. Casual thinking about higher things and reading for amusement or pleasure produce no beneficial effect and serve no useful purpose.

WSD:4:10 The man who is dominated by passion and is the slave of his desires is one whose character is weak. He can serve nothing greater than an earthly end. To serve the Good Religion, a man has to rise above this end, and the means for so doing, the reason and purpose, is the revelation contained within the Sacred Books.

WSD:4:11 The man of defective character seeks to live at the expense of others and does not pull his weight. He takes and does not give; he is a parasite on the body of mankind. Therefore, bear in mind that he who eats from the produce of his own hands is contented in heart and refreshed in spirit. But when eating, do not bring discord to the table or consume food while flies swarm or a dog stands by hungry.

WSD:4:12 Throughout the lands of the old religions, people complain that they have little to live for, but it would be more true to say that they have nothing to die for. They can see no purpose in life, but the truth is they can see no purpose in death. They complain they do not have enough to sustain them in death. The existing religions grow old and weak, not through age, for a religion sustained by Truth is ageless, but through lack of Truth which is the food of good faith. They cannot give sustenance, which provides strength to deal with the times, but the food of the Good Religion must still be withheld from men, for its day remains deep within the womb of time.

WSD:4:13 In these times men lack the strength of character to seek fame, and seek notoriety instead, but this is no more than fame's horribly distorted image. Men are deficient in the qualities, which should spur them to seek fame through service and sacrifice. They lack the driving force and inspiration, which should come from their national spirit. The fertile fields of inspiration are now overgrown with weeds, and the refreshing waters of spirituality are stagnant. The sun of a new inspiration, the dawn of a new day of hope will surely follow this night of darkness. Then, mankind will surge forward once again to storm the spiritual heights, bearing a new standard, a new banner with the device of spiritual inspiration.

WSD:4:14 Pride is a quality of good; false pride and haughtiness are servants of evil. The man who has no pride in himself as a man is weak in character, and this weakness leads him into error and wrongdoing. When a man is without a standard to live by and holds himself in low esteem, any wickedness he does will not appear wrong to him. The laws of men punish the sickness and ills within the nations, but do not cure them. The precepts and moral code of the Good Religion are the medicines needed to prevent and cure; their day will come. If a man is more concerned about what others may think of him than about what he knows himself to be, if he fears their judgement more than his own, then he knows the worthlessness of his own opinion. Man must be made to stand proud in his strength of character and moral integrity. The duty of religion is to make such a man.

WSD:4:15 To be good, a man must not only live a good life; he must also do good deeds. These should not be only such as come his way or result from his inclinations, they must also be the result of effort, search and sacrifice. Doing good when the opportunity arises is not sufficient, for real merit results only from a hard-fought battle with evil.

WSD:4:16 The man of sound character bestirs himself in the cause of good and diligently studies the Sacred Books, to know what is required of him. He accepts with good grace the tasks imposed upon him and does not shirk his duties and obligations. He does not try to interpret the words of the Sacred Books in such a way that things are made easier for him. He does not treat their command lightly, neither does he shun the service they require from him. He knows that no matter how hard he strives, they can still lead him on towards greater perfection. No man is asked to be perfect; he is asked only to strive towards perfection with all his heart and strength.

WSD:4:17 No man can ever be a failure if he strives to do his duty and undertakes all the things he should. But if he turns his back on his duty and shirks his obligations, he is always a failure. A man who seeks to boost himself by displaying his cleverness is like a commander who reveals all the secrets of his defence. He lays himself open to easy conquest.

WSD:4:18 The defects of character are many and varied, but before they can be overcome, they must be discovered. The words written here can be no more than a mirror, which is handed to you. Whether you look at the mere reflection of yourself, or whether you look with deeper insight and understanding, does itself depend upon the nature of your own character. The defects of a defective character may conceal its own deficiencies from itself, but they cannot remain hidden if sought in the light of Wisdom and Truth.

Chapter Five – Within Your Home

WSD:5:1 Though your house is your domain and the stronghold of your privacy, keep it open for acts of charity. Do not close its doors to one in trouble, but let all who need it enter and find sympathy. Let your house be open to receive the widow and the orphan.

WSD:5:2 Maintain your house as a place of contentment and happiness, permitting all members to have their say without interruption or suppression. Uphold its sanctity and the sanctity of your family, whatever befalls, bearing in mind that no sacrifice in doing so is too great. If the sanctity of your home or family has been betrayed or destroyed, do not be passive, for by doing so, you induce the same calamity to fall upon another.

WSD:5:3 Your home is the stronghold of your privacy and ideals, and it enshrines the gentleness of your wife and the modesty of your daughters. Therefore, do not permit it to be invaded by the tongues of lewdness, or allow its air to be polluted by the breath of the foul-mouthed. The man who does so displays his lack of pride and the low esteem, in which he holds his family. If you hear lewdness in the privacy of a man's house, know that he is a weak character whose family is to be pitied.

WSD:5:4 Within your house is your home, and this is the life and spirit of the house. Maintain your home as a hallowed place where all that is finest in mankind remains enshrined. Do not argue except to instruct, and do not chastise without understanding and good intent. Never break the peace of the table, for food should always be consumed in tranquillity and without haste.

WSD:5:5 It is the nature of children to be boisterous and get into mischief, so the good parent tempers discipline with understanding and tolerance. The good parent is never unduly harsh, but neither is he lax and indifferent to the need for discipline. The proper discipline for a child is maintained through example and guidance, not through chastisement. When the need arises to punish a child, never do so without asking yourself where you have failed. If you care enough for the child, you will be diligent in your heart-searching.

WSD:5:6 An unhappy marriage is always the result of haste, thoughtlessness or lack of consideration by both or one. No child should ever suffer for the foolishness or ignorance of a parent, and when dealing with a child, this must be the governing rule. While no one can claim happiness as a birthright, every child brought into the world is entitled to all the happiness possible and all the pleasures of childhood.

WSD:5:7 The sun of a man's home is his wife, but he who takes an unchaste woman to wife is one content to live without the warmth of inspiration. The man whose wife lacks the womanly virtues becomes a prisoner to his own shame, and his house a place of discord and unrest. A faithful wife crowns her husband with a garland of happiness, but the wife who deceives her husband is like a cancer within his heart waiting to erupt.

WSD:5:8 Within his home a man is king, and his wife is queen. No stranger should be permitted to trespass on the domain of their happiness, and prying officials should rightly be excluded. Even those who seek to uphold the laws of men shall not force entry, but all worthy men will deal with them honourably and justly.

Chapter Six – The Treatment of Women

WSD:6:1 No man shall be intimate with a woman during the time of her courses, for this brings about a subtle pollution. However, a man may go with a woman after her cleansing without any fear, for this thing stems from the nature of women and is not uncleanliness. Yet it is to be borne in mind that the sufferings of women at such times are not part of their nature, but a sign of their past failure to maintain the purity of the fountain of life.

WSD:6:2 A man's wife is his own pasture, wherein he may enter as he wills, but he never should be insensitive to her own feelings, for an inconsiderate husband reaps a poor harvest. A wife must not be subjected to harshness, but should be treated with tenderness and affection. She is deserving of consideration, for her feelings are not those of a loose woman, whom men have treated as they willed.

WSD:6:3 Always treat a woman with reserve and respect, for by doing so, you enhance your own standing as a man. It is the men without pride in themselves who hold women in low esteem, and women who submit to such men take a perverted pleasure in their own degradation. When all a man seeks in the company of a woman is frivolity and amusement, he will in the end seek to use her as an instrument of fornication. The wise man keeps well away from the chattering woman, for life with her would be like living at the foot of a sandhill.

WSD:6:4 Every man who follows the Good Religion will treat women with respect and consideration. He will never attempt the seduction of a decent woman, for chastity is the pure blossom of womanhood. Without it, a woman is like a garden tree that never blooms, and she fails to inspire rapture in the heart of any man.

WSD:6:5 Long ages have taught many subtle lessons, and one is that married to a decent woman, a man tends to become better. Married to an unchaste or faithless woman he tends to become lewd, harsh, inconsiderate and rude. The man who is willing to take an unchaste woman to wife gets just what such as he deserves.

WSD:6:6 Therefore, treat those who may become the wives of other men as you would want your own waiting wife to be treated. Bear in mind the ancient words of wisdom, which have stood the test of time, and choose a wife with care. Fortunate indeed is he who unearths the treasure of a virtuous woman, for her value is beyond estimation in earthly wealth. The heart of her husband rests on a bed of contentment, and he sleeps secure in her constancy. She will never cause him to bow his head in sorrow when men speak of women, or to turn his face in shame from the mocking glances of other men.

WSD:6:7 The intelligent man does not maintain his wife in idleness, lest her thoughts stray towards scandal and gossip. When the light of the Good Religion is revealed, it will set the good woman apart from others, and man need no longer walk in doubt.

WSD:6:8 The good woman has pity on the destitute poor, but is not deceived by the wiles of the idle beggarmen. Her children are brought up in the knowledge of goodness, and they reach maturity in honour and uprightness. No songs on the lips of men extol the virtues of a good wife and mother, but the silent, grateful song in the hearts of her husband and children never ceases. It is the holy melody resounding among the universal spheres.

Chapter Seven – Duties, Obligations and Service to Life

WSD:7:1 If a woman is beautiful and gifted beyond other women, then she has been favoured by The Divine and entrusted with life's greatest treasures. Therefore, she should not conduct herself as other women, for many men will seek after her, and she must be discriminating. Her influence on men can be greater than that of other women, so she must always be conscious of its effect. Does it make them better men, and does it serve the cause of good? The attitude of gifted and beautiful women is of prime interest to those who concern themselves with the spiritual uplifting and advancement of mankind. Unlike the religions that will die, the Good Religion cannot ignore this aspect of life.

WSD:7:2 The beautiful woman, if she be good, is proud of being the guardian of such treasure and safeguards it from polluting hands. She dedicates it to the service of good, which also means the service of mankind. She uses it as a spur and incentive in the upward struggle of man towards divinity. She is more modest and reserved than other women, and as this increases her desirability even more, she is absolutely discreet and prudent in all her activities. Her devotion to the cause of good need entail no more than the maintenance of strict female standards of decency in the face of overwhelming temptation and being a good wife and mother.

WSD:7:3 The fires of passion can rage in woman as they do in man, but when they do, it should be borne in mind that such driving forces are to be used for good and not wasted on an evil outlet. Men and women are not alike, and their duties and obligations in the Divine Design are different, even though they share the same urges and desires. The same water is in the river and the irrigation channel, but the millstone and the growing plant do not utilise it in the same manner. The power, which serves best, serves many different ends.

WSD:7:4 The Divine Design sets man and woman apart and prescribes for each a different form of service. Women are not called upon to be warriors, and men are not intended to bear children. Yet, the differences of man and woman complement one another and, coming together, form a harmonious whole.

WSD:7:5 It is the duty of everyone to study the Sacred Books and to try to understand their deeper meaning. All should learn a skill whereby a useful livelihood be earned, and knowledge and wisdom should be increased day by day. As the purpose of life is to develop spirituality and further the Divine Design, it would be utter foolishness to neglect this. Each person should try, each and every day, to become a better balanced being living a more harmonious life.

WSD:7:6 The obligations of men reach out far and wide, while the obligations of women incline towards the beautification of life and enshrine the virtues. The duties of manhood tend to draw men from home and comfort, while those of womanhood tend to draw women to serve hearth, home and family. Man worships at the altar of duty and obligation, while woman worships at the altar of virtue and service. Both bow before the altars of love.

WSD:7:7 It is the duty of anyone who can to set right what another has done wrongly or in error. No one who has the welfare of mankind at heart can say, "This does not concern me," or, "I have no interest in what another does."

WSD:7:8 Do not neglect the welfare of the sick and aged, for this is an obligation each one bears. Visit those who are ill, for visitors break the loneliness of their days. Enter the sick room cheerfully, as though it were a pleasure, and not as if you were fulfilling an obligation. Be considerate of their circumstances, and do not overstay.

WSD:7:9 Each man should clothe his family decently and feed it according to his means. He should never allow any member of his family to become shabby, unclean or indolent. When something goes wrong within a house, it shall be the head of the house who will answer for it. Though every child is born with certain tendencies, the parents incline them as they will and therefore cannot deny responsibility for what a child becomes. When the child grows up to be a worthy man or woman, parents will often hasten to take credit, but when the child turns out to be a disgrace, they are tardy in accepting responsibility. Yet, the bad is more likely to result from what the parents have done or failed to do, than is the good.

Chapter Eight –
Respect for the Rights of Others

WSD:8:1 Do not enter a house other than your own uninvited, and if you have a position of power, do not use it to gain entry into the house of another. Do not enter a house when the occupier is absent, even if it is open. If at any time, you are denied admittance to a house or told to go away, then depart in peace. Only in the interests of justice or peace, or when the safety of another demands it, should the privacy of a home be invaded, and even then only with the greatest restraint and consideration.

WSD:8:2 However, if a house is abandoned or empty, there is no harm done if it is entered for shelter, but it should not be damaged wilfully. Nothing established by the hand of man should be damaged, unless it causes harm or inconvenience, which outweighs its usefulness.

WSD:8:3 When a guest within the house of another, treat his family with respect and his possessions with care. If you damage anything belonging to him, make proper and full restitution. When in the house of a friend, under no circumstances, touch a woman of his family improperly or show disrespect for her modesty by word or gesture. Note the way a man conducts himself in his own home, for this reveals not only his own character but also the character of his womenfolk.

WSD:8:4 If a man greets you with courtesy, then answer him in the same manner, for surliness displays a weakness of character. If a man in difficulty seeks your aid, cheerfully grant him whatever assistance you can. If advice or information is yours to give, do not withhold it when requested, but never press advice upon another.

WSD:8:5 Respect the rights and dignity of the poor, for they may have little else. Those who help the poor or needy with gifts or benefits, knowing they cannot be repaid, are not without gain when their life is enlarged. Receive all comers with a happy smile, and do not look downcast when giving something away; otherwise, you set the gift at nought.

WSD:8:6 Though freedom is the birthright of every man and one of the ideals, which must be upheld, when it infringes upon the freedom of another man, it ceases to be genuine. Therefore, before you talk about your own freedom or rights, consider the freedom and rights of others, for if you are truly good, their freedom and rights are the most important. However, if others come seeking to diminish your freedom and rights by force or legislation, without conferring a benefit of equal value in return, they are to be resisted. But bear in mind that true freedom is another of the sublime qualities unattainable on Earth, where, though man may aspire to it, and must, it is restricted by earthly conditions requiring service, duty and obligation.

WSD:8:7 To be truly free, man must rise above his mortality and become divine. To attain true freedom, he must travel a road of many tollgates, and at each, payment is demanded from his own supply of freedom's gold. Freedom, like perfection, goodness and justice, is an end man must strive for, but he must also realise that its attainment lies beyond the realm of mortal limitations. Like the other divine qualities here on Earth, it is best understood by contrast.

WSD:8:8 Duty, obligation and service are the three inescapable elements of life. On the road to divinity, they are the three burdens, which have to be carried every step of the way. They cannot, of course, be without purpose and so are also the great stimulants, without which man cannot be sustained in his ascent. Take them away, and man slides backwards towards the low ground of the brute beasts which have no awareness of them.

Chapter Nine – People and Places to Avoid

WSD:9:1 Avoid all places and people, which conduce to evil. Keep away from hypocrites, for, having a common feeling of degradation, they will congregate together, and it would be unwise to be numbered among them. Hypocrites tend towards evil because they serve its purpose and, therefore having an affinity with it, they turn away from what is good and just. They are hard-fisted when the poor come discreetly seeking for alms, but are open-handed when approached in a public place. Surely the hypocrite must be the lowest form of man or woman!

WSD:9:2 If you meet a stranger who appears to be filled with extraordinary virtues, or who conducts himself with grace and good manners, do not hastily conclude that this is his true character. Go to the place where he lives and is known. Note his attitude towards his family and behaviour among friends, and listen to what is said about him. Only then will you be in a better position to judge and to weigh him in the balances.

WSD:9:3 There are many persons of a hypocritical nature who reveal their true character in one place, but put on a false display of goodness in another. If you accept a man or woman in haste and are deceived, then blame no one except yourself. The man who accepts another at his own valuation usually gets a poor bargain.

WSD:9:4 Avoid those whose natures are shallow or superficial, even though they be attractive and pleasant. Shallow streams sparkle most, and weakest waters make the most pleasant sound. There are many whose understanding of friendship is mere companionship, and they neither seek nor know anything deeper. Such people should not be cultivated beyond acquaintanceship. No man really knows another until he has seen him exposed to danger and loss. Even then, he cannot know him fully until he has seen him when tested by prosperity and success.

WSD:9:5 Avoid those who are seeking to benefit from your friendship; they are not for you. Friendship is a precious plant, which must be nurtured in the good soil of sincerity and trust, and plentifully watered with loyalty and understanding. The man who presumes too much on friendship is unworthy of it.

WSD:9:6 Avoid the loose woman, for even if she is beautiful, it may be just a lure over the pit trap. Do not become snared by your desires or let your eyes drug your wisdom. The man who claps fire to his chest cannot escape unburned, and he who embraces uncleanliness will be soiled, however delicately it is wrapped.

WSD:9:7 Avoid an evil neighbour and a wicked neighbourhood, bearing in mind that a man is judged according to his associations. There are many weak characters who, while not desiring to associate with the wicked or live in their neighbourhood, will do so for benefit or to advance their ends. Unless they are prepared to freely admit their weakness, they are hypocrites.

WSD:9:8 Avoid the places of pleasure, which attract the weak and bad characters, for if you associate with them you cannot expect to remain uncontaminated. Bear in mind that the best person to associate with may not be the best companion; and evil places are generally more alluring than the good.

Chapter Ten – Neighbourly Living

WSD:10:1 When a man holds views directly at variance with those of his neighbours, they are incompatible with harmonious living. He then has to decide whether the right views are held by himself or by his neighbours and, if by his neighbours, he must adjust his own.

WSD:10:2 However, if he sees that the views held by his neighbours are wrong or corrupt and degenerate, and he fears he may fall under their influence, he must depart without delay. He must go to another place where the conduct and outlook of his neighbours will be more congenial and compatible with his. It does not matter how far he has to travel.

WSD:10:3 Where there is no one ready to take command in an emergency, or no one prepared to concern himself with the welfare of the neighbourhood, then strive to be a man worthy of the purpose. Do this even if it means having to neglect some study of the Sacred Books, for the man who serves his neighbourhood well serves the cause of good.

WSD:10:4 As the whole man suffers for the errors of the hand or tongue, so shall the whole congregation of the righteous suffer for the misdeeds of any one of their number. If a member commits a wrongful act, then the others shall put it right. This is so that every man shall have a feeling of responsibility towards the whole, and that the good name and reputation of the whole shall not suffer for the acts of one person.

WSD:10:5 It may be no great wrong if one neighbour gives comfort to another who has committed some misdeed, but if a neighbour aids another in a wrong or covers it for him, he is no better than the wrongdoer. To comfort and to condone are things far apart.

WSD:10:6 Whatever the problems of your neighbourhood, do not isolate yourself from them, for if they concern the welfare of others, they are your concern. Strive to be on friendly terms with all your neighbours, and if you fail, let it not be said that the fault lies with you.

WSD:10:7 If you have a neighbour in need, do not be tardy in going to his assistance. If you are not in a position to help, show that you are not indifferent to his predicament. If a neighbour falls into ill favour with the law of the land, do not set yourself up to judge him. If you cannot say anything in his favour, then hold your peace.

WSD:10:8 The laws of the land and of your neighbourhood should be framed towards the maintenance of peace and security, therefore it is your duty not only to abide by them, but also to uphold them. Good laws do not need enforcing among the good, for their goodness declares itself to all, but oppressive laws chafe upon the neck like a yoke. The goat does not attack the lion, and sometimes bad laws have to be endured with patience for the sake of neighbourly peace. Yet, if the entrance to its hole is threatened, a mouse will not hesitate to attack an elephant, and men are no less courageous.

Chapter Eleven –
The Cause and its Champions

WSD:11:1 The greatest cause any man can serve is that divinely designed for him and intended to be his. It is the cause of mankind, which operates within the Divine Design and bears man upward to the very threshold of divinity.

WSD:11:2 In these dark days when many gods wage war among themselves for supremacy and man is divided against himself with the many conflicting beliefs, this cause is voiceless and unchampioned. Yet already, the champion is conceived and lies asleep within the womb of time, awaiting the hour of birth.

WSD:11:3 This champion is the Good Religion now safeguarded and cherished by the devoted few during the ages of its conception. This is the religion, which will some day enter the homes and hearts of a despairing humanity. Enshrining the hopes and aspirations of mankind, it will endow them with life and meaning, so that they can rise with man to the mountain tops of divinity. Only the Good Religion will stand forth and declare that man, given a cause sufficiently great, will be unconquerable.

WSD:11:4 While other beliefs appeal for mercy or aid, or beg forgiveness or seek to appease, declaring man to be weak and pitiful, the Good Religion will come to his aid like a life-giving elixir. Its advent will be the morning star heralding a new, brighter day, and, in the light of that day, man will know himself for what he really is and will do the things he must do. He will then no longer be a child walking in darkness and ignorance, wringing his hands and crying because he is so weak and wicked. He will no longer crawl in the dust of servile humility, begging for mercy or for another to bear the burden of his sins. In the light of the new dawning day, man will be shown what he really is, and the dawn heralds will declare his divinity. Then, from out of the dust long-gathered in the darkness, the new man will arise and stride resolutely forward towards the sunrise.

WSD:11:5 In the days of its awakening, the Good Religion will require leaders, and these will need to be men of exceptional qualities. They will have to devote themselves to its cause without any thought of self-aggrandisement. Many men deceive themselves into thinking their desire for leadership is to benefit others, but in fact, they are really seeking self-esteem and power. Some cannot even see their true incentives or read their innermost thoughts, because of the cloud of hypocrisy, which surrounds them. Such men are not desirable leaders.

WSD:11:6 The path the Good Religion must tread will not be an easy one, and all who follow it will need to dedicate every effort and the last reserves of resourcefulness to its cause. The faint-hearted will have no place in it, for a cause so great will need the utmost sacrifice of person and purse.

WSD:11:7 There are men who are vainglorious leaders knowing only outward and superficial values. Many such as these cannot even find the right direction or select the best path for themselves; yet, their vanity and ambition prompt them to presume their qualities of leadership. Still, they may be no more to blame than those who support them and follow a road blindly.

WSD:11:8 When men are half-hearted in a cause or indifferent about the achievement of its objective, they are denied a true leader. If the leader is blind, he and those who follow him will end up in the ditch. The true leader is a man, to whom all who follow him can look up in every way.

WSD:11:9 Where there are no true men capable of worthy leadership, strive to be such a man yourself. Where no one is willing to accept responsibility, or to strive and be worthy of it, then take the initiative yourself. In this, there is no arrogance if you dedicate yourself to service and not self-esteem, if you recognise your own shortcomings and limitations.

WSD:11:10 Leadership and example are essential to the advancement of mankind, and where they are lacking, there is certainly no wrong done in their establishment. The criterion of a good leader is his own integrity and intent.

WSD:11:11 When support is needed for the cause, it will be no betrayal if the infirm, the sick and the incapable remain inactive because of their inability to contribute anything. Their sincerity and moral support may be all they can give. Those who will be blameworthy are the wealthy or those able to serve who seek exemption by excuses. The man who can give most in any way should be forefront; he should not lag behind or be lax in action.

Chapter Twelve – The Good Life

WSD:12:1 Life is not altogether a vale of sorrow, neither is it meant to be a grim, unending struggle. Man is born into the world to make the best possible use of earthly conditions, and this does not mean that effort should be concentrated exclusively on the achievement of spirituality. Things must be kept in the right perspective, and a proper balance achieved. It is unwise to let thoughts dwell exclusively upon the Spiritual Realm, and this was never intended. Only its reality and ultimate attainment should be ever borne in mind.

WSD:12:2 Man is to make the most of conditions as he finds them and get all the happiness he can from life within the framework laid down in the Sacred Books. Not only must he make the best of earthly conditions, but he must also improve them, so that more happiness may be gained. Though this may appear to serve only an earthly end, it is not entirely the case, for in the effort lies the spiritual development. Earthly conditions are not to be accepted passively, for every man has a duty to make some improvement, however slight, upon the earthly state of things.

WSD:12:3 While permitted to seek the greatest amount of happiness, man must bear in mind that the search must not extend beyond the bounds of his duties and responsibilities. When seeking spirituality and knowledge of the Spiritual Realm, man must remember that there are limitations as to what he can experience. The purpose of Earth must, and will, be maintained with all its lack of stability and certainty. No mortal man will ever know for certain what the coming year will bring.

WSD:12:4 The amount of spiritual experience and enlightenment permitted any man is just sufficient not to upset the balance of his life or nullify his earthly existence. This is a fact, which should be clearly understood by those ignorant persons who rail against the lack of divine intervention or guidance. In these times, mankind is not advanced enough for the Divine Veil to be any more withdrawn, and even in the greater light of the Good Religion, it will not be removed. The two realms of spirit and matter, mind and body, must remain separated by a near impassable gulf, which can be spanned only by the utmost effort. When the light of the Good Religion is given to the world, it will not be a world ready to welcome it, or even ready to receive it. The world to which it will come will be a sick, disordered world reluctant to take the medicine, which will restore it to health.

WSD:12:5 In those coming days the desire for the good life will have exceeded its proper bounds and, for many, become the sole objective. It will be a world of spiritual barrenness, a place where discord and disillusion has become lost in a doctrinal wilderness, with nothing more refreshing to offer than the waters of stagnant dogma.

WSD:12:6 What man needs, the Good Religion will be able to offer, but as man is always tardy in accepting what is good for him and seems incapable of diagnosing his own maladies, he is unlikely to recognise the remedy. Perhaps the illness of man will then be too far advanced for the simple cure by herbal potions, and only the agonising knife or cauterising fire will effect it. Meanwhile, wait and watch for the heralds of the dawn.

WSD:12:7 The body of man is perishable and only a speck of dust in the great scheme of things; yet, men believe that the mighty universe was created solely to serve it. Man, the mortal, sadly deludes himself by presuming to think he can bend all Nature to serve his bodily wellbeing. As the fool, seeing trees and mountains shimmering in the waters, thinks their images are dancing for his pleasure, so man, while Nature follows her destined course, believes all her activity is only to gladden his eye and give him pleasure.

WSD:12:8 Nature, like man, is intended to serve an end and purpose, which far exceed any conceivable by mortal flesh alone. Yet it can be said with truth that the eternal universe and boundless Nature exist only to serve man, the greater being. Therefore, this being so, each man has a duty to recognise himself for what he really is and to do all that is required of him. He should strive to improve life, to supply something it lacks, and to leave the world a better place for having passed through it.

WSD:12:9 The man who denies himself harmless pleasure is also a wrongdoer and servant of evil, for such pleasures serve a good purpose and proper end. Happiness is not a thing to be avoided, and enjoyments, which do no harm, are not to be shunned.

WSD:12:10 Desires and ends, which are good should be pursued, but bear in mind that the tree of desire will bear no fruit unless nourished with the waters of effort. Happiness itself is not an undesirable end, but too many pay for it with their contentment and peace.

WSD:12:11 It has been taught that the love of pleasure serves no useful end, and that wisdom comes through pain. This is not true, for the spirit can also develop through pleasure, for otherwise it would be an unjust world. Not all school lessons are unpleasant, though all should be rewarding.

WSD:12:12 It is none-the-less true that of all things man may do on Earth to his benefit, the acquisition of spirituality is supreme. It is in fact the whole and sole reason for man's existence. Therefore, while getting whatever happiness he can, he should never over-indulge his bodily appetites and should shun the frivolities of life. These are earthly seducers, which leave little time for more beneficial things and become more demanding as they gain greater control.

WSD:12:13 Such things as eating, drinking, sleeping and the bodily union of man and woman are meant to be sources of pleasure, when enjoyed in moderation and for their proper purpose. They, too, can serve a spiritual end. The rule is moderation in all things, with consideration for the welfare and feelings of others and a complete disregard of anything, which may serve the cause of evil.

WSD:12:14 Do not fear the onset of old age, for though to the undeveloped spirit, it may be the bleak winter of life, to the developed spirit, it is the harvesting time. Old age is bodily preparation for departure to rebirth. It is the approach to the threshold of a new life.

WSD:12:15 Every man should earn his livelihood by service through toil or skill. The man who wishes to live the good life fully must engage in all kinds of activities, in trade and in various instructive affairs. Life, to be properly lived, must be balanced with a knowledge of many things and a variety of experiences.

WSD:12:16 Man must certainly engage in worldly and social activities for the benefit of his body, for its needs are not to be neglected. Still always bear in mind that this is not the sole aim in life, nor the greatest. Only one aim or objective should be held always in view, and that is the perfecting of the soul. In this way, all activities become praiseworthy and beneficial, since the end lies not in the activities themselves but in their objective.

WSD:12:17 If a man has any talent and fails to develop it, he is unworthy of the gift and, in due course, must make an accounting. The man who does not continually expand the horizon of his life becomes stagnant within himself. The man who does not study and learn places himself on the level of the dumb beasts, though even they learn.

WSD:12:18 The good life is a balanced, harmonious life and a life well and profitably lived. It is a life of many contrasts and experiences, with a steady advance towards spirituality. All earthly goals are elusive, and their attainment may not bring the pleasure and happiness anticipated. There is only one goal, towards which everyone can advance with certainty and assurance, and that is the goal of spirituality. The very things, which defeat earthly ends and render them impossible to accomplish are, if viewed in the proper perspective, aids towards the achievement of spirituality. Out of earthly failure and frustration can come spiritual accomplishment and gain. If you can understand this, the good life is yours.

Chapter Thirteen – The Religious Life

WSD:13:1 Religion is not something alien to the nature of man, but something which supplies a fundamental need. Just as eating is the response to an inner urge, so is religion the response to another. It is only when religion, in a particular form, becomes insipid, ceases to nourish, that it is discarded, and then the nature of man seeks to supply the deficiency from another source. Without religious nourishment, the spirit of man becomes unstable and out of harmony with life. Unless the deficiency is made good the whole being may disrupt into disharmony.

WSD:13:2 The religious urge is as much a part of man as the urge to eat or sleep, though of a much more subtle nature. Some try to suppress the urge, and in such cases, the effects are no less harmful and apparent than when other urges are suppressed completely. Those with a little knowledge and wisdom often turn away from religion, but once they have gained much more, they turn back again. Religion itself can, therefore, never be outdated or outmoded, though its earthly manifestations certainly may be, and so many persons, disillusioned with the image, spurn the reality behind it. True religion deals only with the relationship between man and his divinity and is the stairway for his ascent.

WSD:13:3 Too often, religion is a quagmire, into which the spirits of men sink and are lost, but it is the fault of men and not of religion. Each man has the religion he deserves and not necessarily the religion he needs. When it proves inadequate for his needs and he becomes disillusioned, he seeks to lay blame on the religion and not on himself. Religions which nourished weaknesses of character and ignorance in men have been destroyed by those same failings and are no more, but the religions are no more to blame than those who served them. If a man put to sea in an unseaworthy boat, can he blame the craft if he be cast into the water? Still man is never abandoned and somewhere there is the religion he needs, though he may never find it because of his spiritual indolence.

WSD:13:4 The religious life is not one of ease and indolence, neither is it something to be undertaken half-heartedly. Too often an old man who has wasted his life in worldly excesses and scorned religion, suddenly becomes converted and seeks to imitate the religious life. He imagines he has become good because he performs acts having an outer appearance of goodness. However, he is no more than a hypocrite. The truth is that his abstinence from wrongdoing and conversion to the religious life are directly related to his declining bodily powers. Such men generally become so self-righteous that they readily forgive themselves for their past deeds, which, after a shallow repentance, are quickly and conveniently forgotten. They should read what is written in the Sacred Books, and learn how much more is required of them.

WSD:13:5 Religion is man reaching out towards something greater than himself and attempting to express an indescribable glory revealed just beyond his grasp. It is man's search for greatness, the recognition that he is more than mere mortal flesh, and that above this is a divinity towards which he may aspire.

WSD:13:6 Devotion is not a state of servility, but is actually an attempt to return to man's natural condition. It is a seeking for powers, which, though once possessed, have now been lost. It is a search for the truth concerning man as he really is in his whole being.

WSD:13:7 Incense, fire, candles and ritual cannot increase the glory of The Divine. Certainly they may benefit man and increase his sensitivity, but he should not be hypocritical about their effect or insulting. The sacrifice of bird or beast, the offering of gold and jewels, may assist men, but in no way do they benefit The Divine. All The Divine asks from man is whole-hearted self-dedication to the fulfilment of The Divine Design. The worshipful ritual and devotional acts are the manifestation of man's desire to take an easy path. They are no more than an interlude in his daily life, the acknowledgement that he owes some sort of obligation.

WSD:13:8 The Sacred Books should be read often and diligently, for they are the repository of knowledge transcending that, which can be gained by the senses of men. The Divine knows your heart, your intentions and inclinations, and therefore does not expect you to make the study of the Sacred Books too wearisome. The Divine knows that some are sick while others are handicapped either by a life of movement or a life of restraint. Others are so tied up in the struggle for the cause that they have little time for reading. Many have to depend upon the literacy of others for the learning. Therefore, even one section at a time is enough, if it is studied and meditated upon.

WSD:13:9 Prayer is an exercise of the spirit. It must never be misdirected and cannot be used to change natural laws and effects for the sake of the one who prays. Always pray in a place proper for prayer. Those who say no place is especially holy because The Divine is everywhere, may discover that they are unable to find The Divine anywhere.

WSD:13:10 Prayer is little understood, for it raises the worshipper above a normal state. It is a state of being wherein man loses himself in the Spirit of Divinity. To those great souls who know the true nature of prayer in its highest expression, it seems a miracle that after losing himself in prayer, the worshipper continues to live in the flesh. True worship, however, is not prayer but the devotion of a life dedicated to the fulfilment of the Divine Design and the preparation of the soul for the crown of divinity.

WSD:13:11 Repentance from those who have been doers of wickedness and then repent their deeds or confess their wrongdoing when dying, serves little purpose. Unless some recompense is made by the death itself or by other deeds, mere repentance alone cannot reshape the soul.

WSD:13:12 Worship and devotion require effort, so unless specific times are set apart for reading the Sacred Books, for worship and dedicated service, no time will be given to The Divine. Too often, men devote all their time to the affairs of the body and completely neglect the welfare of the spirit.

WSD:13:13 Ignorant men stupidly stir up many cares and troubles; they confront themselves with pointless problems and add unnecessarily to the burdens of life. They increase the number of trials prescribed by their destiny. They indulge in futile forms of worship and waste time in worthless ceremonial. They delude themselves by placing false values on their offerings, they fast and mortify themselves without gain. They go on timewasting pilgrimages and seek new shrines, but from all this they derive little spiritual benefit.

WSD:13:14 Religious rituals and ceremonies are brought about by a desire for the mutual sharing of religious experience. As words cannot describe the greater glories, which are inseparable from the religious life, the problems connected with belief and faith are no more than standpoints indicating man's limited means of communication. Therefore, let each man find his own path, and having found it follow steadfastly through to the end.

WSD:13:15 The many and seemingly conflicting doctrines, which arise from time to time and in many places, do, if inspired by the urge to spirituality, lead towards the same goal - the One Supreme Truth. They are like the many roads into the city, which convey travellers from all directions. The conflict and discord between the many religions are caused by ignorance, by blindness in the material clouds of illusion and by misinterpretation of basic truths. Rightly or wrongly, each man believes the road he travels to be the best and most direct.

WSD:13:16 A true religion does in fact do no more than supply the medium, whereby man works in co-operation with The Divine. It is the means, whereby the Divine Design is revealed and its purpose interpreted. Whatever goes into the make-up of human nature bearing the impress of divinity, whatever man does to unfold the divinity of his soul, that constitutes the religious life.

WSD:13:17 The religious life on Earth does not lead to any finality. It is no more than the first stage of the journey, but it does lead in the right direction. Death is no more than a movement across a frontier, though the wise man assures that the move improves his circumstances and is to a better place.

WSD:13:18 The course of life is determined by destiny, so pay no heed to those who pretend to read futures in the stars, for they predict only in riddles and what they say may apply to many. No two predictions are alike, except by coincidence, and the planets have no power to determine what a man will become.

WSD:13:19 The origins of superstition and false belief lie in the conceit and presumption of man, but to an even greater extent in his mortal tendency towards deceit and hypocrisy. They also stem from his spiritual immaturity and indifference, for he tries to attain and understand things which are attainable only by the spiritually developed, and interprets them with his inadequate knowledge and inspiration. Superstition and blind faith are pillars supporting the religions of ignorance.

Chapter Fourteen – Personal Conduct

WSD:14:1 Every man should have a cause to fight for and a road to follow. He should fight for the cause until its objective is attained and follow the road until the end. The horizon of each should be outward towards perfection. The causeless man is like a riderless horse.

WSD:14:2 It is better to adhere to one cause absolutely and wholeheartedly than to dabble in many causes without being wholehearted in any. A truly great cause should carry all other worthy causes forward with it, and one great cause cannot fall into conflict with another. A man is judged by what he fights for, or by what he declines to fight for, he must do one or the other.

WSD:14:3 A man must keep careful watch on himself, so he does not wax fat and self-indulgent. Whatever his position in life, he should always be engaged in some worthwhile occupation and never neglect the study of the Sacred Books. Idleness is the mother of miseries. Indolence occupies itself in filling the body with fat.

WSD:14:4 To study the Books of Wisdom is good, for thereby a man learns what to do and what not to do. On the other hand, if a man is busily engaged in earning his livelihood and fulfilling his obligations, it will not occur to him to steal and fornicate.

WSD:14:5 Man and woman are intended to be unalike, and therefore, a man should conduct himself as a man and a woman as a woman. They were made to serve differently; their separate purposes should not become confused. A mannish woman cannot inspire men or serve the cause of womankind. If she serves mankind, it is in a capacity below that of other women.

WSD:14:6 Do not disgrace a man before others or hold any man up to ridicule. The Books of Wisdom say that the only person a man will disgrace before others is his bitterest enemy. Mockery of another discloses the mocker's own weakness of character.

WSD:14:7 Do not be immovable in your ways or set in your circumstances. Be like the reed, which bows with the wind and bends all the way, but always springs up again. Always be alert and ready for whatever may come your way, and above all, do not expect life to deal kindly with you always. Do not envy those who have more than you, but turn your eyes towards those less fortunate.

WSD:14:8 Do not be complacent about your personal attainments, for no one can say truthfully that he has purged his spirit of all disfiguring stains and is now perfect. No matter how perfect a man may appear to himself in any respect, there is still a greater perfection attainable, and that is the goal. The limits of earthly perfection remain unmarked.

WSD:14:9 Cleanliness in all things is essential. If you would not put filth in your mouth, why put it in your mind? No one allows garbage at the eating table, yet many gladly overload their minds with it. These are weaknesses of character, which have to be eliminated. Through long ages it has been known that a foul tongue expresses the language of weakness, and filthy jokes are the consolation of slaves. The nation sinking into the mire is comforted by the knowledge of its affinity to filth.

WSD:14:10 The man who boasts about his prowess as a fornicator does so to hide the secret knowledge of his own inadequacy. His foolish boasting is the source of his satisfaction and indicates the limit of his achievements. Let the man of weak character and weaker vitality betray himself, but keep away, lest you be numbered among the self-deceivers.

WSD:14:11 Let your personal conduct be in all ways above reproach. Strive to be worthy of the respect of all men, though their praise is froth on the waters of life. Live as you should live and not as you would like to live. If you cannot acknowledge your own worth, then recognise your own failings.

Chapter Fifteen – The Spiritual Realm

WSD:15:1 The Spiritual Realm lies between the realm of matter and the realm of The Divine. If your mind is unable to grasp the idea of The Divine and you cannot understand what is meant by spirituality, do not be dismayed. How can an ordinary, unenlightened mind do so when it is shut in by a corrupt material world and enclosed on every side by illusion? Absolute purity cannot be seen amid the clouds of earthly impurity, and in this defiled place, the immaculate is inconceivable. Therefore, if you cannot understand this or perceive the reality of perfection, how much less are you able to comprehend The Divine! Step confidently along the path, guided by understanding companions, who are more enlightened, for they will not lead you astray, and soon the light of understanding will be placed in your hand.

WSD:15:2 The Spiritual Realm is divided into two parts. On one side is the place, where the wicked have companionship of their own kind, and it is a cold place of gloom and darkness. This is the realm of evil containing those who are repulsive even to their own kind. Their greatest punishment may lie in the fact that they retain the memory of beauty, goodness and cleanliness, just as the happiness of those in the realm of good, on the other side is heightened by its contrast with the sorrows and afflictions they have known.

WSD:15:3 The realm of evil is separated from the realm of good by an etheric form of flame, through which communication can be made. Were those on the sunlit side to enquire from the dwellers in gloom what brought them to their deplorable state, if the truth could be found in them, they would reply: "We are those who were heedless of all spiritual and ennobling things. We were those who thought only of their own betterment and not the advancement of mankind and the welfare of others. We were the selfish ones who considered only their own comfort and convenience. Now look at what we have! We oppressed the poor and lowly and exploited the helpless and weak, doing nothing to improve their lot. Now look at ours! We sat on councils and in seats of authority engaging in vain disputes about right and wrong, while the poor, the hungry and the oppressed stood by and suffered in patience. We are, above all, those who could have done much but did little. We were those who, given great gifts, used them for selfish ends. What have we now? We inhabited fine houses and surrounded ourselves with all things to give ease and comfort. Now we are comfortless. We sought out places of pleasure and closed our eyes to the sorrow and suffering of the world. We laughed at those who sought to teach us spirituality and took a base and easy view of right and wrong. There is no laughter here. We doubted that there was any life to come and could not understand the talk about it. Would that the grave had been the end! Talk of duty and service disturbed our ease and complacency, and we let others carry our burdens. If only we could return! Only now when we so miserably exist in the certainty of life after death can we realise our errors and suffer for them. Here the air is filled with the sighing sound of the saddest words we know, "Too late!"'

WSD:15:4 Those words did once span the gulf and were recorded by an ancient seer.

WSD:15:5 On the day when the whole being is split apart by death and the mortal clay is consigned to its proper place, the spirit passes through the great gates into the Spiritual Realm. There it first enters a Borderland, where the floodgates of memory are opened and each and every deed recalled. This is where the newly arrived spirit waits while slowly it assumes its chosen shape and realises the direction of its destination.

WSD:15:6 The spirit does not arrive in a state of waking, but it is like one asleep. It awakes to its new life like a man awakes to a new day. Then, if during earthly life it has doomed itself, this realisation will slowly dawn, and the newly formed being will cringe away from those who came to welcome it. It will indeed wish that death had been the end. The wisdom of ancient times disclosed that the newly arrived spirit stood in completeness for judgement, but what it called the Place of Decision is the Borderland.

WSD:15:7 If, during life, the spirit has beautified and ennobled itself, it will slowly realise its unfolding glory and rejoice. It will rise gladly to its welcome and advance fearlessly into the light of its compatible place. Some, which do not have full affinity with either the light or the darkness depart for the Shadowland, towards which they are impelled by its attraction for one in their state.

WSD:15:8 Within the Spiritual Realm there are places to suit the condition of every spirit entering it, and that is why the ancient books state, 'The mansions of the spirit are without number'.

Chapter Sixteen – The Meaning of Marriage

WSD:16:1 In the eyes of men and according to their laws, marriage is a covenant made between a man and a woman, under which they can enjoy bodily union with the sanction of their religion. This is not the view which can be supported by the Good Religion, for true marriage is not something formed through the words spoken by a priest or through sanction by the laws of men. Marriage is an open declaration, which marks the taking of an irrevocable step by two souls towards a definite end. It signifies their complete surrender and dedication to each other. It is meant to be far more than union of the bodies, it should also be a union of spirits, though this is rarely achieved. True marriage is a union of two realms, it is a twofold union.

WSD:16:2 The marriage ceremony is an announcement made before all persons that a man and woman are setting out on the rocky road of matrimony in search of true love. This is not something which can be picked up like a jewel, it cannot be bartered, bought or sold. The thing which must never be overlooked is that true marriage is not just the union of two bodies, but the first step towards the blending of two spirits.

WSD:16:3 The marriages of humble people, unsanctified by priest, are no less worthy than those of wealthy people of quality whose religion sanctifies bonds of straw. 'Living in sin' means living together without responsibility and for bodily satisfaction alone. Unholy wedlock means being bound fast in the bonds of matrimony without any prospect of advancement to the glory of true love. Wedlock and marriage are not alike, for a true marriage may exist without sanction by the laws of men or blessing of priest, providing a love exists, which can mature into true love.

WSD:16:4 The chain that binds two souls together is forged in the spiritual realm, and no earthly power can ever break it. It is worn on Earth like a gloriously wrought chain of weightless gold, but not one marriage in a thousand is ever blessed with it.

WSD:16:5 Adultery is the defilement of a marriage, but there is a mild form of it when the thoughts of one partner go out towards someone else. Religions now existing do not understand the true nature of marriage and regard it as an end in itself and not as a beginning, a fulfilment rather than a search for fulfilment. The Good Religion will regard marriage as one of the great challenges of life and one of the supreme tests along the road to spirituality. Love is not the end, for love aspires to reach out beyond itself and ascend to the heights of true love, sometimes called 'pure love'.

WSD:16:6 Outside of the Good Religion, union between man and woman has become so tainted with imperfection, so clouded in lewdness, so subordinate to lust and bodily satisfaction, that anyone can readily be forgiven for believing the falsehood that no spiritual benefit can derive from the act; that it has no sanctity, no higher objective and purpose than to meet the demands of the flesh.

WSD:16:7 Man soars on spiritual wings and rises high above the realm of the dumb brutes. Therefore, he can conceive something greater in bodily union than mere satisfaction of the flesh, and indeed it is not meant to be a concession to the flesh but a sublime sacrifice to love. The feelings arising in the body are not, of themselves, servants of evil, this is a wrong teaching. The body is not naturally antagonistic to the spirit, and its needs are by no means incompatible with spiritual needs. As the harp to the harpist, so is the body to the spirit, the instrument and means of expression.

WSD:16:8 Marriage is the fortress of the family, so its safeguarding and integrity is a sacred obligation. The unity and purity of the family is one of the great concerns of men, but though the laws of men may build a wall about it they cannot prevent corruption and decay from within. Only higher laws, moral laws, can deal with this, and these the world sadly lacks.

WSD:16:9 The three earthly institutions a man is entitled to defend, even to the extent of taking the life of another, are: His marriage, his home and his family.

Chapter Seventeen –
The Upbringing of Children

WSD:17:1 To teach a child a readymade code of morality may not be the ideal, but ideals are rarely approachable on Earth and while mankind is so far-retarded spiritually, it is impossible to do otherwise. Yet if a child is also told why there is a necessity for such a code, perhaps in the child's maturity, it will add something of goodness to the code.

WSD:17:2 Children brought up with the very best instruction often become wayward and later disregard all they have been taught. Parents wonder why, for the ancient wisdom states that if a child is properly instructed and good habits ingrained, this will not desert the child when it grows up. Such parents must honestly search their own hearts, because the reason is that they have failed to practise their own teachings, and the growing child resents such hypocrisy. Therefore, as it grows up, it will tend to imitate the parents rather than follow the teachings. Parents should bear in mind that example is the best instruction.

WSD:17:3 A healthier and better upbringing is if parents do not over-indulge their children or play with them too much. A parent is not a playmate, and his or her first duty is to be a parent. A mother should act like a mother, and a father like a father. Read the Sacred Books and learn your proper role in life.

WSD:17:4 Parents get the children they deserve, and the failings of a child mirror the failings of its parents. The children of a considerate and just father are successful. Good children cannot be raised in a house of discord. When the father is hot-tempered and the mother a gossip, the sons are fools and the daughters slovenly.

WSD:17:5 Those who spare themselves the pain of chastising their children display their lack of love for them. Proper and just chastisement is part of a child's upbringing and the duty of every parent. Chastise a child during its childhood, for later is too late. When you were advised against over-familiarity with children, it did not mean that you should be too stern and austere with them.

WSD:17:6 The highest expressions of Justice and Truth and a perfect code of laws are not attainable on Earth. Therefore, the best thing anyone can do for a child is to teach it self-mastery and bring it up in the knowledge of its true nature. The wisdom of the Sacred Books should be impressed upon the minds of children and taught according to their understanding. It is the duty and obligation of every parent to see that their children are properly instructed.

WSD:17:7 Children are not to be brought into the world irresponsibly and parents have an obligation for their welfare. They must see that a child is not left without a craft or calling whereby a livelihood can be earned, There is an obligation upon those who bring a child into the world to see that it does not grow up without learning a skilful and useful occupation, and that it is instructed in the purpose of life and ways of the world.

WSD:17:8 The well brought up child crowns its parents with happiness, but one ill raised weighs heavily upon their hearts. A child may rightly reproach its parents if they fail in their duty or avoid their obligations, for it did not ask to be born. Parents, however, cannot reproach their child, for it came at their behest and is the fruit of their pleasure.

WSD:17:9 Parents should bear in mind that the fruit of the tree of indulgence is bitter and the waters of indifference soon quench the fires of affection. The parent who sows unwisely in the fertile fields of childhood reaps a blighted harvest when the crop comes to maturity.

Chapter Eighteen –
Friends and Enemies

WSD:18:1 The only real enemy any man has is the man he does not understand, and the only man to really fear is the one who is afraid. While it is true that a man can be judged by his friends, it is no less true that he can be judged by his enemies. A weak character does not have enemies, but only those who pity or despise him. A declared enemy is not necessarily a source of constant danger. He is better than a false friend and need not be an object of hatred; in fact, many enemies can be admired.

WSD:18:2 The man who seeks a friend without faults or one without weaknesses and failings, will never have a friend, and he who declares his enemy to be wholly evil is a liar. A man may be poor in worldly possessions but rich in friendship, for true wealth is not the accumulation of lifeless things but the possession of firm friendship. The greatness of a man may be assessed according to his friends, but it may be measured even better according to who are his enemies.

WSD:18:3 True friendship is not given its proper value in times of prosperity, and fair weather friends grow wings when the winds of adversity blow. Though misfortune reveals the friend, it also discloses the enemy. When misfortune strikes, false friends scamper like rats, and enemies gather like vultures.

WSD:18:4 No man can attain full spiritual development until he has learned to respect the rights and views of others. Help others along the path, and the right way will be pointed out.

WSD:18:5 The nature of man is such that while it always tends to resist force and compulsion, it will always yield to gentleness and persuasion. Force is the last resort and an acknowledgement of failure. Power in the hands of a man in all ways strong is always good, but power in the hands of a weak man is a menace.

WSD:18:6 A friend is capable of inflicting greater hurt than an enemy, but both should be chosen with equal discretion. Yet wounds inflicted at the hands of a friend are more to be desired than the hypocritical embraces of an enemy. Let experience be your guide. He who has tested honey knows it to be sweet, while he who has tasted the fruit of evil knows it to be bitter.

WSD:18:7 Do not take a fornicator as a friend, or you admit a wolf into the sheepfold. Enslaved by his urges, he will never be constant and always a weak reed to lean upon. As a dog leaves its kennel to return to its vomit, so is a fornicator drawn back to the woman with whom he relieves himself.

WSD:18:8 Genuine friendship between man and woman is said to be impossible, but this is the talk of weak characters, of whom many burden the world. When the relationship of love between man and woman is hallowed as it should be, and elevated far above sordid relationships, between the two there will be a place for friendship.

WSD:18:9 Do not be lukewarm either in friendship or enmity, for the strong character reaches out afar in all directions. Not all enemies are personal ones, for those who oppose the cause for which you fight are also your enemies, as are all who oppress the weak and lowly. There is everlasting enmity between those who serve the cause of good and those who serve evil, and there can be no reconciliation between the two. To compromise with evil means contamination of the good.

Chapter Nineteen – The Tendency Towards Evil

WSD:19:1 Everyone born to be tested in a mortal world has a tendency towards things, which are evil, rather than towards those, which are good. The material part of man, with its heritage of decay, finds itself more attracted towards evil than towards good. Therefore, it is good, which has to be taught and learned and evil, which has to be put aside and eliminated.

WSD:19:2 When a man delves into wickedness, to satisfy his carnal urges, the body fully supports him, and his mortal limbs and organs readily respond. The bestial desires and urges lurk only just beneath the surface and need little encouragement to bring them up. However, when a man is called upon to do some good deed, his body is reluctant, and disinclination invades his heart.

WSD:19:3 This is because evil impulses range freely through the movement of good impulses. The gross material of the body must be impregnated with spirituality, if the position within is to be reversed.

WSD:19:4 Evil impulses press urgently upon the mortal body and make their demands known in no uncertain manner. Only the best of men are truly free enough to rise above them and stand firm in resistance. Passions and the demands of the body are aggressors from the realm of evil seeking to capture and enslave the spirit. These aggressors must be subdued, put in restraint and made to serve.

WSD:19:5 The tendency towards evil involves not only those who break the laws of men, but also those who break higher laws. The Good Religion should not concern itself so much with earthly lawbreakers, for the laws of men can deal with them, but with greater things, against which the laws of men are inadequate. The number of lawbreakers and outcasts in any nation is the measure of a nation's spiritual deficiency. 'Where there is lawlessness, there will also be injustice, for the two go together like light and shade.

WSD:19:6 The spiritual life is inseparable from daily existence, and a nation becomes spiritually deficient when it tries to separate one from the other. Religions, which stand aloof and permit this to happen, if not servants of evil, are certainly poor champions of good. The laws of men have to be enforced only when people cease to govern their lives by spiritual laws. Therefore, of all laws spiritual laws are the highest.

WSD:19:7 The duty of religion is to concern itself with moral laws and discipline, and when it fails in this duty it no longer serves the welfare of mankind. The laws of men are completely inadequate for this, as indicated by their complexity and multiplicity. The greatness of any nation resides in its national spirit, and the breath of that spirit is religion.

WSD:19:8 The tendency towards evil is opposed by religion, the champion of good, which must prove itself equal to the challenge. A poorly armed champion, ill prepared for combat or defective in resolution, is of no use whatsoever, though the people of few nations deserve anything better.

WSD:19:9 The tendency towards evil includes abuse of the body, for unhealthy excesses lead to weakness, apathy and early death. The body that is overstuffed with food houses a selfish spirit, which has deprived others of sustenance. A body worn out with dissipation hides a spirit, which has surrendered to wickedness. It includes also all things tending towards the disruption of life and the brutalisation of mankind.

WSD:19:10 Yet, to live a righteous life does not mean withdrawal from association with all others. A man should withdraw from life among his own people only when they have turned completely from the path of good and tread the road of evil. In such cases a man has the obligation to separate his family from the contaminating influence of those about him, but he must always bear in mind that his duty is to fight and not run away. Withdrawal to a stronger base, from which to fight is not running away.

Chapter Twenty –
Teaching, Study and Learning

WSD:20:1 Conscience is the best guide, and experience the best teacher. Nature is the best book, and life the highest form of schooling. Death is the great graduation day.

WSD:20:2 Study itself is not enough, for learning without application and practice is futile and leads towards wickedness. The man who studies the Sacred Books as a child and applies their teachings to his life is like one who works with metal while it is still hot. The man who leaves such study until old age is like one who works with metal when it is cold.

WSD:20:3 Study, when not combined with work and practice, tends to lead towards the path of weakness. Unless a man is engaged in a skilled or useful occupation, all his book learning serves little purpose and does not avail him much. Therefore, even the man most devoted to the study of the Sacred Books must also learn a skilled or useful occupation.

WSD:20:4 Practice is of greater importance than study; for of what use is it to study the way for goodness, and being willing to do good, if experience of what constitutes good living is lacking? The good life is a life of action and not a life of passiveness.

WSD:20:5 Yet, study and learning are not to be neglected, for they are part of the discipline of living. Without the study, which leads to knowledge, right living and right action in their fullest expression are very unlikely.

WSD:20:6 In your absorption of knowledge, consider nothing impossible and nothing beyond achievement. Bear in mind that whatever is possible will one day come into being. The road to wisdom begins in attentive silence and passes through study and practice into fulfilment.

WSD:20:7 A teacher's words should be goads to goodness and learning, and not like a salve to the wounds of wickedness or a narcotic deadening the instructive pains of life. As the herdsman's goad directs beasts and urges them along the right road, so should the teacher's word direct and urge the pupil. Words of worth do not fall softly.

WSD:20:8 A teacher may have a pupil wait upon him and attend to his needs, providing it is regarded as an opportunity for training and teaching. The teacher who fails to set a good example, or to abide by his own teachings, is unworthy of his position and betrays his trust.

WSD:20:9 The man who quietly carries out the precepts of the Sacred Books and upholds their teachings is better than he who studies diligently and teaches well, but fails to put his teaching into practice. A hypocritical teacher is the lowest order of hypocrites.

WSD:20:10 A disciple is one who follows a religious master, and it is better to be the disciple of a wiser man than the master of others who are ignorant. Always seek self-improvement and advancement in knowledge, for these are the justifiable aims of the disciple.

WSD:20:11 The man who is diligent and careful in his studies, but not in his deeds or words, is a weak character who tends to hypocrisy. The man who learns but does not practise what he learns is like a man who labours at the sowing, but does not reap the harvest. He is like a man who digs a well and never draws water.

WSD:20:12 The purpose of learning is to know the good from the bad, the beneficial from the harmful. The good and beneficial should not be scorned, whoever dispenses them. Would you take poison even if offered by your best friend, or refuse dressing for a wound because given by an enemy?

WSD:20:13 The man who is filled with learning and knows all the wisdom of the Sacred Books, but fails to put it into practice, is like a many-branched tree with no depth of root. The wind blows, and it is laid low to quickly rot. The man with much learning and knowledge but no strength of character, is like a frail pot filled with precious liquid. If roughly handled, it falls apart, and the contents are lost.

WSD:20:14 Good has its fount in The Divine, and at its source is uncontaminated with evil. It is that which harmonises best with the Divine Design, and evil is that which harmonises least. Good is absolute quality, while evil is not; therefore, even in the greatest concentration of evil there must be some good. So there is no form of evil, whether in man or outside of him, from which some good cannot be extracted, but man by nature tends to overlook this. Entrapped in matter, evil is more easily seen. Bear in mind that, in even the greatest evil, there is somewhere a speck of good which can be of service if extracted.

WSD:20:15 Finally, if seeking a religious master, be careful in your choice. In matters of religion, the whole forces of evil are marshalled to deceive and delude. If one whom you would choose as a master seeks popularity or self-advancement, avoid him like the plague, for he is a false prophet.

Chapter Twenty-One – A Word to Prophets and Preachers

WSD:21:1 The true prophet is a message bearer who has heard a voice crying out across the distances. The message may not be clearly heard and perhaps conveyed with errors and distortion, but if it is the dedicated effort of a sincere man, it must be of value.

WSD:21:2 Because there are many false prophets, the words of a true prophet do not lose their value. No man has ever sought to counterfeit a valueless thing. The vine is judged by the drink it produces and not by its leaves and appearance. It is the end product that matters.

WSD:21:3 The pattern of the Divine Design is marvellous and its working intricate. The threads are many, and their preparation involves countless processes. The weavers are numerous, but few can visualise what magnificence completion may reveal, and none can see the uncompleted whole. Therefore, those who would show others the pattern to follow should not seek to guess at what lies beyond their own range of vision.

WSD:21:4 So if you are a prophet chosen to guide, do not exceed the scope of your authority or seek to describe things beyond the reach of your light. Go forward with courage and confidence, and the voice of The Divine will teach you the signs along the road and make clear their meaning.

WSD:21:5 When you stand up to deliver your message, many hypocrites will gather and declare their belief in what you say. The words they speak may deceive you, for they are a cloak disguising their true garb and, because of their hypocrisy, those who would otherwise listen to your words will turn away in disgust. Therefore, when you make converts, beware of including the faint-hearted and hypocrites, for they will only be a liability.

WSD:21:6 Do not be afraid to speak up when men will listen to what you have to say, but also know when to be silent and hold your peace. It is futile to waste words when you will not be given a hearing. You will have to contend with many false-faced prophets whose words are beautiful baubles falling from silver tongues. They attract the attention of many who listen for pleasure and so are led astray.

WSD:21:7 Some men will come to you declaring that they have been converted to your cause, but the words they utter have no more substance than the breath, upon which the words ride. Their speech does not reflect the image in their hearts, and their hypocrisy places them among the damned.

WSD:21:8 Others will come prepared to accept what you say in part only and to serve with reservations. If good comes out of what they do, they consider the effort sufficient, but if they find the going hard, they will fall away. Those are weak characters who can derive little benefit from your teachings, until they first change themselves. The first duty of the Good Religion is not to preach The Divine, but to teach men to change themselves. Its first aim is to develop a better being.

WSD:21:9 Do not ever tell others the way to live and how to govern their lives, until after you have put your teachings into practice. First practice what you teach, and then, you can instruct others from your experience. The hypocritical teacher betrays his cause.

WSD:21:10 Though you may preach to an audience of allcomers, choose your disciples carefully. Do not waste time on fools or simpletons, or on those unwilling to take the road towards spirituality. Always explain in such a manner that your words cannot be misconstrued. Do not always expect people to ask for further explanation if they do not understand, for their misinterpretation may satisfy them, or they may be reluctant to speak up.

WSD:21:11 Sometimes, a preaching prophet may upbraid his hearers with anger because his heart is stirred up within him, and some may be resentful. They will overlook all his good qualities and search out his faults. Perhaps they will say, "This man preaches forbearance and self-control, while railing against us with hostility and anger." Therefore, before attempting to preach, strengthen your character, so that if you must upbraid people for their ways, you do so with affection and restraint.

WSD:21:12 Do not argue hot-headedly or enter into dispute with your hearers, but talk to them in a kindly, reserved manner. Bear in mind that, whatever their belief, it will contain a large amount of good with which you have no dispute or issue. It is the bad, which taints and contaminates the good, that has to be sought out and destroyed.

WSD:21:13 Do not enter into discussion or argument with anyone well instructed in another doctrine, unless you are equally well instructed in yours and equally well informed on theirs. In disputes and discussions, the ill informed man is knocked over with a straw. In the arena of argument, the man without knowledge attacks with a reed.

WSD:21:14 Other doctrines have their books, and the best book is the one, which benefits the most. In one book, Truth may be described in one way, and, in another book, it may be described differently, but this need not mean that one is right and the other wrong. Truth never goes unveiled, but the wise man seeks her where she is veiled the least.

WSD:21:15 The outward vestments of a religion are unimportant, for gaudy ones may hide a festering body, while unimposing garments may clothe a healthy one. Disregard the bottle and give your attention to its contents. A mis-shapen bottle may hold matured wine, while the well shaped bottle may contain wine newly pressed.

WSD:21:16 If your calling is to preach, then declare to others all the words you believe to be true concerning The Divine and the latent divinity in men. Pay no heed to those who would discourage you, and follow the footsteps of Truth unflinchingly. The least enlightened are those who close their ears to the voice of wisdom.

WSD:21:17 If you have been granted the gift of speech so that your opponents are routed under a hail of words, do not proclaim a victory. A man is not converted because he is silenced. The advocate who presents the best argument may not have the best case, and he who speaks the right words may not be on the right side.

WSD:21:18 Though you cannot reveal the Divine Design, you can point out the order in the Divine Dominion. All about, the signs are manifested in the order and procession of the stars and the succession of the seasons, in the abounding beauty and bounty of Nature and in the laws that govern growth and decay.

WSD:21:19 When the call to the cause is sounded in the dawnlight of the day of Truth, preaching prophets will fare forth as harbingers. If it falls to your lot to be numbered among them, then consider yourself honoured among humanity. Summon others to tread the way of Truth with you, but do so in simple words and with enlightened argument and wisdom. Do not enter into time-wasting disputes, but use gentle persuasion and kindly guidance to put the feet of your followers upon the right road.

WSD:21:20 Those who answer the call to the cause cannot expect to escape the conflict unscathed. If you are among those who suffer, do not take reprisals, but only such steps as will prevent a repetition. Display your strength of character in patient endurance and cheerfulness, but you are not expected to be meekly submissive.

WSD:21:21 Endure whatever trials come your way with patience and fortitude, for they serve you well. Do not be unduly disturbed if you are not believed, or troubled because so many betray their own nature and destiny. You can do no more than warn them and call upon them to fulfil their duty and obligations. Do not let your heart be troubled by their subtleties of arguments, and bear in mind that deluded men always believe in the reality of their delusions.

WSD:21:22 Concentrate on teaching the young, for this is like engraving words on metal, while teaching the aged is like writing words on the seashore sands. But instruction should be given by the aged, for he who looks for wisdom in the young is like a man who eats unripe fruit from the vine or drinks unmellowed wine from the cask.

WSD:21:23 The Good Religion will not concern itself with moneymaking for profit; though, if it is made to serve a good end there is no harm. With moneymaking and profit, it is the objective that counts. Those who preach the Good Religion will take no money for themselves in such a way that people might come to regard it as no more than another means of livelihood. The praiseworthy teacher will earn his livelihood through his skill or labour.

WSD:21:24 However, if a man devotes himself to furthering the cause, and sacrifices opportunities in other directions, he shall not be denied a fair return for his services. A man who dedicates himself wholly to the service of a cause can rightly expect that cause to supply him with the necessities of life.

WSD:21:25 The preacher dedicated to service must not be too fastidious, for to give battle to the muck wallowers, the muck heap must be entered. Neither must he be intolerant with those who hold to the most outlandish beliefs, for each man's belief seems right in his own eyes.

WSD:21:26 The harbingers of the Good Religion must be men of strong character and integrity, for a fortress cannot be built on shaky foundations, or stout walls erected over a bog. The preacher who is truly dedicated to a Divinity of Love and Goodness becomes, himself, a manifestation of those qualities.

WSD:21:27 Man is not expected to achieve perfection here on Earth, but only to seek it. What is expected of him is a sincere and honest effort without any hypocritical or deceptive reservations. The Divine Design requires that man make a conscious choice of right under the constant pressure of temptation to do otherwise. This also leaves man free to choose wrong.

WSD:21:28 Man chooses wrong instead of right for just two reasons; either it is the easy path of least resistance, or it is the most alluring. Consequently, the Good Religion must first concern itself with establishing strength of character and moral backbone, for these form the only foundation, upon which the palace of spirituality can be erected.

WSD:21:29 Long ages ago, man took the wrong path and was led astray still further by guides with insufficient knowledge of the way. They knew the general direction, but their maps were faulty. Now, man is lost in the swamps of spiritual barrenness and the marshes of moral decay. His vision cannot penetrate the thick mists of mortal and material illusion, which have closed in upon him. He has lost all confidence in his guides and feels betrayed, abandoned and lonely.

WSD:21:30 The lost wayfarer must be revived with a draught of moral courage. He must be strengthened and revitalised with a belief which gives him spiritual backbone. The religions, which pander to the weak characters, to the meek and servile, the ignorant and unthinking, must be discarded. Man must be given what he needs, not what he deserves. He must be taught the meaning and purpose of life, so that he no longer wastes it. He must know that whatever befalls him on Earth is either decreed or the result of his own actions, but that it may be utilised to his benefit elsewhere. Now, as always, man is taught to seek inspiration outside himself. In the light of the new dawn, he must be taught to seek his inspiration from the divinity within himself.

WSD:21:31 This is not the hour of dawning, for it lies still distant, and therefore, these words are no more than an arrow shot in the direction of the rising sun. He who writes them now will never put them into effect, for a child born prematurely has little chance of survival. A ship is not launched on the floodwaters, and a harvest is reaped only when the seed is sown in its proper season.

WSD:21:32 Do not be downhearted if the results of your preaching cannot be seen, for be assured that if good is sown well, it will surely take root. When your hearers are men of intelligence, speak to them profoundly, but if they are men who toil, men not gifted with intellect or well endowed with words, instruct them by parable and with tales drawn from their own background and turned to account.

WSD:21:33 When The Divine intends to call a man to high service, that man is certain to be the first disciplined by suffering. He may be tested by bodily labour, by hunger and privation, or he may be tried in the fires of trouble and distress. His every undertaking may be confounded and every effort frustrated. By such means his character will be strengthened and his resolution intensified. His understanding and compassion will be increased.

WSD:21:34 Men have to make mistakes to learn, and reformation of character often commences under duress. Yet, it does not follow that all derive benefit from the tests of life, for many weak characters succumb before them, and then, their weakness swallows them up. The benefit comes to those who realise benefit is to be gained and who look for it, or to those who, unconscious of benefit, still rise above their trials,

WSD:21:35 Nothing is wrong with the Spiritual Realm, and nothing is wrong with the world except through man's own actions. What is wrong and must be remade is man, himself. The Good Religion must, therefore, teach man to be happy and contented within himself and to rise above his environment. Too many lack this ability and are happy only when circumstances and surroundings are favourable, but they soon become depressed and sad when things go against them or are not to their liking. Despondency and worry arise when a person's thoughts are completely self-centred, and harmful desires arise when they seek selfish gratification. To seek the things and circumstances that please and to shun those that do not is taking the slippery path leading to the pit of sorrow. The road to degeneracy is wide, smooth and downhill all the way.

WSD:21:36 Men must learn that, while they traverse the arid desert of materialism, they must expect to suffer the thirstpangs of unquenchable desires and unsatisfied urges. Their feet will always drag heavily through the sands of sorrow and suffering. Only when they come to the cool waters of spirituality can they rest, refreshed and satisfied. The duststorms of passion, the mirages of deception and illusion and the dark cloud of mortal ignorance must be penetrated in order to glimpse the Light of Divinity beyond. The phantoms of sense fallacies must be recognised for what they are, unimportant things without substance.

WSD:21:37 Things come into being because they are needed and necessary, and when the Good Religion opens its arms to men, it will be for this reason. Until then, it is not harmful for them to worship the awe-inspiring symbols and indulge in the spirit-stirring litanies conceived by the many existing religions. These do serve by assisting the spirit to purge itself of grosser attractions and to elevate the soul. In such elementary forms of worship, the object of homage does not matter, for each worshipper forms an image in his own mind of what lies behind it according to his own state of development. In this manner, the way is prepared for the coming of the Light.

WSD:21:38 No activity of man is so wrapped in ignorance, so inept and harmful as religious intolerance or prejudice in favour of one outward form of worship as against another. All who worship are seeking the same destination, and each takes the road he thinks most suitable. Men are led by phantoms to fight for dimly-revealed causes and end up consumed in fiery pits of hatred. Why have they chosen one side rather than the other? Only because the particular religion they support is an accident of birth and upbringing. Man weaves his sorrows from the very materials given for his adornment and glorification.

WSD:21:39 The answers given by all true religions are inspired by the desire to meet particular needs. These needs differ according to time and place and the condition and development of men, but all true religions have this in common: they come in response to something upsurging in the nature of man. When the rites of a religion are performed without thought and its ceremonial becomes meaningless, then that religion is ready to die.

Chapter Twenty-Two – The Good Religion

WSD:22:1 This is not a recipe for salvation, nor a formula for blind belief. It is not a matter of doctrine alone, and dogmatic belief must not be rigidly imposed, though loyalty and unity are certainly to be expected from those who follow its light. The Good Religion is not so much a belief or doctrine as a way of living. It is the way of life of a company of kindred spirits headed for the same destination and all sharing the same adventure, with its hazards and excitement, all seeking the best road together.

WSD:22:2 It is not a religion of gloom and despair. It does not seek to placate or coerce any Being, for it serves a Divinity above such things. It is not a religion revelling in servility and meekness; instead, it seeks to reveal the greatness of man. It is a religion of joy and hope, of high ideals and aspirations. It adheres to the highest principles of Truth, Justice and Goodness. It aspires to the greatest good for all mankind and believes in the sanctity of life, love and family. It hallows hearth and home.

WSD:22:3 It is a practical religion teaching the doctrine of evolving betterment. It establishes a standard for men to live by, which will make them better men and permit them to live in peace and harmony with others. It values the qualities of courage, audacity, fortitude and steadfastness. It upholds the virtues of modesty, patience, purity and gentleness. It is not a religion of undue restraint or narrow dogma, and it does not believe in the futile mortification of the body. It takes full regard of man as a twofold being and maintains the dignity of the mortal as well as the spiritual body. It makes no empty promises of salvation or redemption and is not founded upon a system of indulgences, rewards or promises. It expounds the principles of personal responsibility, obligation and effort. Its prime objectives are to the carrying out of the Divine Design and the service of mankind. It is a religion to be lived by and not just believed in. It demands to be expressed in deeds and not in words, in beneficial action and not in blind conformity. It is more interested in bringing out the hidden good than in outward display and pomp. The Good Religion concerns itself with whatever is necessary for the unfolding of the spirit, and its aim is to spur man upward to divinity.

WSD:22:4 The purpose of a religion is to serve, and it cannot do this properly by concentrating on spiritual matters alone, for it also has the obligation of setting a moral standard. A worthwhile religion cannot permit itself to be shut out from everyday life. If it does so, it is undeserving of its status. It must concern itself with the way men live, with the conduct of their daily affairs, with their relationship with one another.

WSD:22:5 Religion is man's response to his existence in earthly conditions and the answer to the challenge of his environment. Therefore, it is in religion that he finds the most satisfactory outlet for his feelings and the best way of expressing his inner yearning. The soundless, insistent voice of The Divine calls out to man from the depths of his being, and that which guides and directs him towards it is called 'religion.'

WSD:22:6 The Divine is hidden from men and veiled behind the firmament, and this separation, this feeling of being cut off, is the source and basis of religion. The Divine and man, fire and spark, now sundered apart, crave to be united, and this craving expresses itself as religion.

WSD:22:7 Man, the person, is like a lamb separated from its mother, the source of its life, and lost in the mountain mists. He is a lonely creature pulled and pushed around by urges and desires, dragged onward by the remorseless chords of time, heavily burdened with fragile mortality and always haunted by the accompanying phantoms of decay and change. His only encouragement is the light of divinity just dimly glimpsed in the distance, and his only consolation and comfort his religion.

WSD:22:8 But religion too often gives cold comfort and little encouragement; therefore, the Good Religion must be a truecomforter as well as a champion. It will teach man that there is a happy haven and worthwhile destination at the end of the road. It will show him that it is futile to try and run away from life and that its trials are inescapable. Life is given to man with intent and purpose, and he can achieve divinity only by first experiencing the realities of existence here and rising above them.

WSD:22:9 The standards imposed upon those who follow the light of the Good Religion will be those already set out in the Sacred Books of times gone by, for wisdom is not a callow youth. Such standards should not weigh too heavily on men, as do some enforced under the cloak of ignorance. This is the Religion of the Light, and it accords with the natural tendencies of man. It declares every man to be heir of divinity and, therefore, capable of living a righteous and upward-tending life.

WSD:22:10 The concept of righteousness held by the Good Religion is not one of external display, for it preaches that goodness is expressed in deeds and in a way of life, not in the holding of barren beliefs and purposeless ceremonial. It is like a mighty oak, always shedding leaves and replacing them in the proper seasons. Its roots keep spreading out into new ground, but its trunk is always strengthening and growing greater.

WSD:22:11 The Good Religion believes that man is the instrument of The Divine and His deputy on Earth; that man is entrusted with certain responsibilities and duties, which he can shirk only to his cost; that the soul is immortal and the body mortal and that man can achieve divinity only through his own efforts. He can be saved by no one except himself.

WSD:22:12 There are those who prefer the worship of many lesser divinities, and those who divide their belief so from one come many, and each is content with his portion and derides that of others. The many divinities are like mirages across the sands, which appear to offer cool waters, but no man ever found refreshment there. When darkness falls, the mirage disappears, and he who trod the sand towards it is lost.

WSD:22:13 Men have to be organised in worship as in all things, but this is not so much for their own good, though this is often made the excuse, but to check man's inherent tendency towards irresponsibility and apathy. While it is true that the less responsible and resolute men are the more they have to be organised and controlled, it is also true that the more they are organised and controlled, the less responsible and resolute they tend to become. In this as in all things a balance must be struck. Therefore, when a religion teaches that men should be responsible and resolute, it should not seek to organise and control them too much. However, it must also be remembered that without leadership, organisation and discipline, no battle was ever won.

WSD:22:14 The Good Religion must do more than produce good men. The popular religions within the confines of civilisation already produce good men, but they do not produce divinely inspired men or men who rise even above goodness.

WSD:22:15 The Good Religion will not accept the doctrine now preached that the man who suffers is one who has done wrong or offended some divinity. Instead, it will declare that the man who suffers is undergoing one of the inescapable tests of life and may be one chosen for higher service. However, it should acknowledge that this should not lead to suffering being accepted passively. Not only must suffering be struggled against, but every effort must be made by others to help the sufferer. The trials and tests of life are not things to be endured with passive patience, they are challenges to be met and overcome.

WSD:22:16 The Good Religion must establish a tradition of service, which it can hand down from one generation to another. It must also establish base within a compatible body of people, from which it can be propagated, not only by preaching and teaching but also, more important, by example. To each of its followers, it must declare the message: "Whether a man does much or little is not as important as to whether he always does his best and directs his actions towards the fulfilment of the Divine Design."

WSD:22:17 The Good Religion exists even now, for it is the faith of the few who cherish the seed. It is limited to a small number who hand on the torch, and this must continue until the day already appointed. Meanwhile, mankind is not ill served by its many religions, but the day comes when they will no longer serve, and that is the day the child of man's ancient heritage will be born.

BRT:4:2 After our Lord died, having been hung on the cross outside the city walls of Jerusalem, Joseph of Abramatha took Mary, the mother of Jesus into his home until John could make suitable arrangements. Then he was called Guardian of the Lady, which title became confused in Britain with that of Guardian of the Sacred Vessel.

Table of Chapters

BRT:1:1 – BRT:1:21	Chapter One	133
BRT:2:1 – BRT:2:18	Chapter Two – Jesus - 1	135
BRT:3:1 – BRT:3:58	Chapter Three – Jesus - 2	137
BRT:4:1 – BRT:4:26	Chapter Four – The Writings of Aristolas	142
BRT:5:1 – BRT:5:36	Chapter Five – The Writings of Abaris	145
BRT:6:1 – BRT:6:72	Chapter Six – The Writings of Emris Skinlaka	148
BRT:7:1 – BRT:7:70	Chapter Seven – The Corrygorsed	155
BRT:8:1 – BRT:8:36	Chapter Eight – Nobility	158
BRT:9:1 – BRT:9:20	Chapter Nine – Shards of Wisdom	161

The Britain Book

Chapter One

BRT:1:1 To my stalwart son, always well beloved. I greet you heartily, desiring to hear of your welfare. Be not displeased at my going from Kelshaw or my manner of departure, for I first gave your mother and sister over to good keeping in the hands of the goodmistress Cotter.

BRT:1:2 Verily, such tidings were brought to me by diverse persons of the Craft on matters of our abiding concern, that I was beholden to come hitherwards. Nor durst I now go hence, for the charge remains, lying heavily upon my breast.

BRT:1:3 As for Hempshill he lied to us, for he is a knave and a churlish one, and we were fools to be deceived by his wiles and his tongue speaking such wild language. I will entreat with the bailiff, and mayhap he who stands in the lord's place will abide my supplication.

BRT:1:4 As we planned, you do thereafter, but I pray you beware in what manner you walk, for those, among whom we walk are full black-hearted and enwrapped in the ways of wickedness. They desire an end to all things, in which we hold fast, but are not as staunch that they will set upon you in a manly way but will start out upon you like lurking footpads. Beware, too, what you eat and drink, and trust not even they who speak fair unto you, for the hands of all outsiders are against us.

BRT:1:5 Send me tidings of Long Will and goodwife Abigail, and of John the Cordwainer and John of the Wildwood band, and others who stood in at the tithing ere you departed. It is to my abiding contentment that we have been able to acquit the Wanderers in full good measure, for their braziers did their work right stoutly in a cunning manner. Had we a clerk among us, then it could have been wrought to more avail; but no matter, for their hand was firm, and they faithfully followed the marks.

BRT:1:6 Now, take you the secured budget and go against Lewlaw, and leave it there in the cell under the Grimsbarrow where Alain the Pedlar secured his hoard.

** ** ** ** ** ** ** ** **

BRT:1:7 In the Books of Britain it is written: Ilyid came seaborne in a ship of Tarsis from across the sea of Wicta, setting up at Rafinia in the land of the Wains. From thence to the river Tarant, which flows between the Kingdom of Albany and the Kingdom of Korin, Albany being the land between the Isen and the Ikta. Passing Ivern and Insels, south of the Kathebelon, and then past Dinsolin to take water at the town where ships traded, standing at the foot of the red cliff between the two white ones around the extreme of the world to the northern Ikta in Siluria. Here, they were unwelcome, but were permitted to take water and wood and to trade for meat and grain. Sailing thence towards the rising sun, they came to the place beyond Sabrin called Summerland.

BRT:1:8 They were coldly welcomed by Homodren of the Chariots, but in the Kingdom of Arviragus they came under the mantle of the High Druid of the south, whose ear was inclined towards them, for he understood full well the nature of the three-faced god. The king heard their words but did not take them to heart, saying they differed little from what was there.

BRT:1:9 Then were the shipborne wanderers given land over from the Isle of Departure, saying that, could they live where no one else could because of the spirits, then their holiness would be established before all the people. The strangers were sorely tried by the Druids, but the spirits troubled them not. Nor did the sickness of the place come upon them, and the people wondered. They were troubled because of where the strangers were and were stirred up by the Druthin, but the shield of Arviragus protected them.

BRT:1:10 Now, eastward and to the north there was a lake, and between this and the Isle of Departure, there was a swampland and there was a village of houses that stood out above the water, and the moonmaidens and moonmatrons who served the dead dwelt there. Among these was Islass the Dreamer, who was sacred to the guardian of this place.

BRT:1:11 Islass was the daughter of the queen's youngest sister and a holder of the king's favour, and when she attended him, she divulged her dreams. It happened that she dreamed the same dream thrice, and this was its manner as she told it to the king: "Behold, I saw a moon which had three changing faces, and, as I watched, the changes the moon itself changed and became a sun, and within this sun was a face of a god. As I looked long on this sun, another sun appeared, and such was its brilliance that the first sun appeared inferior in brightness. Then, the two became one and its brilliance filled the sky. In the midst of this, I saw the king and many Druthin and priests of the strangers. Then I saw a great battlesword, and the brilliance faded, as did the figures, and only the sword remained, from which blood dripped drop by drop. Then, too, it faded.'

BRT:1:12 The king took heed of the dream and gave the strangers land beside the Summerhouse of the King, which could be reached by ships. Inland from here, the gifted land extended to the tree now called the Great Oak, which still stands, and thence to the hill south of the residence where Ilyid, being wearied, rested against a great stone. Beyond this was an avenue of standing trees and oak trees placed one and one, and the gifted land came up against this.

BRT:1:13 It extended southward to the holy vineyard, which was fenced about. The fruit of these vines was small and bitter in the mouth. The strangers built huts for shelter on the hillside, high enough to be free of the tides. They settled down and learned the language, though Ilyid and two of the women spoke it strangely.

BRT:1:14 The words of the strangers fell on deaf ears, for the people were content with the gods they knew and did not wish to weary their minds with the words of the new ones. When the strangers gathered in praise of The One True God, the tribesmen stoned them and shouted abuses, but Ilyid persevered, and while later the people still would not believe that The God of whom he spoke was more powerful than their gods, they would sit around and listen to his stories.

BRT:1:15 Now, when the strangers were granted the land, the Druthin disputed this with the king and said that they wanted a divine sign that their gods approved. Ilyid said, "Give me but half a year." At the witnessing of this, the Druthin set up a holistone, and Ilyid struck his staff into the soil to mark the covenant.

BRT:1:16 The following Eve of Summer there was a gathering and it was found that a small green shoot was coming up from the ground beside the staff, which was an offshoot of the staff. The king decreed that this was a sign that the land accepted the strangers, but these took it as a sign that what they taught fell on fertile ground and would take root.

BRT:1:17 Here, the strangers, now called the Wise Ones, were free from the yoke of Rome and from the intolerance of the Jews. They were not subject to immoral customs and were among the right-living people, simple but pure in mind and body. Close by was a place for trading in metals, slaves, dogs and grain. Here, Ilyid built himself a house unlike any others, for it was square and in two parts, more stone than timber. This place was called Kwinad.

BRT:1:18 Here, on twelve portions of land, the wise strangers dwelt in peace and they built a church which was a full sixty feet long by a full twenty-six feet wide. At one end was a statue four feet high, carved from a beech trunk. The roof was thatched with reeds, after the manner of the Britons. The walls were of wicker overlaid with plaster of chalk and mud.

BRT:1:19 Ilyid is buried outside the forked path before the church, and on his tomb was written, "I brought Christ to the Britons and taught them. I buried Christ, and now, here my body is at rest."

BRT:1:20 Islass was the first convert, and it is said that she alone knew the secret of the Holy Hawthorn. What this may be, none can know now. It is said that, when the Druthin murmured against the staff of Ilyid, she placed a twig in water and it flowered.

BRT:1:21 Here, in this holy place, under the direct guidance of God, our father founded the first church in Britain. It is said it was not built by human hands, which is true, and from here shall come that, which will be the salvation of mankind in the years to come. Here was the resting place for the souls of the dead, where they received their last sustenance before passing through the glass wall. From here ran the old road to the place of light where the bright-winged spirits flew freely in the place called Dainsart in the old tongue.

Chapter Two – Jesus - 1

BRT:2:1 This is the true record of events concerning Jesus, son of Joseph and Mary, which we have received by the hands of several who have lived within the circle of His Light, and more especially from one who is our earthly father in the faith. He being not the least among the articulate ones who knew Jesus, and a person of no mean estate, both in the distant land from whence he came and in this more virile land.

BRT:2:2 For Jesus came to fulfil the desires and longings of men expressed in certain Holy Books, but more so in many unlettered hearts. For it is written that such is the nature of things; the tree springing from the yearning of men shall not fail to bear fruit. For the Holy Books can be likened to an egg containing the embryonic hopes and desires of men.

BRT:2:3 In the Sacred Books of the Idewin it is written: 'The Son of Man is the shepherd of men and we know how diligently a shepherd tends his flocks.' Jesus came not as a shepherd to drive, but as one bearing a guiding lantern to show the way. It is also written: 'The Son of Man is the deliverer of men,' and while we know from what we have to be delivered, those who lived in His land misunderstood the meaning.

BRT:2:4 From the Book of the Holy Mark (whose wife was one of our own fair race, her father being a Roman waykeeper whose wife was barren, and having this homeborn lady, her mother, as a slave, had by her a child whom he later adopted and raised as a lady of estate), we learn much. But clearer to our understanding is that knowledge concerning Ilyid imparted to us by our earthly father.

BRT:2:5 Aristolas taught that Ilyid had been one who commanded with the ships of Rome, but was not without ships himself. So it was that, when Jesus went down to the Western Sea of the Jews, which is not the Sea of the Setting Sun, He being one skilled with His hands, worked on them. Jesus was brawnily built and not one to take money without labour.

BRT:2:6 Jesus, our Master, Light of our Life was hung on the shameful cross in His twenty-seventh year, this being the one thousand and ninety-ninth year of Britain, in the reign of Tiberius, ruler of the Roman lands to the east.

BRT:2:7 Within a year, Ilyid and others departed from their homeland shore by ship, and though this was demasted in a heavy storm, it made safe haven in Sankel. There, he and his son were joined by several other holy persons. They tarried awhile before crossing to Laidlow, from whence they took a ship to Tarsis.

BRT:2:8 In the year of Britain one thousand one hundred and twelve, our father came from Rome with others, because of the decrees of Claudius, ruler of all the Romans to the east, seeking refuge beyond the oppression of Roman might, where the true light could burn undisturbed. But the circle of Roman might spread ever wider, like a thrown fisherman's net.

BRT:2:9 Thirteen years after our Master was hung on the cross, the Romans came to the fair land of Britain, and the might of their legions prevailed over the brave Caradew, great battleking of all the Britons. He was the leader of fighting men such as will not be seen again. He was carried off, betrayed by an irrational woman, an honourable peace offering to appease the argument of might, together with the British fount of knowledge and wisdom. With him went the allwise Fran, being held in honourable captivity until returned to the land of light at the intercession of our father, for those whom he befriended had not forgotten him. For Ilyid taught that the greatest wrong man can commit against man is the betrayal of a friend.

BRT:2:10 Now, the daughter of Caradew was Gladys, red-haired, blue-eyed and slim, who married Pudens, Commander of the Legions, beloved of Paul the Martyred in God, who died in the one thousand one hundred and thirty year of Britain. Lein, son of Caradew, brother of Gladys, being the first Christian in Rome.

BRT:2:11 In the year of Britain one thousand one hundred and twenty-seven, there was a great outbreak of fighting, and many men sought refuge within the enclosure of Ilyid, for the free Britons had risen, having been given an assurance of victory by no less than the battlegoddess herself.

BRT:2:12 Calling on Amaraith and Kamulose, the Britons followed their battlequeen, whose heart was afire because of the rape of her daughters. She stood tall in stature and was serene of face, speaking deep but melodiously. She knew the mastery of letters and spoke three tongues. She had fair hair hanging to her hips when not battlegirded. Her head was circled by a golden war coronet and her tunic was of green and brown interwoven in the manner of men. She wore a short cloak of purple. Thus she spoke before the battle:

BRT:2:13 "I speak to you as a woman whose house has been violated and her daughters dishonoured, We have been dealt with unjustly and I appeal to you not only as a queen but more so as a woman. Britons who honour their womenfolk cannot regard this lightly. Unlike the squirming Roman Nierotes, I do not rule over servile and docile unmanly men who are less than men, nor like he who rules over pedlars and hucksters. Nor am I like the cowardly man/woman, Nero, who surrounds himself with perverts and half-men and slaves who satisfy obscene desires. Such is the nature of the vile culture these foreigners have introduced to our fair land."

BRT:2:14 "I am not such as these whose minds are fevered with an evil ferment. I rule over true men, little schooled in craftiness and deceit, real men born to fight and withstand adversity. The code they live by is that of manliness. True men indeed who, in the cause of freedom, willingly heed the call to arms and stake their lives on the outcome. They willingly offer themselves as a sacrifice for the future of their womenfolk and children and their lands and property."

BRT:2:15 "As the leader of this brave breed of men, I fervently plead for the assistance of your strong right arms. Let us not shirk the task or shun the opportunity to strike a blow for freedom. I pray the gods of war, the overseers of battles, for victory. We have the duty to stamp out these infections on our land, these ruthless enemies whose reputation is infamous. They are perverters of justice, promoters of depravity and servants of greed."

BRT:2:16 "They are a race who enjoys unmanly pleasures, who delights in the infliction of pain on the helpless but cringes like a dog at the prospect of its own suffering. Whose approbation is more to be feared and its friendship more to be shunned than its enmity. Never will I surrender to people whose ways I abhor, nor will I ever desire to live to see my countrymen treated as servile serfs. May the Great Godly Powers be with us now in the great testing time, as we gird ourselves to face the issue."

BRT:2:17 Those brave, inspiring words were of no avail, and Britain was lost, but the spirit could not be quenched, and manliness was maintained. It is not in victory that a race finds greatness but in defeat. The knowledge of Christ came, not through peace and prosperity but through persecution. That, which is written is not a tale of victory, but of the glory that resides in defeat. The books, which are the recipe for victory are written by defeated men.

BRT:2:18 I, Elfed, write these things, but they are not from my own heart but come from the hand of others. This is that Elfed who married Marcella, maid of Ilted, after the death of her husband who tripped over a stone and fell on a spike and died bent like a bow.

Chapter Three – Jesus - 2

BRT:3:1 Jesus was the son of Miriam called Mary, by Joseph. His brothers were Jacob, Joseph, Simon and James. He was born at Bethlehem. In the days of His youth, the land rang with the exploits of Judas the Galilean, who preached that there was no ruler but God; he was called the Teacher of Righteousness in his day.

BRT:3:2 Joseph, Jesus' father, died when Jesus was sixteen. Mary, His mother, did not like His inwardness, His long silences and His solitary habits. She rebuked Him for being a tardy breadwinner, but this was unjust, for He excelled in His craft. She could not understand her strange son who was unlike the others, and she wanted a practical man, not a dreamer and preacher.

BRT:3:3 Jesus had spells of rapture, and His male kinsfolk declared He was out of His mind, so they sought to have him put under restraint. But the womenfolk said He was harmless, and in cases such as this, their words coloured the law of the land. Jesus loved His father, who had taught Him His trade. He consoled Himself with the scriptures which said, "I will become His father and He shall be My son."

BRT:3:4 Jesus early became a wandering carpenter and then joined the Nasarines. There was excitement in the land because it was said that the prophesy of Daniel was to be fulfilled in these times. The conditions of the times fulfilled the predictions.

BRT:3:5 Then, Jesus went into the wilderness beside the Jordan. He joined the Society of Saints, which was beside the Sea of Heavy Salt. When He came back to the Jordan, He no longer retired within Himself, but was a man of direct and forceful speech. He was decisive and commanding.

BRT:3:6 The people called Him the Galilean because He was raised in Galilee, and they sought to name Him the Man of Messianic Hope and the Suffering Just One, when Judas the Galilean was dead. Some thought He was the warrior messiah, but He rebuked them, saying, "I am He of whom it is written 'He shall judge the poor rightly and reprove those who oppress them. He shall smite the Earth with the rod of His mouth and slay the wicked with the words that issue from His mouth.'"

BRT:3:7 He wrought cures, as did many others in those times. The Levites put out that He did not as they, but by the power of the Prince of Darkness. But Jesus said that such was blasphemy, as the healing spirit of God was strong within Him. Therefore, such an accusation was a sin, but they mocked Him.

BRT:3:8 He was a true man, a good organiser, strong, alert and resourceful. He had determination and courage, though withal, He could be gentle and compassionate. He was inflexible in purpose, yet, He could bend before the storm and survive where the stubborn man would go down.

BRT:3:9 He stood firmly against the holy men of the Jews, whose seeming holiness was but a cloak, for it was something that flourished only in the public eye. It was woven with self-righteousness, lined with intolerance and sewn with threads of sadness. Good men do good deeds out of the sight of others and gain merit from their selfishness and sacrifices.

BRT:3:10 One came to Jesus, saying, "Lord, I give many gifts and alms to the poor. I am ever giving to the needy. I am a rich man, but my riches have come by lawful means. I have traded with ships and encountered dangers to accumulate them. Having gained wealth, I live in moderation, supplying only my moderate needs. I give the rest to the needy poor, and I am ever ready to serve the deserving. Am I then a sinner?"

BRT:3:11 Jesus said, "No, by giving with discretion and making such sacrifices, you gain merit, and there is no harm in seeking riches for worthy ends. It is the love of money for its own sake that is productive of evil. The evils of riches arise from their misuse. If a man gains wealth in a lawful way and does not live in luxury, supplying no more than his moderate needs, serving the poor and deserving with his surplus, then he does no wrong."

BRT:3:12 A teacher of the Jewish way said to Jesus, "If God is so great and all knowing, why does He not strike down the wrongdoer? Why does He withhold His justifiable wrath when the wicked man swallows up the man who follows the path of goodness? Is he not the God of justice?" Jesus replied, "Justice is not a thing of the time. Though the mills of God grind slowly, they grind to perfection. Life itself metes out justice. The justice of God adjusts the injustice of men. Were this not so, I would not have come."

BRT:3:13 Jesus was then asked if He was one with God, and He answered, "It is not in Me to state that, which I know to be untrue, and truly there can be but one God alone. Because I have been granted visions and insight into things unseen and unknown to other men, what manner of man would I be did I claim equality with God? I have spoken only that which I am bidden. I have said, 'Worship God who is My Father and your Father.' Does this then raise Me above other men? I have proclaimed all men My brothers, and if I have said I am even as God, then truly I have raised them up also. Yet, this they cannot see, or is it that they fear the burden of their own godhood?"

BRT:3:14 Jesus came and was like the slasher, which clears away the useless undergrowth in the forest of life. He uprooted and burned that, which was unproductive. He planted good trees, but the undergrowth returns. It is a time for the activities of good men. Jesus found pearls by the seashore. He sowed the good seed in the hearts of those who followed Him closely. For his sake, many of the rich became poor.

BRT:3:15 He came and separated men out from the errors of the world. He brought men a mirror, into which they could look and see their own divinity. He opened a door now open to all, and those who choose to pass through stand on the road to the eternal. He raised up the fallen and healed the afflicted.

He woke those who slept and reminded those who had forgotten. He enlightened the righteous and gathered in those who were lost.

BRT:3:16 To what can He be compared? To the great sun that shines down, giving joy and life to all living things. To a great river giving gladness to men and the waters of life to beasts. To the good husbandman who cherishes his fields and tends his flocks. To the men of the forests who care for their trees and thankfully gather the fruits thereof.

BRT:3:17 The sun shines today, and the air gleams with light. The Earth puts forth blossoms, and the seas are calm. The waters flow clearly, the birds sing and the gloomy Winter has gone. Hope dawns, and so it is with the Son of Man.

BRT:3:18 The tree of glory has been planted and will survive, for it is well serviced. Its servants are dutiful. So let it be like the holly, whose leaves are not shed in Summer or Winter, which stands with weapons ever ready in persecution or freedom, in good days and bad.

BRT:3:19 He who neglects these scriptures is like the branch of a fruitless tree; his life is fruitless. Blessed are those who seek fruit that grows out of our good deeds. He who copies a book is like a maimed man who gives his weapons to a whole and healthy man. The lettered man resembles this good land, which takes the seed and nourishes it. The rains fall plentifully and the crop is good.

BRT:3:20 The life men live is like an inn where they dwell shortly, or like a house rented for a limited time. Vessels of metal and earthenware are to them like borrowed utensils. Their riches are held in trust. The wise man uses them and they serve him, but he does not set his heart on these or hug them to his bosom.

BRT:3:21 Who is most praiseworthy for his goodness, the son of a rich man or the son of a poor man? The rich son gives only what he himself has been given, so surely it is the son of the poor man, for he has overcome the temptations of poverty and satisfied the cry of hungry mouths with the earnings of his own labour. It is the poor who help the poor, for the rich help themselves.

BRT:3:22 There are those who fast for the sake of Heaven, but Jesus said it were better did they devote themselves to learning the scriptures and to good works for the sake of Heaven. Yet, it is useless to merely read the scriptures, for unless they be taken into the heart and lived by, then they are things of little value and use. The value of all sacred writings lies in what people do with them. More important still is what the scriptures do to the people.

BRT:3:23 A man asked Jesus, "Lord, what does it mean when it is written that the iniquities of the fathers shall be visited upon the children?" Jesus said, "When a man commits a sin, for which he does not make full recompense in his lifetime, then the same temptation is placed in the way of the son, for there is a bond of family blood between them. Is it not manifest also that the wrongs a man does within his own household become the sins of the sons within their households? Wrongful living is the heritage of generations.

BRT:3:24 A man asked, "Where is God?" Jesus took a piece of bread and gave it to the man, saying, "Take this and hold it." Then He said, "Put out the other hand." He poured a little water on the upturned palm and said, "Now you have felt the power of God, for without His spirit in the bread and in the water, these would not exist for you. Split a billet of wood, and God will be there. Lift up a stone, and you will find Him."

BRT:3:25 Another said, "Tell us how we may best serve God." Jesus replied, "Talk not of serving God as you would serve a king. In serving God, man serves himself. You ask in your heart, shall you be this or that or a priest. Let your own heart point the best way, and having chosen it, follow it with devotion and fortitude."

BRT:3:26 At a wedding feast, Jesus was asked, "Master, why do You come to this place when it is a gathering place of those who seek only their own pleasure and will drink to excess if it is provided?" Jesus said, "Our purpose here is to make glad the hearts of the hosts and to share in their enjoyment, blending their pleasure with ours. There will always be those who are neglectful of their obligations and who concern themselves only with their own wellbeing. Yet, is this reason enough not to bring happiness to those who have invited us?"

BRT:3:27 One day, Jesus and those with Him came upon an old man playing with childish things. A bow and arrow-bearing huntsman passing by mocked him, saying, "Behold the old man playing as a child." Jesus called him over and said, "Do you always keep your bow bent, the string under stress?" "Of course not" replied the huntsman. "To do so would be foolish, for the bow would become useless were it not unbent from time to time." Jesus said, "Just so is it with the old man, and you should know better."

BRT:3:28 The bowman strings his bow before he shoots and, when the shooting is over, he unstrings it. A bow kept always strung will break and be useless when needed. So it is with a man who never relaxes. He is ever taut within, and when the testing time comes, his stomach turns to water.

BRT:3:29 Jesus taught that there are things, which should be approached with humility of spirit, they are: holiness, wisdom and nobility. Humility bestows upon the soul the benefit of harmony and attunement. A man once said to Jesus, "But who can define these things; that which is holy to one man can be unholy to another. The thing, which one man holds sacred, another holds to be an abomination. That, which one will bless another will curse." Jesus said, "The many nations and men, because of the diversity of their natures, hallow many different persons, places and things, apart from their gods. But nothing can be made holy by men alone, neither can anything wholly of Earth be holy. That, which is wholly of and for God is holy, the place wholly for God is holy and the person who lives wholly for God is Holy, but where on Earth can such absoluteness be found?"

BRT:3:30 "If by gathering in a temple, men feel they can better commune with God, then He will be there, and that place will be holy. If within a circle of stones or before a symbolic image, the soul of man may be stirred to attunement, then God will not absent Himself because of the Nature of the Place. He will meet man wherever man earnestly prepares for His coming. Though the temple may be holy to one man and the circle of stones to another, both places will be hallowed by God, if therein, the souls of men are elevated to commune with him."

BRT:3:31 "A structure of splendour, magnificent in its architecture, called holy by men who worship there, if their spirits remain asleep and unstirred will not be hallowed by the presence of God. He does not honour places where men just congregate, where their voices alone are raised in worship. He hallows the place where their souls and spirits are uplifted as they seek communion with Him. A Holy place is where the uplifted spirits of men blend with the nature of God."

BRT:3:32 A man asked, "What of wisdom? Has this not been plentiful in the world since the days of the Great Enlighteners, of whom Solomon was deemed the greatest? Even before him, there was much wisdom, yet is Earth a better place for this? What has it contributed to progress?" Jesus replied, "Alas, never has there been a shortage of wisdom in the world, but always there has been too little in the hearts of men. Wisdom is not something written in books, but that, which is conveyed from the book of the heart. It is a way of life."

BRT:3:33 All the wisdom of the past, held in reverence by some, was easier to write than to live by. Yet, following it is the only wisdom. Wisdom, however, is more than the thoughts of the wise, it is the accumulated philosophical knowledge of mankind winnowed by the wind of practicality.

BRT:3:34 Nobility is an attribute of the soul, and no man has this by right of birth. Nobility demonstrates an ability to live and act according to the high principles. It is expressed in deeds, outlook and bearing, in the manner of life and relationship with others. That, which ennobles a man is his recognition of something to love and strive for outside of himself. Nobility is the subordination of self to principles.

BRT:3:35 Jesus was One, in whom all the virtues came to fruition, and His gentleness drew to Him all His neighbours. In His presence, even enemies were reconciled, and this presence alone brought tranquillity to a restless and sorrowful heart. In the street, even the little children followed Him, just to touch His hand.

BRT:3:36 His reaction to injustice and insult was a sorrowful compassion. He neither sought to acquire anything beyond His immediate needs nor treasured what he had. Beneath His soft exterior was a rock-like, immovable determination immune to oppression and suffering alike. Despite His gentleness He could act decisively and swiftly, and when He had cause to strike in the name of justice and right He never avoided the issue.

BRT:3:37 His mind and wit were like the lightning flash. He was always keen and alert, and His face never lacked the calm beauty of cheerfulness. He was friendly towards all and acted so as not to annoy anyone. Only in the face of great injustice to another or oppression of the weak, or in the presence of gross hypocrisy did His wrath boil up and overflow; but never was it other than righteous. Though always compassionate and sympathetic, He was never sad or downcast. He rose above all suffering and pain, and ever seemed at peace within Himself.

BRT:3:38 Mary said to Jesus, "To whom can Your Disciples be likened?" Jesus said, "They are like children at play in a field, which belongs to a stranger, and when the owner comes, they say, 'This is our field, therefore convey it to us.'"

BRT:3:39 Thomas said, "If the spirit brought the body of flesh into being, it is a marvel." Jesus said, "It would be a much greater miracle had the body brought the spirit into being, for the lesser cannot create the greater. I marvel how this great wealth of beauty can dwell in such a mean habitation. But to he who has goodness in his heart, goodness shall be given; he who lacks goodness shall be stripped of what he has."

BRT:3:40 Jesus also said, "Just as it is impossible for any man to stretch two bows or mount two horses, so is it impossible for a man to serve two masters."

BRT:3:41 The disciples asked, "Is circumcision a good thing?" Jesus replied, "If it were would not children be born circumcised from the mother's womb? Only circumcision in the spirit confers true benefit."

BRT:3:42 When asked concerning accounting, Jesus said, "Give to Caesar that, which is Caesar's and to God that, which is God's. Give Me what is justly mine, and keep for yourselves only that which is rightly your due. Deal fairly with all men, and shun the morals of the marketplace. Do not become like the Samaritans who, loving a tree, hate its fruits, or loving the fruit, hate the tree. The Pharisee is like a dog sleeping in the manger, from whence the oxen eat. It cannot eat what is in the manger; neither will it let the oxen eat."

BRT:3:43 Jesus said, "The Kingdom of Heaven is like a woman carrying a jar of good wine. Being careless, she puts the jar down heavily and crashes it, and when she resumes her way, the wine spills out behind her on the road, but she blithely continues on her way, unaware of the spillage. When she enters the house, the master takes the wine jar and finds it empty." The disciples asked what this could mean, and Jesus replied, "When you possess the good things of the Kingdom of Heaven, do not let them slip away."

BRT:3:44 "For the Kingdom of Heaven is neither here nor there and contains all good things. It is in the hearts of men and exists where God reigns. When the lion lies down with the lamb and peace reigns over all, there shall be found the Kingdom of Heaven. Yet truly, Heaven and the Kingdom of Heaven are not the same." These things were said in the forecourt of the temple.

BRT:3:45 Jesus took the disciples who were with Him into the Court of the Hebrews, which was an inner place, and a warden, a priest named Levi, stopped them, saying to Jesus, "Are You an ignorant man? Do You not know it is forbidden to walk here in the presence of holy things without first purifying yourselves? See, those who follow You have not even washed their feet. They enter here defiled by the world."

BRT:3:46 Then, Jesus stopped and said to Levi, "Concern yourself with your own state rather than with ours." The priest replied, "I am clean. Having bathed in David's pool, going down by one set of steps and coming up by another; only having done this and donned clean clothes have I come here." Jesus said, "Lord, have mercy on the blind! You have washed in standing water, which may have been befouled by dogs, and scrubbed your outer skin as harlots, singing girls and vain men do who are full of vileness inside. But My disciples and I have little need for outer forms of ritual cleanliness, being clean within, for we have washed in the living waters of the spirit."

BRT:3:47 Having departed from the temple, Jesus said, "Do not the guests assemble in the antechamber before entering the feasthall? There, the hands and feet are washed, the head anointed, and small foods to whet the appetite are eaten. Even so is the Earth the antechamber of the Kingdom of Heaven."

BRT:3:48 "Live your lives in the world as men who journey through a strange land, marvelling at its wonders, tasting its pleasures, but ever on guard against dangers, for undue love of the world is a doorway to evil. There are those who derive pleasure in being what they are not, but as their hair turns grey, they suffer sorrow and frustration. Be ever true to yourselves and to your natures."

BRT:3:49 It came to pass, at this time, that many said that Jesus was the Messiah, but this was a manifest falsehood. Jesus, the son of Joseph and Mary, was an inspired prophet, a teacher who held the hand of God and there had been others before Him. His mother was a decent woman; both ate food as humans do. Mary did not set herself up as a goddess, neither did she preach.

BRT:3:50 It is of no moment to those who are not Jews whether Jesus was the heralded Messiah or not, so believe as you will, but were He born of a Holy Ghost and not of Joseph, then He did not fulfil the prophesy. Men step outside the bounds of truth in their beliefs, but this, too, is of little moment unless they impose their beliefs on others.

BRT:3:51 Jesus was not a sorrowful man, for greatness cannot be downcast. Always, he brought strength to the disheartened and was not influenced by the despondency of others. When Peter was dismayed and shut his sorrow within, Jesus said, "If My friend will not admit Me into the antechamber of his sorrows, how can I ever sit in the reception room of his affections?"

BRT:3:52 Jesus set His face against all forms of melancholy. He said, "The man who cannot rise above the burden of his sorrows or the trials of the day shall not know the Kingdom of Heaven; nor can he know the love, which is the cornerstone of life."

BRT:3:53 There was a Greek scholar in the crowd, who said to Jesus, "Your never-rusting tongue wearies me; words neither make men nor change things. It is the sword and spear which are all powerful and raise kings or cast them down." Jesus replied, "Truly, the words of scribes are greater than the commands of war chiefs. That, which is written and read can not only change things but also endure forever. The sword gains prestige through destruction, but the pen of the scribe gains prestige through creating. That, which destroys will be destroyed; that, which creates shall be preserved."

BRT:3:54 A Roman soldier who hailed from Gaul spoke up, saying, "Let scribes do what scribes do best and swordsmen do what they do best, but it is foolishness and futile to set one against the other, for men cannot write with swords, or fight with quills or writing reeds. Let men become brothers, as they await the day of the Awakener. Tell me, good Master, when shall the end be?

BRT:3:55 Jesus answered. "There will be an end to the beginning, and men will know this by the spirit of the times. Men will no longer be as brothers; nor will they be manly. Women will be as men and men as women. Adultery will not be condemned, nor will fornication; therefore, these will flourish. Men will not honour their homelands, and there will be no discrimination among them, nor will they maintain the purity of their races. Fathers will not be honoured, nor mothers respected, and children will be raised to be wayward. Perversions will be encouraged, and criminals will mock the law. There will be incest and rape and it will be unsafe to walk abroad. Floods, famines, droughts and earthquakes will cause death and destruction: Strange sicknesses will smite the people, and there will be a denial of God. Babes will be slain in the womb."

BRT:3:56 "Men will lust after the wives of other men, and marriage shall lose its meaning. Women will go to the marriage table unchaste and with deceit in their hearts. Their husbands, creatures of pity, will hear the mocking voices of laughing men. Priests will defile their altars with their impurity, and the rulers will be held in little repute. It is not God who marks the end days, but men who lives as though setting a pitfall for himself."

BRT:3:57 Jesus saw a man ill-treating a horse, and He rebuked him for his cruelty to a dumb animal.

The man became angry and said, "This is my beast." Jesus said, "You are wrong, it is God's creature, and I, as His servant, am here to protect it. For no man can wholly own any living creature except it be in the name of The Great God of Life."

BRT:3:58 This has been copied and edited as found. It appears to have been preceded by a document entitled, 'The Sayings of Jesus.' For some reason, it has been cut up into pieces, each containing just a few paragraphs. Included were other scraps from some much later source, which, for various reasons, are suspect. The latter part of this manuscript is probably a late if not modern addition, but it may have been re-written from some older material. This has not been altered and is included under the authorisation given to the compilers.

Chapter Four – The Writings of Aristolas

BRT:4:1 This is an account of the coming of certain Wise Strangers to the sea-girt realm of Britain. Taken from the Books of Britain and re-written into the appendices to the Bronzebook. This being that part safeguarded by Rowland Gasson.

BRT:4:2 After our Lord died, having been hung on the cross outside the city walls of Jerusalem, Joseph of Abramatha took Mary, the mother of Jesus into his home until John could make suitable arrangements. Then, he was called Guardian of the Lady, which title became confused in Britain with that of Guardian of the Sacred Vessel.

BRT:4:3 Aristolas wrote these things in the Sacred island, and this is his prayer: "In silence, hands uplifted, heart humbled and mind stilled, Your servant presumes to come into Your Presence, Great Understanding One. Grant me the abounding joy of union with Your Spirit. Grant that all my deeds be in harmony with the Great Law and that I learn to acquire wisdom, so I may illuminate the hearts of men."

BRT:4:4 "Let me embrace Your Spirit in full knowledge of my twofold nature. Guide my feet towards the Great Law, by which all true seekers find the light. As long as my body and spirit remain together, so long will I preach to men, seeking always to awaken a response in their hearts. Bless me with sweetness of speech and harmony of voice. Help keep me from the grip of greed and from the loud-mouthed futilities and frivolities of illiterate men. Spare me the sad companionship of the sanctimonious ones."

BRT:4:5 "God of my heart, Sun of my life, Keeper of my circle of content, fill this place with the divine emanations from Your Being. Attune with the Circle of Truth and the Circle of Light. Make me receptive to the lessons and inspirations of life."

BRT:4:6 Joseph, our father in faith, came across the storm-tossed seas to the place called Balgweith, and from thence to Taishan, where he met the envoy of the king who was sorely troubled. For the Chief of All Druthin, called Trowtis, was away at the meeting place of his god, where he came in a wondrous way every nineteen years. There, the ceremony lasted three moons.

BRT:4:7 When Trowtis returned, he met Joseph at the place now called Henmehew, because of the strange tree that grows there. The Druthin held a feast of welcome in the place called Nematon, which is below the great hill. The Chief of All Druthin washed his face, his hands and his feet, then a white goat was led out and sacrificed on a four-horned altar. Trowtis washed his hands again and made an offering of salted barley cakes and gave some to Joseph, called Ilyid by the people here.

BRT:4:8 Then, the goat's thighs were burnt on the altar while a lesser priest mixed the sacrificial blood with water and black wine. Then barley cakes and a chalice containing the blood, wine and water were passed through three sacred horns before being given to the chiefs present. Then, youths danced around the fire over the sacrificial pit.

BRT:4:9 Then, priests of a lower order prepared tables for a feast while the common people sat around on logs made smooth at the top. The sacrificial beast, having been first offered to the gods of this place, was eaten by the common folk. All except the liver, which, being the seat of blood and life was kept for the diviners. These found that the right wing of the liver was broken, so they prophesied that no enemy would enter the land.

BRT:4:10 Now, the king called together a great conclave of the people, and the Druthin were there. The king said to our father, "Speak now before the people. Tell us of your ways, and we will judge whether they be worthy." Joseph spoke a tongue understandable to these people, but he spoke slowly and not after their fashion.

BRT:4:11 Our father said, "As the light came first and called the eye into being to see it, so it is with God, who is the already existing light. The heart does not create the thought, but the thought produced the heart. This, so it could manifest, for the heart is created to serve thought in the world of effects. The world of causes lies in another kingdom." The Druthin said, "The light we know and have, these things are not strange to us. All light comes from an original crystal, which is always virgin, and we say the behaviour of light is the fore-ordained symbol to man."

BRT:4:12 Joseph, our father, said, "I have not come to batter down your house of hope, for it has many pleasing features, even as ours. So let us not disagree, but take the best from both and, discarding what is less good, fashion something of value to all. Let us weigh one thing against the other, rejecting that, which less clearly shows the way."

BRT:4:13 The king said to the Chief of All Druthin, "Do we not have the source of light in a grail egg?" The Druthin replied, "The sun shines not, and the Esures (servants of Light) will not come without the presence of the Great Gleamer, which provides their sustenance. There can be no incarnation of light on Earth unless there be, behind it, a greater light."

BRT:4:14 Joseph said, "When I was shipbound, I had a vision of God; the eyes of my spirit were opened, and I saw Him in all His glory. Then, I understood that there was no difference between the nature of His Spirit and the spirits of men, only that His was of an infinitely greater purity. This I knew for sure: God and man are of the one essence. I knew we are all rays of the One Light, sparks from the One Flame. Yet, the flame is not the fire, for what flame can call itself into being?"

BRT:4:15 Joseph said, "If fire can be contained in wood, to leap forth when two pieces are heated through rubbing together, yet remain hidden within the wood, then surely it can be so with the soul within man.

BRT:4:16 The Chief of All Druthin said, "Often have I thought on this. All men are alike in nature and all aspire to the same goal. All seek to make the same journey's end; only the route differs. Therefore, let us not argue whether men should follow your road or mine, but find between us a path better than either."

BRT:4:17 One priest said, "What of the worlds within the ever moving circles?" Joseph replied, "The hidden worlds are numbered as sands on the seashore. If a man concerns himself with many things, he benefits none and derives no benefit, himself. Let us concern ourselves with this world first."

BRT:4:18 The Druthin said, "Who can change the natures of men, for these are fixed by the gods." Joseph answered, "All things can be changed, but not always for the better. Change and life are inseparable."

BRT:4:19 Joseph went on to say, "Because you are folk who work the land, bringing it to fruitfulness, you are not to be despised. Let the newcomers with their armed might say as they will; you are workers with God. Were not the Sons of God also called the Sons of the Plough? Did they not fight against the Sons of Men who were hunters eating raw flesh like the beasts and worshipping serpents, which crawl on their bellies? Always there have been some who worship things of insensitive wood and stone, grovelling in the dust at their feet, and those who worship the highest they can see, the sun and the stars. Others reach out even beyond these."

BRT:4:20 One of the Druthin asked, "What know you of the Eye of God in men?" Joseph replied, "What is written in the heart is the Eye of God in men; this sees everything. Knowing right from wrong, it puts things in instant perspective. Men, in whom this eye is closed, are little better than the beasts of the field and forest. I come as one who opens the eyes of such as these."

BRT:4:21 In the beginning, the king had listened in silence and was tolerant, because he felt he could indulge these strangers. Now, as he saw that their teachings might prevail, he became angry and unreasonable, as it happens in instances such as these. He said, "Who gives you authority to speak in this manner? Who sent you, and do you come to spy on us? To whom do you make report?"

BRT:4:22 Joseph said, "Know this, great king. I am a servant of The Great God of Light. I am sent in order to build a church here, where it will serve your people well. I will establish a place of light unto them. I come to teach the perfect commandments. Ask among your own about me, for I am not unknown to them. I have no human teacher, from whom I learned the wisdom, from whence I got these things. I lived in the light of Christ but learned tardily. Then I had a message from God Himself, 'Go preach to those who dwell at the edge of the Earth.'"

BRT:4:23 The king said, "How comes it that these things have been revealed to you, while the same God who reigns here has not revealed them to us, even though we were the lords of this land? Are you a man of significance this side of the wide waters?"

BRT:4:24 Joseph answered, "Those who are established in The God of Light need no mentors, and they take pride in their insignificance, for it is said, 'The first shall be last and the last first. The lowly shall be raised up and the haughty cast down.' We do not seek after gold or worldly possessions. Of myself, I have no power, but I have power from God. It is God who commands, and it is He who makes a true man of God."

BRT:4:25 There was much talking and long discourses on the nature of God, and the Druthin challenged Joseph to produce Him, saying, "Though you decry our images, yet we do have likenesses of our gods, while you lack even these. Your words are mere puffs of wind."

BRT:4:26 These things and more were said, and the Druthin believed, but tardily. Then, at the midsummer festival the Chief of All the Druthin collapsed on the processional walk, denying himself the reviving draught prepared by Islass, his daughter. He died in the arms of Joseph our father. It was he who received the moon chalice and the light of Britain. The

Druthin held the secrets of the Great Temple of the Stars, and theirs was the royal isle in the Kingdom of Kevinid.

Chapter Five – The Writings of Abaris

BRT:5:1 I write in terrible times. My people have been driven to black despair, and the most cruel of foes has taken our fair land. The wisdom which flows through my pen, tutored by Isbathaden the Younger, is as set into writing by our father Aristolas and by the great ones who gave us the Annals Romanorum which we hold in part, clinging like the thundervine to what is left.

BRT:5:2 I am no weaver of words and if fine phrases bedeck what I transcribe, they are the work of better hands than mine. I am not as a teller of tales who sits before the hallfire, a waster of words like women over the fuller's tub. Those who wear the red robes of nobility have passed over the misty seas, and the land lies barren of learning. The Firthreig have taken over the dwellings of the wise, and the three pillars of progress - wisdom, courage and beauty - no longer stand against Maermagic.

BRT:5:3 I speak of one named Jesus who was Hesus come to Earth as a godling, the much abused One, but does not the lawman whose case is bad abuse his opponent? I speak of those who followed Him and suffered in the dark days of oppression. The anger of the people smouldered against the just ones, as Jesus had foretold while still in the body. Then, the time came when the dragon of disaster awoke, thirsting for blood, and it began to stalk its prey while liemongers fanned the smouldering embers of hatred into flame.

BRT:5:4 The king of the land was stirred up to anger, and the hatred of the people became an all consuming fire. The wolves came out of their dark forest and suddenly fell upon the flocks of innocent sheep and rent them apart. Wild bears burst among the sheepfolds and ravaged them. Evil-motivated ones came and cut down the apple-bearing trees, and the starglint nights were woeful. Beasts trampled the flower gardens while eaglehawks swooped down among the dovecotes. The earthen ones broke.

BRT:5:5 The culled-out servants of The High God entered the arena of vile entertainment, like children before their teachers. They were thrown into the path of the lions. Some, they equipped with weapons and forced to fight with bears. Women were scented with the smell of heat-angered beasts, and children stood frozen with fright. Their bodies were shredded like the paper of Egypt.

BRT:5:6 They moaned pitifully, like oxen awaiting the slaughter, and their children were murdered before their eyes. They were raised up by throngs on the wrists, their feet pressing on thorns or on heated plates, or over small fires. Many were thrown into prisons to die of hunger, thirst and cold.

BRT:5:7 In the days when the Druthin looked darkly on the enlightened ones, the Hammer of God said to the king, "It is in the nature of people placed such as we to fear those who wield the weapons, but we have One who is more to be feared than you, and He is One to whom I look up. I stand in awe of The Great One who is strong enough to overlook your present power, but who will surely call you to account in the life to come." The king said, "Where is your temple?" The reply was, "A true servant of God has no need of a temple built of wood and stone."

BRT:5:8 It was to tell of such things that the Anointed One came, to awake sleeping men drunk with the heavy droughts of sensuality and lewdness. He came to open the eyes of men to their carnal degradation, which corrupts their spiritual natures. He came to open their eyes to their divine destiny and to show them the hidden sparks of divinity captive and suffering in the carnal natures of apathetic men.

BRT:5:9 There are those who prefer the dregs of darkness to the living power of light, which flows from Jesus, Son of Dewi, Sap of the Trees, Sweetness of the Fruits and Perfume of the flowers, Bread of Heaven and Shepherd of Souls. He is the River of Sweet Waters arising at the Spring of Truth.

BRT:5:10 I am an unworthy one in the telling of these tales. Great Inspirer, give me a ray of inspiration to raise my voice, as it were, from the mystic cauldron, sister vessel to the ice-clear chalice. I will lay the dowry of the mystic maid at the feet of the discriminating ones. The smoothness of my lay flows from the bubbling brew from out of the great cauldron. I am one of God's inspired and not numbered among mere poets yapping at the heels of high-browed bards.

BRT:5:11 I am not one aspiring to the noble chair, whose words must be proved by privilege and truth. Where are the grave, high-browed druids of the past and the wonder-making bards? Those who thrive today cannot rise to the sky heights of song, even though their melody-making wings ache with fluttering. They are like the food pot placidly bubbling over the red greying coals.

BRT:5:12 O Comforter of the comely tribes, welcome me into the lush dominions of field and forest. O Champion of the thrusting sharp spear, hear my petition thrown out into the three-circled expanses of power. Let us feast at the overflowing cauldrons of peace and let us, your people, sleep in the downy, heather-scented beds of tranquillity. Protect the holy sanctuary of the blue-gowned bards where valour is honoured and chastity cherished. The raging assailants, protectors of slothful ways, labourers of concealed mysteries, surround us. We call on the guardian bulwark of celestial power to become the smasher of shields.

BRT:5:13 How straightly comfortable a scribe am I, who reconciles the mystic daughter with the lowly mother! Who places the crystal-clear chalice beside the blood-filled golden cup! Who combines the divine circle with the eternal cross and the sorrowful son with the triumphant fighting father!

BRT:5:14 In the beginning, only the Absolute existed in the firmament, called Nuvrie by the Britons and Kewgant by the Welsh of the west. The Spirit of Life spread outwards from the hub to form Gwinvidon, the region of light and the circle of spirituality. This opened out to Anton, which is the circle of germinal existence, at the inner edge of which was the circle of corporeality. This spread out to Abred, which is the material plane and the circle of trial, testing and tribulation. It is a place of experiment and experience for gaining knowledge, wisdom and spirituality. Below this is Anoon, the sea of souls. Here is the lake of unspecialised soul stuff, which is forged and fashioned in Abred and perfected in Gwinvidon. In Abred was the Garden of Karahemish,

through which flowed the river Nara. Here dwelt Keili and Kithwin. Here were born Derwiddon, the first of the Druthin, Gwinidendon who composed the first song, and Tydain who was the first bard.

BRT:5:15 It is said that there were two classes of druids: the Dryones who were masters of medicine and divination, and the Druthin who were superior and gifted with twinsight and magic. The first had their seat at Abri, while the Druthin had their seat at Innisavalon, the island of indestructible apples.

BRT:5:16 The druids believed in the One Supreme Being, but also held that there was a body of lesser Beings. They believed in a fairyland of Nature Spirits, which manifested to mortals. All happenings were motivated by an interplay of unseen rays from The Source. Therefore, the running of a hare, flight of birds, fall of leaves, patterns in sand, the sound of waters, were meaningful.

BRT:5:17 Their seven deadly sins were: hypocrisy, theft, cowardice, fornication, gluttony, indolence and extortion. Above all precepts were the three manly qualities: honour, courage and manliness, and the three womanly qualities of decency, decorum and chastity. There were female temple attendants, but no female druids. The druids who taught were called Nemids. There were Waiths who knew the secrets of Nature, and these would not eat birds. Once every three years there was a firewalking.

BRT:5:18 Under the great night reflector, only four animals appear as ghosts: the dog, cat, horse and hare. The ghosts of these could be forewarners of the crack of doom. Will-o'-the-wisps haunt the marshlands, but few are enlivened by ansis. Nick-o'-the-nights haunt the stony places and fells.

BRT:5:19 Joseph Idewin and his brave band came to flowering Britain three years after the death of Jesus. He converted Gladys, sister of Caradew, who married a Roman, and her sister Aigra who was the wife of Salog, lord of Karsalog. After landing, he and his band passed through an avenue of oaks and standing stones. They first built huts over against the holy vineyard where the fruits were bitter.

BRT:5:20 After all the saints had gone to their rest, the first church and its surroundings became a wild place, a refuge for wild creatures. Then, as the land remained holy, saints came from Gaul, who restored it, and one was Fairgas the Briton, who had served at this place as a youth. Idewin was buried in a shirt of fine linen, which he had worn when burying Jesus, and which was stained with three spots of blood on the chest. He was buried by the two-forked cross. The saints had lived in twelve huts around a never diminishing well at the foot of the holy hill.

BRT:5:21 Joseph Idewin was related to Avalek, whose kingdom bordered that of Arviragus, through Anna the Unfaithful. He converted Claudia Rufina, the daughter of Caradew previously called Gladys, who married Pudens, a Roman, and had a daughter Pudentia. In his twenty-eighth year, Caradew was betrayed to the Romans by Arisia, queen of Bryantis. He married Genuissa, daughter of Claudius, to bind the peace agreement. The name 'Caradew' means 'filled with love,' but he preferred to use a warrior name.

BRT:5:22 Gladys, sister of Caradew, married Aulus Plautius, a Roman commander. Caradew held an estate in Siluria, and he was made warchief when Guiderius, son of Kimbelin, was slain by a slingshot, near the river Thames. In the year 59 of our Lord, the British rose up tinder Woadica, the horsefighter, who died nearly three years later when Gulgaes became warchief.

BRT:5:23 Caradew went forth with the bright, flashing, sharp pointed spears of war. Bards, renowned judges of excellence, sang his praise. Even druids of the three great circles launched their eloquence in the five dialects and four tongues. Dancers from the steep mount gaily preceded him, and diviners from the high-pillared gates declared wise oracles.

BRT:5:24 I am one who lived in those brave days. It is my right to be the master singer, for I stand in the last line of blood from the golden strong-armed kings of old. My fathers father was a bard of the high enclosure, prince of the true tribe, high-caller of the Kimwy, a giant of song born of melodic race, light-tongued, harp-voiced.

BRT:5:25 Well fitted am I to sing Caradew's praise. Excepting great Keili and the all-seeing diviners of the land, and sagacious druids of the fine woven gold chains, and chiefs of the splendid wars, I am first above all to open his mouth in honour. He honoured all blue-gowned bards, singing bards of the land, guardians of the storehouses of winged words. Guests such as I were never wanting for provision while Caradew reigned, a high king over the wide land of heroes. He paid them well in sleek, fleet-limbed coursers, chasers of the wind-borne hare.

BRT:5:26 The valorous druids, feared by foes, the flowing-robed judges of disputes, said, "Let songs be composed with melodious refrains to praise the savage-subduing heroes."

BRT:5:27 The power of the bard is in the uplifted shield shaking before the tumult, high-riding on the battleleader's shoulder. It is in the quivering hare crouching in the bracken-buried hallow. It is in the soft-sighing promise of a fair-skinned maiden. In the finely-shaped form of the terrible spear-blade. In the bright-bladed sword clashing in the heat of the conflict. In the homely, comforting abode of the family.

BRT:5:28 I have sung my last day, the wonder days have gone and strangers walk the land. The high-hearted bards have gone to their rewards and the diviners mouths have been sealed. Now it is the fashion to hear the babbled words of Brandigan of Walsogo, which stand before the Resounding Halls, by the stream of sorrow, at the very gates of hell.

BRT:5:29 The purifying Kolgarth fires remain as transmuters to Heaven. Happy is the flame-borne one. Our fathers of old believed that fire was a form of creature, which had to be fed with fuel, given share of the food and in stressful times the sacrifice of a human. They who read the flames and embers are no longer with us, for they have been supplanted by the omen readers.

BRT:5:30 As dogs can see happenings in the world of spirits, then whatever they do is important, and a wise man watches them and takes heed. For if a dog sleeps before the fire, all is well, be at peace. If he sleeps on a bed, then beware. To sleep in a corner means strife, and to howl means a death. To crouch and whimper indicates the presence of a spirit.

BRT:5:31 Happy are the bright spirits in Elendon, the glorious sky isle where they await their call to return. All here have the Kailight around their heads. Come night, and they visit Earth in their dreams. If there be confusion in dreaming, then there is confusion in the daily round of life. Dream without confusion, and see clearly and know you live well.

BRT:5:32 Seek not to dream through the spotted elfincap, though it give enormous strength, visions and the gift of prophesy. Do not dream with the dungchild, as did the seers of olden times. Do not look through the window of the egg vessel. These things are forbidden to you. Nor may you consult the tree-bound maiden who, in truth, is the viper-blown Glainid. That, which was done on the high night of Summer shall be done no more.

BRT:5:33 Gems from the serpent must not be sought, nor may you follow the swanship, though that, which it bears within itself may be yours. Even so, it is unwise to bring the majestic sun down to incarnate in a stone. Know the secret of the sunship and all wisdom will be the reward. Seek it at Karelen.

BRT:5:34 Those worthy ones who could drink from the Gloryglian are no longer a voice for the land, but there is a new chalice at the well. The phoenix sleeps in the holyhole of Karperal. If a man would know the mystery of life, the secret of these things, he must climb the Mountain of Tears in the Vale of the Dead, at the trysting place of the sun and the moon chalice. Thence must he go to the Place of Brandigan, following the path of mysteries. If he does by the wanderer's way, he is lost.

BRT:5:35 The secret of Dwyva is known to the Knights of Karwidrin, who sit within the Sacred Circle. They fight the never-ending war with the Powers of Darkness. It is victory in the conflict of the soul, which entitles the warrior to drink the cup of immortality. The Knights of Karwidrin seek in a never-ending quest. The wisdom of the way by which knights and their ladies live is, 'Let men follow the natures and ways of men, and women follow the natures and ways of women, and let each serve the other rightly.'

BRT:5:36 The heart of Britain is the moon chalice, which was brought here by the hands of the Chief of the Kasini. He came shipborne to Rafinia, which is by the Mount of Lud, against Ardmoal. Passing Insdruk, he came to Itene where he hid the treasure in Trebethew. It was not captured, as men say, nor could it decay. In the fullness of time, it came to Kargwen. There it was kept secure with the Grailstone and the ever-virgin vessel which was brought down the rays of the sun. Thus it was that these treasures of Egypt came to Britain. This was the secret of Britain.

Chapter Six –
The Writings of Emris Skinlaka

BRT:6:1 The master was born under the sign of the Churlswain, at Dinsolin, called Insel by the Sons of Fire, in the year that the warwolves drove back the Children of the Horse. His father was one of the ornaments of Hew. In his youth, he was a battle-blooded warrior.

BRT:6:2 He was a dashing leader into the thick of the fray, a dauntless captain in the heat of the battle. The bearer of the battle-hammer was the great-hearted valiant warrior. He stood stern and steadfast in the grim work of bloodletting. Proud as the high-flying death eagle he stood.

BRT:6:3 A dark doomsbird flew over the land when the daring hawk gave battle. Behind came the sharp extractors of blood, the thrusting spears darting eagerly to the thrust. Like ripples across a pond, further and further spread the dying groans of doom-gathered men. The spear horde stood firm to protect the Vale of Tadwylch. It was a testing time of manhood.

BRT:6:4 Knightly men will read these words with a swelling heart. They will feel for the heroic brides of bloody spears, for the shattered shields and splintered hafts. The valiant captain of men sounds the red horn and sweeps over the fearsome foe like foaming seas. They were consumed by his bright-burning breath, like the fierce bush flame raging through the brown bracken.

BRT:6:5 The horse-vaulting warriors rode in for the final assault. The patron of the blue-bound bards swept the foe before him. Raising the red shield, holding high the sharp-slashing sword enjewelled with the ruby-red blood of warriors. It was a proud day for the ruler of the battle, the leader of strong, mail-clad spearmen, the scion of an illustrious race.

BRT:6:6 Only real men know the exultation of victory. They cheered the battlechief irresistible in the war rush. His spears dismayed the blood-thirsting, frightening foreigners. He wielded the dreadful blade of battle, which tested the manliness of men. Those were brave days. Now, only mean-minded, faint-hearted buffoons lampoon the heroes of renown. Where are the manly men; where the chaste ladies?

BRT:6:7 We were blameless for the outflowing tide of blood and entitled to the peace of the plough. The reward of the warrior is the tranquillity of old age. The pillar of battle, whose hands once wielded the hard-downslashing swords, the dragon chief, is due the peace of aged infirmity. If he is found among the gentle women, is it of any account? For he has established his manhood before men.

BRT:6:8 Thus spoke the master in the court of the king: "I am a man who has never shirked his duty. I have stood fast in the fray. I have struck many a mighty blow. Am I any less qualified to speak on things of the spirit because I was what I was? I have stood at the gateway of the grave and I have slept the sleep of inspiration. As my arm weakens, my spirit strengthens. I am no longer a man of war, but a man of peace. But let no man say before me that I am a shirker at the manly test. I am no lesser a man now. Hear my words, and let your heart judge."

BRT:6:9 "If a man followed a sunbeam to its source, he would find the sun; and likewise, if he followed his mind, he would find The Divine Source from whence it came. From The High God flows the inspiring spark in men which kindles the flame of Wisdom, Truth and Goodness. Likewise does the mind project its thoughts and plans, which are given form when expressed in words. When a man's thoughts come from a spiritual mind, they reflect the nature of The Spirit Above All Spirits. When they are stimulated by desires, feelings and urges, they reflect only the influence of matter on mind."

BRT:6:10 "Individual man is not a separate being cut off from all others, living isolated in his own enclosure. All things are in unity, and the thoughts and feelings of others, living or dead, pass through men like water through the gills of a fish. No man is cut off from the free flow of life, which purpose is to bring forth new forms of life, absorbing the old and outworn and replacing it with the new."

BRT:6:11 "Have faith, for this is the child of study and diligence. If, however, adopted by credulity or apathy, it becomes a useless thing. Faith is not an excuse, but an expression of hope. If made the refuge of the gullible, it is a thing of little moment. Faith is the spear of the wise and the crutch of the foolish."

BRT:6:12 The king said to the master, "Why do you, who are of warrior estate, entertain uncouth and ignorant men? Some say you even prefer their company to that of the wise and highborn." The master replied, "Sire, I will tell you how a Teacher greater than I dealt with such a question. In a land across the waters, a wealthy man gave a feast, to which this Great Teacher was invited. As was the custom there, outside the feasting place was gathered a motley crowd of hangers on, drunkards, thieves, deceivers and harlots. Now, when the prime feast was over, the Teacher went and sat among the outsiders and talked to them, in a manner to their understanding, concerning uplifting things."

BRT:6:13 "Those within and the disciples of this Man were aggrieved because of this and sent out two men who said to the Great Teacher , 'Tolerant Master, is this a wise thing You do?' The word of such doings will spread quickly and when they hear of the company you keep, prudent men will shun You.' The Great Man replied, 'A worthy man never fails to do his duty wherever he may be, and what I am entails a duty to minister to such as these. As to My reputation, have I not taught that reputation is subservient to service? These, being God's children, are our brothers, yet their lives contain more problems unknown to you. Because you have no knowledge of the nature of their burden, you, considering yourselves wise, cannot disclaim understanding and sympathy.'"

BRT:6:14 "These sinners are openly guilty, but such honesty is capable of transmutation into shame and shame into remorse. Those within are clever enough to cover up their guilt, and their duplicity and dishonesty cannot lead to shame and remorse, for they believe only that they are more clever than those here. Suppose those within, who despise these sinners, were to stand forth stripped of the hypocritical overlay covering their sins? What do you think you would see? I tell you, the inner aspect of many of those within is more hideous than that of many here without.'"

BRT:6:15 "'For those within have much and therefore should be above temptation, yet I tell you that the man with most is often the most avaricious. The distortions of sin are not caused only by deeds done, but also by the suppressed wish and desire.'"

BRT:6:16 " 'I say to those who sit at the fleshpots, you covet the wealth of others. You envy the house or wife of your neighbour. Lewd thoughts burn in your minds when you gaze on the figures of women, so that your bodies lust after them. You practise deceit every day, wishing for wealth, position and fame. The man who covets in his heart suffers as a thief, and she who lusts in her heart is a harlot.'"

BRT:6:17 Those within heard these words, but held their peace and were silent. The master said to those who were beside him, "Their own hearts accuse them, for the hearts of the pure do not make such accusations. The impure cover the evil polluting their hearts with hypocritical displays of righteousness. They hide their true thoughts by displaying loathing for things their hearts long to do. They revile others for their sins, but this is hypocrisy. They hug their worldly reputations won by deceit, but were the mask to be torn aside, they would be seen as wallowers in the mire of secret sinful thoughts and hidden vices."

BRT:6:18 One day, the master went to the encampment of the idol worshippers and said to one there, "Why do you worship images of wood and stone?" The idol worshipper replied, "So that it will provide me with food and shelter and keep me from harm." The master said, "How can it do this when it cannot even move of itself?" Said the idol worshipper, "Whom do you serve?" The master answered, "I serve The Great God Above All Gods who can feed His worshippers everywhere." Said the other, "See now, your own actions contradict your words, for if your God is everywhere, why have you left your home beyond the great forest to wander here?" The master replied, "I am not here to serve God alone, but also to serve you. I bring wholesome fare as a gift of comradeship."

BRT:6:19 Wayfaring with some waytamers, the master looked into a pool with all its life and said, "What an imagination God has!" They said to him, "You have been taught in the shadow of the Great Master and may gaze on that, which casts the shadow, but how will it go with our children and their children who know only the shadow of a shadow?" The master said, "Behind every shadow, there is substance. If you see a shadow, believe there is substance somewhere."

BRT:6:20 There was a dyer with them, and he used the unripe berries of the buckthorn, which were for dying, as a purge. Dyers' greenweed gives a yellow dye, and wood mixed with this and lime gives a good green. The waytamers had a nightlight, which they made by heating a few oyster shells in the fire until they became white. Then they heated them in a container with double their weight in brimstone, for three hours, until they became red. This made a light in the night.

BRT:6:21 Many times, the master spoke wise words, and his followers wrote them down, for he knew the way of words. He said, "When the wind blows it discovers every opening. Keep your eyes and ears fully open before marriage and half shut afterwards. Even a thief does not steal from his own neighbours. What does the wolf care if the sheepfold be destroyed. Progress is the creation of discontented people. A wise man learns to love the lovable and to hate the hateful, but more important is to know the difference. A child should behave towards his parents so they have no anxiety except as to his health, and confidence in the wisdom of his actions."

BRT:6:22 "No law whatsoever can ever unman a man or devirtue a woman. For the waywenders, the old law holds good. It is said that he who kills another unlawfully, who steals or robs with violence, or rapes or seduces a maid or matron, shall be placed in a wicker cage with others and burnt. Now this does not apply, but he shall be hanged at the crossroad."

BRT:6:23 "It is not unlawful for a husband to kill his wife's seducer. It is unlawful to require that a wife shall lick ash off a spearhead to establish her virtue. The first God-given right of man was the right to maintain his family inviolate; and it is the duty of the rulers to uphold that right. The seven qualities of manliness are: courage, fortitude, kindness, integrity, truthfulness, consideration and protectiveness."

BRT:6:24 A stranger accosted the master and said, "I don't like Your methods." The master answered, "Is that so? Well actually, I am not too satisfied with them myself. Tell me, how do you inspire men to live in harmony among themselves?" The stranger said, "I don't." Said the master, "I prefer the way I do it to the way you don't."

BRT:6:25 The stranger said, "You are unbending in Your teachings. Is it not wise to follow the path of moderation?" The master answered, "I am not interested in moderate faith or moderate goodness, moderate honesty or moderate virtue. There can be no moderation in things of vital importance. The moderate man is not for me. Would you eat a moderately fresh egg, or want to live in a house that keeps out most of the wind and rain? Would you be satisfied with most of your wages or with moderate work from your servants? I am not a moderate man, but one who plants his standard firmly. A standard of moderate morality is no standard at all. Could an army of moderate fighting men secure the land?"

BRT:6:26 The master went on to say, "Man lives for two things: the acquisition of knowledge and skill, and the refining of the spirit through experience. He who commands by his integrity is like the pole star, which remains constant while others revolve around it. To give you the essence of my teachings, I would say: Let all your thoughts be wholly good."

BRT:6:27 One asked of the master, "Who shall be our teachers?" The master replied, "They who, by revitalising the old wisdom of their forefathers in this land and adding to this new knowledge, are suitable." When they asked who should preach, he said, "He who should not preach what he desires others to practise is one to whom these practices are not normal. To learn without thinking is futile; to think without learning is profitless."

BRT:6:28 "Wisdom does not consist of what a man knows, but of recognising the limits of his knowledge. Listen always, but speak seldom. Maintain silence when in doubt, and you will seldom get into trouble. Keep your eyes open, but forget what you should not have seen. Never gossip, and shun all gossipmongers."

BRT:6:29 The master was asked, "How should a master deal with his servants," and he replied, "Promote those who are worthy and reward their loyalty, and train those who are incompetent. To know what is right and not to do it is cowardice. Wealth and station are desired by every man, but if these can be acquired or retained only to the detriment of his service to his creed, he must relinquish them. Poverty and subordination are disliked by all, but if they can be avoided only to the detriment of his creed, he must accept them with good grace."

BRT:6:30 Become paladins among the people, making the words of these writings the cause you serve. The inspiration is divine, but the medium is human. In the past, the pure light of Truth was concealed, from the multitude of the people, in riddles and a fog of jargon. Parables satisfied the people's understanding. Religion degenerated because in its higher aspects, it was not understood by the mass of the people, and there was a fear of casting pearls before swine, hence the mysteries and the need for ceremonial, images and symbols. People more readily worship representations of God, because they cannot comprehend Him and shirk the effort of trying to. God cannot be represented by things of this world to the understanding of the aristocratic soul.

BRT:6:31 There are Adamites whose souls slumber within, and Godmen who are the ultimate earthly beings. These are mysteries held close and safeguarded by the Knights of Karwidrin, but which came to our master through Gwalgwin of the white hawk crest, and Gwalanad the Summer Hawk. Also, through Palader of the spears and Lancelot, he who carried the mystic spear of Lot. They who are ready will read these things with understanding.

BRT:6:32 Words are mysterious things, within which can be hidden profound things, but enlightenment does not come easily or from mere reading of what is written. Greatness declined during the great peace, when knights were lax and pleasure-seeking. Men forgot their past unity and there were quarrels and rebellion. Peace is a fatal sickness to the Sons of Brittania. It was said of their battlechief that he lost every lesser battle and won every big one.

BRT:6:33 The art of the scribe came to Britain with the highbrowed one who taught Gwilidun of Ivern, who had seven sub-scribes. He said to the king, "This strange art will make the Britons wiser and will improve their memories, for it is the very essence of memory, which has been brought to this island." The king said, "Most wonderful, but while you may be prepared to bestow this, have you the ability to judge the worth of this art? Should not this be with another? The potter lacks the ability to judge the worth of his own pots, or the knight his own horse. Therefore, the ability to judge the usefulness or harm of this new thing should surely lie with another. Now, you who are the master of letters have been so swayed by your affection for them that you endow them with powers quite the opposite of what they actually possess. For this new thing will not increase the range of memory, but will lead to forgetfulness in the mind of those who learn this strange art. It encourages men to cease to practise their memory. Are the legs of a horseman equal to those of a man who walks? With time, men will put their trust in writing, and these strange signs will discourage memory. They are not instruments of memory but of reminding. Those who learn to read many things without proper instruction will then give an appearance of knowing many things, of which they are in fact ignorant. They will be hard to get along with, since they will not be wise but only appear so."

BRT:6:34 So it was that the art of writing did not come easily to Britain. Yet always, there had been the letters on stone and the brand sticks, but these were not for ordinary men. Give an ass oats, and he will run after thistles. Such is the nature of man, and never went out an ass that came home a horse.

BRT:6:35 The king had imprisoned one of the master's followers, and when the master sought the king's ear, his retainers drove him off. He returned, but this time, they turned loose the hunting dogs upon him. The master stood firm and made no move, saying in his heart that if God decreed that the hounds should maul him, so let it be. The hounds stopped before him and refused to obey the urging of those who trained them. This filled the heart of the king with wonder, for he knew the nature of the dogs of Britain, and he released the prisoner.

BRT:6:36 It was at this place that the master was challenged to produce his God. They said, "Though you decry our images, yet do we have likenesses of our gods while you lack even this. Your words are no more than puffs of wind." The master said, "These are the words of the report; to few has the arm of God been revealed. Did it not shoot up before your eyes as a sapling from a staff, and did not the withered staff take root in alien soil? Even so will it be with my words."

BRT:6:37 "I heard the Spirit of God in the nightwatches, saying, 'Go, carry My words of Truth to the unbelievers, and it will be like the rain that ends the drought. My words shall strike deep into fertile soil. Its beauty shall be like the holly tree. Its fragrance shall fill the land like the scent wafted from a new-mown meadow. You, My servant, will plant a tree, which shall shelter all nations.'"

BRT:6:38 "You say, 'Show us the road', and I say go a little way and you will come to a fork in the road; take the turn to the right. Go awhile along this until you come to an inn. Pass this and take the next road bearing left. A little further along this road you will come to a village, and beyond this a lane to the left. A mile along this lane is a rise, from whence you will see your destination ahead."

BRT:6:39 "A man who has been provided with this most complete directions possible from my intimate knowledge of the area, may lose his way and become lost. Another man comes along later and is given exactly the same information, and he reaches his destination. No doubt, the first man will revile his informant and seek to place blame wholly upon him, declaring the directions to have been misleading. The other will declare how comprehensive they were."

BRT:6:40 "My words direct those, who listen with understanding, along the road of man's destiny. This road will not change about and will always be there. Here, too, there is one who knows the road well and gives clear instructions. Yet, some become lost while others get there safely. I am only the shower of the way, the light on the path. I instruct all the same."

BRT:6:41 "Did I ever say to you that, if you followed me, I would make every secret known and reveal every hidden mystery? I did not, for this is not for all men. Suppose a man was pierced in the breast with an arrow, and his friends were to summon a physician skilled in such matters. What if the man said, 'I will not have the arrow withdrawn until I know who fired it and from what manner of bow it came; whether the archer be fair or dark, tall or short. I would know his name and his tribe; I want to know whether the arrow is fletched with feathers of a goose or of a fowl.'"

BRT:6:42 "Such a man would die, and all his queries would serve him not one jot. The man's life would come to an end, but still the great question which he overlooked would go unanswered: Why was the arrow fired? It is equally foolish to say, 'I will not accept the teachings of this man until I know from whence he came, who is his father, what is his estate.'"

BRT:6:43 "A man wishes to know what the land of Egypt is like, but does not wish to endure the discomforts and dangers of the voyage. Yet, when others who have made the journey tell him about it, he says, 'I will not believe this until I have seen it with my own eyes.' So there is only the choice of making the voyage or accepting the word of those who have done so. None can justly say, 'Because I have not seen it for myself, because I decline to face the dangers and discomforts, the place does not exist.'"

BRT:6:44 The master was asked, "How shall we live to be in accord with the way of God?" He replied, "Say not that you live for God, for whatever man does serves man; God is served only by serving men. Follow the words of the wise, and do not chase after fools. Learn about the ways of life, and enjoy them to the full. Life is meant to be lived with excitement and joy, but never for mere pleasure or self-satisfaction. Discipline your daily doings, and let these not become burdensome. Earn a congenial livelihood, and in all things you, do be honest, diligent and careful."

BRT:6:45 "Let not your thoughts be the sport of every wind that blows. This thought may come to you: 'I know imperfect conditions may be put aside. I know impure things can be discarded.' But a man may even be blessed with the good things of life and yet remain sorrowful and melancholy, for this he is by nature. Happiness and cheerfulness are not things flowing from affairs of the day or through circumstances. The sorrows of a sad man come from within."

BRT:6:46 "Things of the daily round of life should be directed in the knowledge of what is for your own good. There must be an understanding of the way of the path. Be upright, conciliatory in speech and rational in bearing; mild but not meek and with no vain conceit. Be content, having few material wants, frugal and composed in mind. Be discreet, neither insolent nor avaricious. Do no mean thing, for this is not the way of a knightly man. Never act deceitfully or scorn another unjustly. Be free from sloth, and spread goodwill to all."

BRT:6:47 "Many will merely read these things, which will go in one ear and out of the other. There is no virtue in just reading them; they have to be lived by to be of value. Wisdom can be given to men, but this, of itself, does not make them wise. Wisdom is like a handful of seeds plucked from the seedbag. There is no value in them unless they be sown, nurtured and reaped."

BRT:6:48 "Be ever mindful of what is done. Know the body as it deals with the outside. A man thinks to himself, 'This body I wear as a garment is what I make of it.' He does not neglect the body and is always aware of its existence and activities. This awareness is called mindfulness. Through bodily contemplation, a state of mindfulness is reached."

BRT:6:49 "The mindful man is ever conscious of every action and its consequences. He knows what he does, whether standing still or engaged in some activity. Whatever the body does, he is aware of it and he has it under control. He knows his body to be filled with a variety of contents, he regards it as a pedlar's bag. Examine the body daily, in contemplation, and thus develop mindfulness."

BRT:6:50 "Contemplate the body made of earthly elements in solitude and know that, which contemplates is the spirit. Think of the body as if dead. What enlivens it? What is life? Be mindful of all your feelings. If experiencing something unpleasant,

BRT:6:50 ...be mindful that this is so. Be mindful of all the activity about you, of the sighing of the wind, of the song of birds, the rustle of grass and the whispers of leaves."

BRT:6:51 "Know the difference between that, which is generated by the body and that, which is generated by the spirit, Abide in the mindfulness of feelings. Teach the body to know itself more fully and to comprehend more of its surroundings. When a man is mindful of what flows from the body and what flows from the spirit, then he knows he is body and soul."

BRT:6:52 "Be mindful of what is good and what is bad. Thoughts become confused when undirected; so, like horses, they must be kept in hand through the restrictions of bridle and reins. There are lofty thoughts and base thoughts, thoughts which arise through the prompting of the body urges and thoughts which arise through the purifying prompting of love."

BRT:6:53 "The wise man dwells in mindfulness of all things, not overlooking the urges towards indolence, ill will, resentment, worry and wavering indecision. Be mindful of ideas and ideals. Be mindful of the full working of the eyes, the nose, the mouth, the ears and the skin."

BRT:6:54 "The true way is the overcoming of self and the mastery over earthly conditions, for as a man changes himself so does he change his condition. Man must be able to say, This is of me and this is not of me. This is me or this is not me. He must divide himself in two in mindfulness, knowing what is of the Earth and what is of the spirit."

BRT:6:55 "He must travel the great path, conscious of his twinself. He should observe others, whether or not they have the quality of mindfulness. He must be self-possessed by his own spirit. The self-possessed man acts with composure, is mindful and self-aware. The man of turmoil is he who goes abroad with senses unguarded. Without mindfulness, he is unsteady and unstable in thought.."

BRT:6:56 "The godly life is one, which attracts friendship, which is the appreciated revelation of beauty. It is the search for beauty in all things. The holy prophet, in his austere, dank, dark cell, is not truly holy. The long-faced preacher is not truly holy."

BRT:6:57 "The godly life is associated with beauty. Whenever a man reaches out after the beauty found in purity of spirit, he is uplifted. It is by not understanding the true nature of godliness that men have become entangled like fowls in a net. They are like leather covered with mildew, like logs encased with moss."

BRT:6:58 "Godliness is attained by abandoning worthless things, by not falling into the fallacies of unchastity, by the repulse of sensuality and the repudiation of evil. This can be done by mindfulness of such things."

BRT:6:59 "When a master takes an apprentice, he gives the first lesson: 'Come and be disciplined, learn restraint and obligation. Learn right behaviour.' When the pupil is controlled, then he gets the second lesson. The master says, 'Seeing things with the eye, do not be misled by their outward appearance. Be mindful as to what they do to you. See with your mind all that the eye sees, and so it is with all the senses. Be aware of everything; experience all things, but do not become immersed in anything.'"

BRT:6:60 "For man is shut off from the spirit by mindlessness. As he becomes more aware of the material things and happenings about him, so does he more and more become mindful of the spirit. He who says, 'I have no feeling of the spirit,' is a man of small mindfulness. He is mindful of what is at his hand, but unmindful of what lies beyond. What lies beyond forms a veil, through which he cannot see. How can a man mindful only of what holds his immediate attention be aware of the world beyond his narrow confines?"

BRT:6:61 "Be like the spirit-filled Earth, who accepts unto herself all the foulness, which you cast out of your body and cleanses and purifies it. She is neither disgusted nor delighted, but transmutes it. Water accepts both foul and fair, for from its embrace, both emerge together in goodness. The wind is not disgusted with the foul smells of Earth, but mixes them with the essences of earthlife so they are sources of fragrance."

BRT:6:62 "Practise kindness, compassion, poise and decorum. Contemplate beauty and banish ugliness. Contemplate virtue and goodness, and banish carnality. Contemplate the eternal and banish impermanence. For all things of Earth must decay and pass away, and it is the destiny of every human being to embark on the dark adventure."

BRT:6:63 Thus, the master spoke and he said, "You must accept any intelligent person into the sheepfold. Accept all who are willing to follow the light of our way. I say this, not desiring to win followers or wishing to turn others from their ways if they walk in light. I seek only those who walk in darkness or seek a better light."

BRT:6:64 "For all journey towards The One Light, but not seeing it in its perfection, they must travel by the reflection they see. Each sees a different reflection, and therefore, men dispute among themselves as to the nature of the truth behind it all. Be not one who indulges in such futile foolishness."

BRT:6:65 "Never judge virtue by outward appearance, for then, the evildoer as well as the saint may lay claim to it. An artful imposter may gain more admiration than is given to the zeal of a saint. Do not nourish the cankerworms of malice, hatred, envy and jealousy within your bosom."

BRT:6:66 "It is truly said that the heart of man is a labyrinth. Goodness is not merely a matter of right action, it includes bravely enduring and surmounting difficulties. The final test of character is when trouble comes in strength. Then, the question is not so much whether a man does what is right, as to whether he can stand up, with integrity, to what life does to him. The anvil stands steady when the hammer falls."

BRT:6:67 "Manliness involves recovery from every moral failure. It involves the retention of honour. What honour is to man, chastity is to woman. Honour and manliness endow a man with inner strength. His slightest word, his very presence, bring peace and leaves others strengthened. No man or woman, no matter how humble, can be really good without the Earth being better for it, without someone being helped and comforted by that goodness."

BRT:6:68 "Words such as these blow against the whirlwind of human nature; yet, they are the stuff of the spirit. When the breaths of the multitude blow back the whirlwind, then has life fulfilled its purpose. Say not that the days of victory of good will be brought in with a griffin's egg."

BRT:6:69 "No man is free who does not control his own movements. No man is free who is not master of himself. Fear is the tribute the mind of man pays to guilt. He who has never been guilty knows no fear. To see the path of duty and not to follow it is the way of the coward. A man tarnishes the lustre of his greatest actions when he applauds them himself."

BRT:6:70 "No man is more vile than he who causes a woman to shed tears from the heart, tears generated in remorse and regret. Every maid has the potential for ladyhood. A lady never flaunts her estate, but ever remains modest and reserved. She covers her virtue with ladylike ways, for as a veil adds to beauty, so is chastity enhanced by being veiled. The wise woman pays no notice to the spider's lullaby from the lips of hypocritical men who speak of love. The spider loves its prey."

BRT:6:71 "Babblers are not wanted. Shun the Sophists and their sophistry, and be chary of divinators. Avoid the Paynim, and be as strong as a bull, light as a hawk, swift as a deer and tenacious as a salmon. If things go against you, never despair. To be vanquished and still not surrender, that is victory indeed! Avoid the talebearer, and do not listen to the witches' whisper. Be prudent; giants step off the path in the realm where a dwarf is king."

BRT:6:72 "Avoid the daydreamer and the moneyluster, the vagabond and the woman fascinator. Avoid the honeytongued hypocrite, for it were better you took a viper to your bosom than to open your heart to one such as these. Do not become a griffin."

Chapter Seven – The Corrygorsed

BRT:7:1 To you, Nathaniel, son of my brother Will Smith, and to Andrew, his half brother, I leave two books of integrity and others in portions. The bare words are unimportant, but what they convey is as jewels in a crown of gold. Yet, even this is not the crown itself, which should be sought in the Karnamard at Nantladiwen. I am not an unlettered man, but I lack the virtue of subtleness in writing of things best hidden.

BRT:7:2 Inasmuch as the ferocious bloodseekers close in upon us and Christian folk do in their zeal deem it fit to claim for their own persons of innocent blood, persecuting them with ratchet, rope and brand even unto death, I charge you, my assigns, to protect the several holy Books even unto your death. Believing full well that evil cannot triumph over good and the dark days of fearborn hatred will pass, keep them secure under the most sacred oaths now foresworn.

BRT:7:3 The said Holy Books, of themselves innocent, fill the base hearts of our enemies with craven fear, even as the lamp-bearing lackey causes scuttling among the rats in the larder. What dire secret do they hide closeted within their breasts, occasioning such terror that limbs quake when innocent wisdom is mentioned in their presence?

BRT:7:4 In all the land, no place remains comfortable and the free-spirited are as hares hunted by whippets running into the talebearing wind. Before the doomsmen come, we make our peace and can await our call to sacrifice in patience. The jewels are safely hidden. These things, which follow, are found in The Book of Recitals.

BRT:7:5 There are three adornments of life: Love, Truth and Beauty.

BRT:7:6 There are three things, of which God is The Source: Life, Wisdom and Power.

BRT:7:7 There are three things, which men must get from living: The greatest benefit, the greatest knowledge and the greatest experience.

BRT:7:8 There are three causes, in which it is fitting that men should risk their lives: In establishing Truth, in upholding Justice and in seeking Liberty.

BRT:7:9 There are three paramount qualities, to which all else should be subordinate: Love, Truth and Good.

BRT:7:10 There are three things men should place above themselves: Their faith, their race and humankind.

BRT:7:11 There are three things a man should value above his life and possessions: His family, his honour and his reputation.

BRT:7:12 There are three principles of government: Effective security of life and person, security of possessions and dwelling, and security of personal rights.

BRT:7:13 There are three things a government must hold inviolate: A man's family, his dignity and his opinion.

BRT:7:14 There are three things the government must provide: Education, Justice and Safety.

BRT:7:15 There are three pillars of the state: The questing scholar, the diligent craftsman and the incorruptible official.

BRT:7:16 There are three unities: One God, One Truth and One Creation.

BRT:7:17 There are three things, for which the Earth exists: The development of souls, the fulfilment of the destiny of man and the manifestation of life.

BRT:7:18 There are three things man must give to life: Beauty, Stability and Harmony.

BRT:7:19 There are three things woman must give to life: Love, Goodness and Compassion.

BRT:7:20 There are three things only God can do: Constantly renew Himself in the infinite Circle of Eternity, remain unchanging while impregnating every state of changeability, and encompass everything existing.

BRT:7:21 There are three things required of men: The ability to change that, which is changeable, to accept that which is unchangeable and to know the difference.

BRT:7:22 There are three virtues of maidenhood: Prudence, Modesty and Decorum

BRT:7:23 There are three virtues of wifehood: Faithfulness, Industriousness and Motherliness.

BRT:7:24 There are three graces: Faith, Hope and Love.

BRT:7:25 There are three things to know about God: He must be sought for, He cannot be given anything by man which increases His Greatness and He dwells within His own Law.

BRT:7:26 There are three rights of man Freedom to move, to enjoy privacy and to speak his mind.

BRT:7:27 There are three things God requires of man: Effort, Courage and Reverence for the sacred.

BRT:7:28 There are three duties of woman: To reproduce the race, inspire mankind and beautify life.

BRT:7:29 There are three duties of man: To protect the race, strive for progress and elevate humankind.

BRT:7:30 There are three things, which distort the soul: Malice, Deceit and Sensuality.

BRT:7:31 There are three rules, which govern a man's relationships with others: What he requires in another, what he forbids in another and what he regards with indifference as being entirely the concern of another.

BRT:7:32 There are three things, which shatter a man's life: An unfaithful wife, invasion by foreigners and a crippling disease.

BRT:7:33 There are three principles of greatness: Obedience to the law, concern for the welfare of the community and the ability to suffer with fortitude all the blows of fate.

BRT:7:34 There are three states of being: That of God in the Great Circle, that of Spirit in the Outer Circle and that of Matter in the Inner Circle.

BRT:7:35 There are three duties of parenthood: To protect, to cherish and to educate the child.

BRT:7:36 There are three duties of a child towards its parents: Obedience, Respect and Loyalty.

BRT:7:37 There are three qualities of a husband: Consideration, Protectiveness and Care.

BRT:7:38 There are three essentials of manhood: Courage, Fortitude and Honour.

BRT:7:39 There are three qualities of womanhood: Loyalty, Decency and Gentleness.

BRT:7:40 There are three jewels of womanhood: Modesty, Decorum and Circumspection.

BRT:7:41 There are three prime qualities of the Real Man: The ability to maintain self-control, the ability to remain calm under stress and provocation, and the ability to not stand too rigidly upon his rights.

BRT:7:42 There are three things in men that other men hate: Saying one thing with the mouth while holding something quite different in the heart, withholding evidence in favour of another to the detriment of another, and spreading scandal and gossip.

BRT:7:43 There are three things that hold the state in cohesion: Effective protection for everyone and their property, just punishment when due, and a proper blend of punishment and mercy.

BRT:7:44 There are three obligations of men in war: To kill and not be killed, to destroy the enemy and his possessions, and to survive the onslaught.

BRT:7:45 There are three types of persons who cannot bear arms: A bondsman, a boy under fifteen and a public idiot.

BRT:7:46 There are three kinds of stone, for which removal is death: A council stone, a session stone and a guide stone.

BRT:7:47 There are three things, the punishment for which shall be greater than a simple death: Killing a kinsman, killing a child or virgin, and killing an idiot.

BRT:7:48 There are three things, for which the trumpet sounds three times: The counting of heads and numbering of families, the horns of harvest and the horns of war.

BRT:7:49   There are three persons who can demand hospitality: The traveller from afar, the afflicted or orphan and the bard.

BRT:7:50   There are three groups entitled to freedom of movement and maintenance: Chiefs of tribes and their retinue, druids and their followers, and judges and the retainers of their courts.

BRT:7:51   There are three types who can claim citizenship: Those who bring new land under cultivation, those who work with metals and those who bear arms.

BRT:7:52   There are three basic protections: Protection of life and person, protection of possessions and dwelling and protection of natural privileges.

BRT:7:53   There are three types of persons who forfeit life: One who betrays his country, race or kindred, one who kills another through viciousness, lust or gain, and one who injures a child for life.

BRT:7:54   There are three things, which are indivisible and unchangeable: The Supreme Being, Truth and Reality.

BRT:7:55   There is one God, one Truth and one Reality.

BRT:7:56   There are three necessities of man: Change, Suffering and Choice.

BRT:7:57   There are three tests to determine a free man: He has equal rights with every other man, he has no more obligation to the government than it has to him, and he has freedom to come and go.

BRT:7:58   There are three things essential to united nationhood: The same language, same rights for all and the same race.

BRT:7:59   There are three things, which are private, untouchable and sacred to every man: His wife, his children and his tools of trade.

BRT:7:60   There are three persons in the family exempt from menial or heavy work: The small child, the aged man or woman, and the sick and afflicted.

BRT:7:61   There are three civil birthrights: The right to free movement, the right of protection for family, possessions and liberty, and the right to equality in privilege and restriction.

BRT:7:62   There are three requirements for social stability: Security of life and limb, security of family and possessions, and security of traditions and culture.

BRT:7:63   There are three foundations of the nation: National solidarity, national courage and national pride.

BRT:7:64   There are three things a man can legally be compelled to do: Fulfil his family obligations, attend a law court and serve in the military in times of national peril.

BRT:7:65   There are three things, for which a man can be called a traitor: Aiding the enemy, meekly submitting to an enemy, and betraying his race.

BRT:7:66   There are three things no law can deny: Water from a spring, river or lake, wood from a decayed or naturally fallen tree or branch and unused stone.

BRT:7:67   There are three forms of sonship: A son born within a marriage, a son born outside a marriage but publicly acknowledged by the father and a son by adoption.

BRT:7:68   There are three types of thieves not to be punished: A woman compelled to steal by her father or husband, a young child and a starving person who steals to eat.

BRT:7:69   There are three things, which must remain open and free to all: Rivers, roads and places of worship.

BRT:7:70   It is said that Alfred the Homeborn rewrote these things, but it is also said that what was is lost, and he put this in.

Chapter Eight – Nobility

BRT:8:1   Nobility and honour are words much abused, but in truth nobility is not bestowed by birthright, but resides in the soul, and honour is not a thing bartered among kings, but comes from a sense of goodness. Men sell their honour for gold, and nobility is conferred on those who have done nothing more than their duty. This is wrong.

BRT:8:2 When titles are given as the reward of true, selfless service, when he who serves his fellows well is ennobled, both giver and receiver are raised in stature, and the realm benefits.

BRT:8:3 When they who inherit titles also inherit the virtues, which earned these, then all is well; but when he who inherits, to whom they descend, is unlike he who earned them, then they can no longer be borne with honour.

BRT:8:4 Honour and nobility, in their true sense, are not things which can inevitably be inherited; they are not in the blood. The man who, being without merit himself, appeals to the actions of his ancestors, for his justification is like a thief claiming justification in possession. What good is it to the blind that his parents could see, or what benefit to the deaf that his grandfather heard? Is this more foolish then that a mean-hearted man should claim nobility because his forbears were noble? A man who serves the people well has no need of ancestors. The noble mind does not derive pleasure in receiving honours, but in deserving them. Is it not better that men say, 'Why has this man not been honoured by the king?" than to ask why he has been?

BRT:8:5 I speak to knights who, surely of all men, are the most noble. Eat slowly and with good manners, even if alone at the table. Do not gulp down ale or water, for food hastily eaten sits on an uncomfortable stomach. Though we must feed our bodies, even as animals have to, we are not as they and must do so with good manners. This is also a knightly discipline, which will enhance the light of your soul.

BRT:8:6 This soul has an inner stronghold, an unassailable keep, which remains impregnable against all outside influences. It is an inner zone of silence, so that even in the most crowded street, amid the din of commerce, the hustle and hassle of everyday life, in joy, sorrow, success and failure, there is always an inner sanctuary, a place of retirement, a retreat, to which one can always retire, assured that no intruder can assail anyone there. This is the citadel of the soul, against which all the tempests and turmoils of life's storms may beat in vain. Within, all will be serene, peaceful and secure, and if it be well built, nothing can ever overthrow it.

BRT:8:7 Loyalty is an attribute of the knightly man. It is expressed in deed and service. Be audacious in confrontation. It is a bold mouse that pulls the cat's whiskers. Be renowned for what you achieve, not for what you are. The renown of a bowman is not earned by his bow, but by his aim.

BRT:8:8 Those who seek to shun the battle of life because of cowardice or selfishness find that their attempts to run away are in vain, for the Law compels them to engage. Because human destiny, individual and collective, is bound to the rock of the Law, that which is avoided is enforced.

BRT:8:9 I come before the dire days to carry a sword against evils, which threaten our race, and to direct the struggle of man into correct channels. Be true to yourself, and answer accordingly to your own inner knowledge. Are your God-given qualities, which all possess, marshalled to carry out the Designs of God?

BRT:8:10 The rallying call has sounded, and it echoes in every responsive heart. Arm yourself for the fray with the God-given powers within. Align them to fight on the side of good. The call has gone out, and the inner forces of every Real Man are required to rally to the cause of humankind.

BRT:8:11 If everyone in the world would rally their own special forces within and throw these into the battle on the side of good, the Earth would overflow with goodness.

BRT:8:12 Men and women are apathetic; instead of taking up the sword against evil, they stand aside like menials. So evil grows, and the main cause of the present sorry state of the people is man's lack of fighting spirit. In war, it is the cause that counts and it is not enough to resist evil. It must be attacked.

BRT:8:13 When you have conquered the weakness within yourself and assumed full control, you are a true knight ready to go out and fight. The trumpet has sounded, and the rallying cry rings out, so do not seek the place of protection. Do not hesitate in this dramatic hour. Say not that these things foreshadow things in days far ahead, or that they are residue from the past.

BRT:8:14 Cease all disagreement among yourselves. Unite as comrades in arms. There will, of course, be arguments and differences, but be men enough not to let them divide you. We are in our present sorry state because of past disunity and disobedience to the Law. Do not allow the knights of right to be disarmed, and fight against the Realm of Darkness.

BRT:8:15 It is a manifest thing that kingdoms divided against themselves are destroyed by more united forces. Yet, is not the Kingdom of God divided against itself?

BRT:8:16 Truth and faith are the handmaidens of love. They bring confidence, and how can a man stand steadfast unless he has confidence, for in confidence is strength. The qualities of knighthood are such that those who have them can look the world in the eye. They have no furtive deeds to hide within where they eat away at a knight's integrity.

BRT:8:17 Praise no day until nightfall, no wife until she is buried, no sword until blooded, no maid until married and no ale until drunk. Never be a talebearer, for this is despicable in a man.

BRT:8:18 Persons who, within themselves, are really enemies often come garbed as friends, and among these are the following: He who takes little care to hide his intentions to rob or violate and does it brazenfaced, he who gives a little with the intention of getting much back in return; he who puts on a friendly front out of fear and he who acts friendly to serve his own ends.

BRT:8:19 The man with the well greased, mobile tongue can be distinguished in this manner. He is inclined to talk much about himself and his past accomplishments, or he will fill your ears with boasts about his future deeds; he assails your ears with empty words and with the sweet draught of flattery. Walk warily, for these are false-fronted friends and when their friendship is put to the test, it falls apart like rotten wood. When called upon for assistance in time of need they plead their own misfortunes and handicaps as excuses for standing aside.

BRT:8:20 The smooth-tongued hypocrite glosses over the misdeeds of others. He excuses unworthiness and sings your praises before your face, in your hearing, but reviles you behind your back. Avoid all such as these, for their friendship is worthless.

BRT:8:21 The other to avoid is the wastrel. He will be a pleasant companion in the drinking parlours. He will be your amiable companion in the places of pleasure, where there is gaiety and laughter. He will be a charming companion at feasts and festivals. He will be quick to suggest gambling and dissipation and all things that lead to sloth.

BRT:8:22 Here are the earmarks of a true-hearted friend: He will help you when help is really needed and requires real sacrifice on his part; he remains unchanged amidst the fluctuations of fortune; he is the one who is not afraid to tell you what is for your own good; he is the one who declares his friendship and loyalty in the company of those who condemn you.

BRT:8:23 True friends are few and are treasures indeed. A true friend watches over you when you falter on the way. He keeps a watchful eye on your property and interests when you are indisposed. He is your refuge in times when you are in fear, and your consolation in distress. He is your reassurance in doubt. He never deserts you in need.

BRT:8:24 A true friend tells you his secrets and never under any circumstances reveals yours. He never forsakes you in times of trouble and would sacrifice almost anything for you.

BRT:8:25 In earthly armies, rules and commands must be obeyed; there is no other way to conduct a campaign. It is so in the army of good; each and every man can rise by his own efforts and perseverance.

BRT:8:26 Be as ready to take orders as to give them, for no man has the qualities of leadership who cannot also obey. All soldiers in the Holy Army must be well disciplined. How otherwise can the battle be won? If we falter in this, the infidel and heretic will prevail and the long, weary journey be abortive.

BRT:8:27 Be ever loyal to your comrades placed in authority. Trust them, and change only when, by direct and personal contact and knowledge, you find them false and wanting. True friendship is the greatest of all gifts.

BRT:8:28 In the courts and castles of the land, women, as apart from ladies, because of their physical weakness have been made to appear of lesser importance; but a true knight, while honouring ladyhood, treats all women with respect and chivalry. It is chivalry, which distinguishes our times from all others.

BRT:8:29 A true knight is decorous at all times and circumspect in the presence of womenfolk, for he honours the delicacy of their ways. Always, however, womanliness is required to respond to and foster the chivalry in men. A mannish-mannered woman is the declared enemy of chivalry.

BRT:8:30 A knight embodies the criteria for manhood. He concentrates on mannish things and mannish ways. He does not meddle in the affairs of womankind.

BRT:8:31 A true lady is a rare and lovely jewel. What the word 'lady' means is hard to define, but one meaning is that a lady is a woman, in whose private presence, a man acts with decorum and reserve. He shields her from crudity and lewdness.

BRT:8:32 A knight understands the economy of life. It is too easy to long for a certain conclusion, perhaps that the suffering of a loved one will end. However, it may be a case where only endurance and fortitude will heal and benefit the spirit. Pain purifies and strengthens, and sometimes it is better to suffer than to sleep.

BRT:8:33 True knighthood demands not only nobility of spirit, but also nobility in attire and manners. It is an attitude towards others. The duties of man to man are almost as important as those of man to God where the obligations entail the stewardship of God's earthly estate.

BRT:8:34 Man chooses as he will, and it is entirely up to him whether or not he does a thing. Of what benefit is a high position to a man who uses the power he has over the lives of others only for purposes of boosting his own arrogance and false pride; who uses it only for his own pleasure and not to serve others.

BRT:8:35 God has given man shepherds to guide him and indicate the path. But these shepherds cannot, of themselves alone, gain such leadership and guidance, unless inspired by the Spirit of God. Man must be guided according to his spiritual needs and not according to his worldly needs.

BRT:8:36 Therefore, God has ordained a means whereby these shepherds may be found, and He has told them what to teach the people and in what manner to accord with their understanding and acceptance. The way is complex, as can be seen through these writings.

Chapter Nine – Shards of Wisdom

BRT:9:1 In the days when Lucius Clorus was named King Coel and lived at Karcolwin, Enisivorwin served the good Queen Helena, and from her to her husband, Kambord, by whose hand these things were written, came words of wisdom. There is that, which is old and that, which is new, but old and new are one in the eye of time. Therefore that, which is first might be that, which was written last, for now, among the pieces, none knows which should be where. In truth, none knows when these things were written, but what has just been said was found as a broken piece, and where else could it be?

BRT:9:2 Of the druids, it is said that Pair Keridwen, the Cauldron of Higher Love, represented to them the womb and that the fire, with which it was associated, was the lifeforce. It is said that the representation was in more than one form, but what this means none now knows. To become a druid required immersion in a bath with a decoction from the cauldron. After immersion for a prescribed time, the residue from the bath, infused with the man's evil, was poured into a pit. His spirit was thus cleansed and renewed, but henceforth, any wrongdoing would have a twofold effect.

BRT:9:3 A band of Troubadours, being people who held some secret of life, came to Britain in the days when England was Saxonised. They had a secret book said to explain all the mysteries of life, but the book itself explained little; yet, they who followed the secret book became the wisest among men. Written words, when read without thought, are valueless, and this is how most men read. Troubadours have a secret place in the Ogmosian hills.

BRT:9:4 Emris said, "The people are entitled to the consideration and care of the rulers who direct their days. Men are entitled to the peace of the plough unless their lands and families are under threat. No man who is a man slumbers under threat, and the reward of the warrior is tranquillity in old age."

BRT:9:5 "The foolish man who sacrifices his peace of mind and happiness to seek wealth is like a man who sells his home to buy furniture."

BRT:9:6 "If there is anything more powerful than fate, it is the courage that bears whatever fate decrees unshaken. The dispensations of life favour the courageous man."

BRT:9:7 "Within the wider world, responsible procreation and selectivity play a spiritualising role, while on another level, they preserve the diverse racial and cultural heritages. Racial pride is a positive quality which has nothing to do with racial prejudice. Pride without prejudice should be the watchword."

BRT:9:8 Thus, it is written: 'They who inherit and inhabit the kingdom, in which irresponsible procreation is condoned prepare for themselves the path of degeneration. They do not hold human sexuality sacred, enshrining it in the family and placing it in the guardianship of women. They do not honour the mistress of the house as the vigilant guardian of their racial heritage. The worship of ancestors sprang naturally from the pride and reverence, in which people held their forebears. It indicated their gratitude and understanding for the sacrifices the ancestors made in being selective and responsible.'

BRT:9:9 'When the selection of a marriage mate can be left to the sense of responsibility in the couple primarily concerned, then civilisation has taken a big step forward. But who is wise enough to determine when this wisdom is present and expressed? Where are those prepared to uphold responsible breeding habits?'

BRT:9:10 As found written, these are the accomplishments of a lady: She should learn the following: Cutting, sewing and making of garments. The arraying of garments and adornment of the body. The toilet of the hair and the art of hairbraiding. The art of motherhood. Housewifery and cooking. The preservation of fruits, meats and herbs. The growing of flowers and herbs. The stringing of necklaces and the making of ornaments. The making of pottery and the preparation of perfumes and ointments. Singing, if she have a sweet voice and melodious speech. Writing and drawing with paints. The art of archery with the little bow and small swordsmanship. The knowledge of jewels. The making of lace and knitting of wool and weaving. The use of herbs and simples and small leechcraft.

BRT:9:11 Her teacher in the ways of life should be her mother's sister, should she be married, or a sister who is married; or a female friend of her mother who is of long standing and in good grace with her mother; or a female tutor or female nurse who is attached to the family.

BRT:9:12 Concerning women, there are petty maids and maids (both of these categories being virgin); unmarried matrons, wives, widows, cast out women, women of no repute and harlots.

BRT:9:13 A woman living as married but not actually married is not inviolate, nor is an unmarried matron. Those may be sought for pleasure. An unmarried matron having been enjoyed by others is available for a man's pleasure.

BRT:9:14 These women are not to be touched in lust: A madwoman, a woman with running sores, a woman with child and a wife. No child shall be touched in lust. A man shall not display his nakedness before his daughter, nor a mother before her son.

BRT:9:15 After the days of Emris, it was written: 'Never give up; where there is a will there is a way; while there is life there is hope. Never leave your friend in the lurch, but support him with might and main. Do not be half-hearted or run with the hare or chase with the hounds.' Those are things said in our days.

BRT:9:16 These are the qualities and attributes of trees, as revealed by the ancient lore of our fathers, the usage whereof is known to the wise: The providing apple, the winsome cherry, the soporific ivy, the comforting elderberry, the holy oak, the sorrowful willow, the compassionate ash, the protective yew, the happy birch, the companionable holly, the lively hawthorn, the mystic hazel, the sedate pine, the wish-granting sallow, the healing heather, the age-consoling alder, the youth-giving waywithy, the generous broom, the helpful furze, the spirit-strengthening beech, the soothing windrake, the laughing aspen, the gentle junapah, the reliable wayfaringbeam, the cunning hornbeam, the flighty gadberry, the ominous dogwood, the jumping buck-thorn, the light-hearted maple, the direful slaethorn, the angry parbeam, the wilful kartakbush, the haunted banbeam, the frightened witchbeam.

BRT:9:17 They who are at one with the trees understand the nature of the life within them and make much of such things. There is a mystery here to be worked by those with understanding, but to others, it will be meaningless.

BRT:9:18 These are the useful herbs to be found in field, forest and wayside in the days gone by: Wolfbane (which guards against wolves and dogs), barroweed (which grows only near the dead), harwort, witchweed, tinkerbells, wayweed, skullcap, featherflowers (which cure the stone), blackberry, sundew, deadly dick, celandine (which cure the piles), windweed, moonflower (which works a spell), witchhead (called blackspear), asproot, drudbalm (which brings sleep), witchbane (which is put above the door), hawflowers, ellenberry, wimberry, dradsweet, elfeyc, fairyfern, witchwhispers, quickenbush, sowerseed (which purges), bardberry (for lovers), amarinth (it never fades), windflower, goolflower, weggrig, blowderbud (which heals all wounds), levenshade, layganleaf, hokanmil, rillweed, boonberry, hatherswed (which women use), esislip, fullerswort, withrinweed (which makes blue dye), canweed (which quiets the heart), mayslip, kodecreeper, slanlus, sewd, (which cures men of madness), mothan (which only grows on cliffs), arkiesene, dafblowder (which cures stomach sickness), malbrig, maisbel (which heals the stomach), bormowed (which soothes burns), selerweed (which gives visions), tianwed (which heals the skin), kaincop (which makes a brew), cowslip, waybroad, satyrion (which overcomes impotency), dwail, corncockles (which men call tares), dockumdick (which gives men virility and only grows under the shivertree).

BRT:9:19 These things serve well, but some are lost to the knowledge of men: Herb beer, made of yarrow and riversweet, soothes the spirits of men. Red clover cures the small cancer, if the suffering one be a man of self-control. The herb called 'mothan' is drunk with milk at childbirth.

BRT:9:20 Sickness is first a malady of the mind.

Index

A

Abaris 145
Abigail 133
Abred 146
Abri 146
Absolute 116, 146
Adamites 151
Adultery 117, 142
Affinity 67, 77
Afterid 5
Aigra 146
Airana 10
Alain 133
Albany 24, 133
Alcuth 5
Alfing 13
Alfred 158
Allgood 65
Alone One 6
Amalugad 7
Amaraith 136
Amerith 7
Amon 24, 26, 39, 48, 134
Amorika 13
Anarath 8
Anath 8
Andrew 155
Angel 42
Anger 101

Anna 145, 147
Annals Romanorum 145
Anoon 146
Anton 146
Apathy 55
Arayan 17
Ardan 18
Ardmoal 148
Ardpeth 5
Ardwulf 5
Arinrada 8
Arisia 147
Aristolas 135, 142, 145
Aristolio 25
Arkist 17
Arviragus 134, 147
Asterith 7
Athlan 8
Aulus Plautius 147
Avalek 147
Aveg 7
Awakener 69, 142
Awamkored 14
Ayed 8

B

Babes 142
Bagut 22
Balgweith 143

Balings 10
Bamlod 14
Baradon 10
Bards 147
Baruts 23
Basabrimal 13
Basgala 14
Battleblooded Northrider 12
Battlebook 25
Battlechief Kumwa 20
Battlekings 7
Battlemaster 26
Beauty 8, 30, 67, 89, 156
Being 13, 29, 38, 66–69, 71–72, 88–89, 125, 141, 143, 146, 158
Bel 7–8, 13–14, 53, 146, 156
Bele 7–8, 13
Beledon 13
Beledon the Thrummchinned 13
Belesetin 7–8
Belinos 8
Belishmer 14
Benlanda 14
Bethbal 7–8
Bethlehem 137
Bilew 11
Bitterbiting Sword 27
Black Brood of the North 16
Black Bull of the North 5
Blackbannered Chief 18
Bladud 8
Blasis 9, 11, 16
Blissful Generations 6
Bodiless Body 82
Body 82
Bond 69–70
Bondage 70
Book 8, 70, 76–78, 80, 85–86, 89, 100, 102–104, 107, 109, 111, 113–115, 118, 120–121, 126, 133, 135, 142, 156
Book of Recitals 156
Book of the Holy Mark 135
Books of Britain 133, 142
Books of Wisdom 115
Borderland 116
Bramathamlin 8
Brandigan 147–148
Brandigan of Walsogo 147
Branwen 8
Bread of Heaven 145
Bread of Heaven and Shepherd of Souls 145
Bright 8, 18
Brim 16, 18
Brimcofer 16
Britain 5, 9–10, 14, 16–17, 23–25, 133, 135–136, 142, 144, 146, 148, 152, 161
British 14, 136, 147
Briton 5, 18, 25, 135–136, 146–147, 152
Bronzebook 142
Bronzefinder 16
Bryantis 147
Brydin 8
Brythonic 24

C

Caesar 140
Cauldron of Higher Love 161
Central Flame 66
Chaisite 23
Chamber of Eternity 67
Chariots 134
Chastisement 99
Chethin 9
Chief of All Druthin 143–144
Chief of the Kasini 148
Chief of the Wellborn Ones 17
Child 9, 11, 22, 118, 148
Child of the Landholdingers 22
Child Protector 11
Children 9, 118, 148
Children of the Dusk 9
Children of the Horse 148
Choice 158
Christ 5, 135–136, 144, 156
Christian 5, 136, 156
Churlswain 148
Circle of Eternity 156
Circle of Light 143
Circle of Truth 143
Circumspection 157
Claudia Rufina 147
Claudius 136, 147
Comforter 70, 72, 146
Commander 27, 136
Commander of the Legions 136
Compassion 89, 97, 156
Consideration 81, 157
Coppersmiths 5
Courage 157

Court of Splendour 6
Court of the Hebrews 141
Courtesy 101
Cowfeeding Pastures 23
Creating Divinity 97
Creating God 23, 50
Creating Intent 40
Creation 66, 68, 156
Creativity 30
Creator 76–77, 82

D

Dainsart 135
Dancers 147
Daran 22–23
Dardanos 29
Dark One 17, 38
Dark Ones 17, 38
Dark Spirits 90
Dawndays 9
Day of The Awakener 69
Days of Decision 53
Death 44, 77, 114, 120
Deceit 157
Decency 157
Decorum 156–157
Dektire 18–19
Derwiddon 146
Design 45, 76, 107, 110, 113–114, 121, 123–125, 127, 159
Designer 45, 76
Designs of God 159
Devotion 113
Dewa 7
Dianket 9
Diligence 49
Dinsleir 5
Dinsolin 133, 148
Director 76–77
Disciples 54, 140
Discipline 153
Disobedience 102
Dispensations 99
Divine 6–7, 29, 35, 37–38, 40, 52, 76, 95, 97–100, 102, 106–107, 110–111, 113–116, 121–127, 149
Divine Design 76, 107, 110, 113–114, 121, 123–125, 127
Divine Designer 76

Divine Essence 38
Divine Hymn 6
Divine Inspirational Source 37
Divine Intent 40
Divine Justice 38
Divine Melody 7
Divine Mindfulness 95
Divine Source 149
Divine Spiritual Fountainhead 35
Divine View 102
Divine Will 52, 97
Divinity 43, 97, 99, 114, 123, 125
Divinity of Love and Goodness 123
Dona Smiling Eyes 8
Donardkath 25
Doomdragon 14
Doomsong 14
Dread Rites 37
Druthin 134–135, 143–146
Dryones 146
Dunmerkil 20
Dunvarmod 25
Durain 29
Duties 106
Duty 29, 87, 108
Dwarf Isle 9
Dwyva 148
Dylan 8

E

Earth 6–7, 10, 14–15, 18, 20, 29, 37, 39, 43, 46, 53–54, 59, 66–68, 70–72, 75–76, 78, 80, 82–87, 95, 97–100, 108, 111–112, 114, 117–118, 123–124, 126, 137–141, 143–145, 148, 154–156, 159
Earth Burner 7
East 5, 7, 24
East Saxondom 5
Eastern 7
Eblana 17
Education 156
Edwin the Elder 5
Edyfrabandy 17
Effort 157
Egfrid 5
Egypt 145, 148, 153
Elan the Sea Smith of the Floating Forge 8
Eldiwed 10
Elendon 147
Elfed 137

Elfingers 12
Elidor 37–38, 41, 44, 48, 51, 54, 58
Elsis 10
Elvira 12
Endlings 10
Enelek the Potter 5
England 162
Engling 13
Engravers 5
Enisivorwin 161
Enlightener 140
Enok 7
Erigen 8
Erim 17–19
Esures 16, 143
Eternal 66, 85
Eternal All 85
Eve of Summer 134
Ever Broody Hagmother 12
Ever Broody Mother 12
Evil 11, 74, 76, 80, 119, 145
Eye of God 144
Eye of Heaven 25

F

Faidlimid 14
Fairgas the Briton 147
Faith 8, 17, 23, 59, 149, 157
Faithfulness 157
Far Away Formless One 89
Far Western Land 15
Father 7, 11, 65, 138, 142
Fermadamid 8
Feymin 16–17
Filistis 8, 24
Finkera 8
Firstfaith 5, 17, 23, 25
Firstfaith Bringers 23
Firthreig 145
Flood 13, 142
Floodtale 13
Forest Fighter 12
Forest Mission 73, 75, 77, 79
Forestmen 22
Formless One 89
Fortitude 157
Fran 8, 136
Franan 8
Frans 8

Franwy 8
Freedom 80, 108, 157
Frewil 13
Friends and Enemies 118
Friendship 108
Frokith 12
Frolga 10, 13
Fronwin the Swordmaker 5
Frugality 36

G

Galilean 137
Galilee 137
Galo 18
Garadon Pankris 5
Garden of Karahemish 146
Gatuma 7, 13
Gatumugna the Skyfighter 7
Gaul 142, 147
Generation of Change 6
Generation of Fire 6
Generation of Grass 6
Generation of Light 6
Generation of Stone 6
Generation of the Axe 6
Generation of the Bow 6
Generation of the Chariot 6
Generation of the Helmet 6
Generation of the Shield 6
Generation of the Spear 6
Generation of the Sword 6
Generation of Trees 6
Generation of Water 6
Generation of Wood 6
Generosity 101
Gentleness 157
Genuissa 147
Gilamish 7
Gladys 136, 146–147
Glainid 148
Glason the Inglinger 5
Glenapton 13
Glorygleamer Folk 17
God 18, 23, 25, 28–30, 38, 46, 50, 65, 67, 134–146, 149–154, 156–161
God in the Great Circle 157
God of Life 142
God who is My Father and your Father 138
Godling of Greenness 18

Index

Godward 67
Godward Road 67
Gold 18–19
Golden Faced Skyspirit 18
Good and Great Being 67–69, 71–72
Good Books 70, 76–78, 80, 85–86, 89
Good Books of the Ancients 78
Good Religion 101–104, 106, 110–111, 117, 120, 122–127
Gorwel 10
Grailstone 148
Grakenwid 9
Great Being 67–69, 71–72
Great Chief 8, 16
Great Chief of the Upright Ones 8
Great Design 45
Great Designer 45
Great Enlighteners 140
Great Gleamer 143
Great God 25, 29, 136, 142, 144, 150
Great God Above All 29, 150
Great God Above All Gods 150
Great God of Life 142
Great God of Light 144
Great Godly Powers 136
Great Gods 25
Great Hewe the Strongarm 17
Great Holy One 23
Great Inspirer 145
Great Law 142
Great Light 88
Great Man 149
Great Master 150
Great Milk Giver 23
Great Name 67
Great Oak 16, 134
Great One 145
Great Path 58, 66, 98–99
Great Path of the True Way 58, 98–99
Great Protecting Spirit 25
Great Protecting Spirit of Britain 25
Great Stone Chambers 37–38, 47
Great Stone Chambers of Initiation 37–38
Great Teacher 149
Great Temple 145
Great Temple of the Stars 145
Great Understanding One 142
Great White Goddess of the Cowfeeding Pastures 23
Greater Beings 88
Greater Law 70

Greatness 151, 157
Greece 24
Greengod 23
Greengod of Life 23
Grimsbarrow 133
Guardian 8, 71, 142
Guardian at the Gate 71
Guardian at the Gates 71
Guardian of the Gate 8
Guardian of the Lady 142
Guardian of the Sacred Vessel 142
Guiderius 147
Gulgaes 147
Gwalanad the Summer Hawk 151
Gwalgwin 151
Gwidonad 6, 23
Gwilidun of Ivern 152
Gwin the Fairfaced 7
Gwinidendon 146
Gwinon the Welcomer of Warriors 8
Gwinvera 19–23
Gwinvidon 146

H

Haltraith 13
Hearth Hallower 11
Heaven 6–7, 14, 25, 40–43, 85, 139, 141, 145, 147
Heaven-sent 7
Hefa 17
Hegrin 9
Helaf the Carver 5
Helen Bloderwed 8
Helith the Lifebringer 7
Hell-formed 15
Helva 20–23
Helwaren 14
Helwed 20
Henmehew 143
High Druid 134
High Priest 25
Higher Spheres 66
Hilderith 10
His Greatness 157
His Spirit 143
Holbon 10
Holiselder 25
Holy Army 160
Holy Books 135, 156
Holy Ghost 141

Holy Hawthorn 135
Holy Mark 135
Holy Spirit 65–68, 70–72, 74–75, 79–80, 82–84, 88, 90
Homeless Generations 6
Homodren of the Chariots 134
Honeyladen Isle 13
Honour 29, 155, 157, 159
Hope 137–138, 157
Hovenlee 13
Hurash 10
Hypocrisy 101
Hypocrite 108

I

Iberis 11
Idewin 135, 146–147
Idunings 13
Ifananud 25
Ikta 133–134
Illuminated One 82–84, 89
Illuminated Ones 82, 84, 89
Illusion 14
Ilyid 133–136, 143
Inawk 18
Inawk the Collector 18
Inconceivable One 6–7
Indrud 10
Industriousness 157
Inheritor of the Ancient Wisdom 37
Iniseug 9
Inisgwin 23
Innisavalon 146
Insels 133
Instructing Voices 40
Ipedruad the Grinder 5
Isbathaden the Younger 145
Isen 133
Islass the Dreamer 134
Isle of Departure 134
Itene 148
Ivern 133, 152

J

Jacob 137
James 137
Jerusalem 142
Jesus 135, 137–142, 145–147

Jewish 138
Jews 135, 137, 141
Jezel Bethamin 25
John of the Wildwood 133
John of the Wildwood band 133
John the Cordwainer 133
Jordan 137
Joseph 135, 137, 141–144, 146–147
Joseph Idewin 146–147
Joseph of Abramatha 142
Jova 7, 10
Jovan 7
Judas 137
Judas the Galilean 137
Justice 30, 38–39, 48, 52, 89, 118, 125, 138, 156
Justice and Truth 118

K

Kadwilan of the Firstfaith 5
Kailight 148
Kailwardens 5
Kair 25
Kairhen 25
Kal 7
Kalesdrid 7
Kamailas 8
Kamba 8
Kambord 161
Kamelognatha 9
Kamledis 9
Kamulose 136
Kamwird 11
Kamwird the Wrinkled 11
Karboska 16
Karcolwin 161
Karelen 148
Karguthrin 8
Kargwen 148
Karkilgule 14
Karkol 25
Karnamard 156
Karperal 148
Karsalog 25, 146
Karunas the Hornheaded 8
Karwidrin 148, 151
Kasini 148
Kastira 17
Kastwelan the Invader 8
Kaswalen 25

Kathebelon 133
Kathlon 9
Kathon 17
Ked 6
Keili 7, 146–147
Keili the All Knowing 7
Kel 5, 7–8, 11, 13–14, 20, 24–25, 133
Kela 8
Kelefa 7
Kelglain 14
Kelnahilene 13
Kelshaw 133
Keltic 24–25
Keltica 24–25
Kelwin 5, 8, 25
Kelwine 25
Kelwinith 8
Keningwed 13
Kents 5
Kerirway 7
Ketwin 5
Kewen 25
Kewgant 7, 146
Killen 11–12
Killen the Northrider 12
Kimbelin 147
Kimwy 147
King 5, 22, 98, 133–134, 141, 145, 160–161
King Coel 161
King Ifor 5
King of the Howan 22
Kingdom of Albany 133
Kingdom of Arviragus 134
Kingdom of God 160
Kingdom of Heaven 141
Kingdom of Kevinid 145
Kingdom of Korin 133
Kingdom of the Spirit 98
Kithwin 7, 146
Klude 5
Knights 148, 151
Knights of Karwidrin 148, 151
Kolehan 8
Kolehan the Teacher 8
Koles 24
Kolgarth 147
Kolwader 13
Korin 133
Kostain 29
Kratalinth 8

Krisnakel 25
Krisura 24
Krowkasis 13
Kudira 17
Kumbirgels 14
Kwasir 9
Kwetana 17
Kwicta 16
Kwinad 135
Kwits 5, 16

L

Ladore 17
Lady of Life 18
Lakes of Light 37
Laledkin the Larger 8
Lancelot 151
Land of Manan 16
Last Forest Teachings 88
Law 43–44, 51, 66, 69–70, 72, 76, 96, 142, 157, 159–160
Law of Nature 66
Leir 8
Lemany 24
Lengil 29
Lengilwin 29
Levi 137, 141
Levites 137
Lew 5, 8, 133, 150
Lew Dewtears 8
Lewin of the Gutradors 5
Liberty 156
Life 6–7, 18, 23, 44, 55–58, 75, 83, 85–86, 88, 90, 97, 99–100, 106, 111–112, 126, 135, 138, 142, 146, 153, 156
Light 6, 37, 88, 125–126, 135, 143–144, 155
Liky 18
Linleon 16
Lir 19
Lodgrains 23
Lodmor 11–12
Lokrinos 8
London 19
Long Will 133
Longaset 18
Lopik the Blackbannered Chief 18
Lord 7, 68, 137, 139, 141–142, 147
Lord of Battles 7
Lord of Creation 68

Lot 5, 151
Lothir 5
Love 6, 10, 30, 89, 99, 117, 123, 156–157, 161
Loyalty 157, 159
Lucius 161
Lucius Clorus 161
Lude 12
Lugad 7, 9, 16
Luk 9
Luk the Arbitrator 9
Luktin 9
Lum 11

M

Maermagic 145
Magilmish the Wanderer 7
Magog 7
Maid of the Morning 12
Malice 51, 157
Malvas Anshriver 8
Mamagog the Fertiliser 7
Man of Messianic Hope 137
Manwidan 8, 16
Marcella 137
Mark 135
Marriage 117
Mary 135, 137, 140–142
Master 55–58, 135–136, 139, 142, 149–150
Matter in the Inner Circle 157
Maya 16
Meany 11
Meditation 95
Men of Isolia 72
Merkings 16–17
Messiah 141
Midsummer Festival 23
Mire of Matter 68
Miriam 137
Moderation 86
Modesty 156–157
Modren 8
Molmed 8
Molmed the Wise 8
Mooney 11
Morals 95
Morigu 8
Morkoravit 17
Mortality 65–66, 68, 70, 75–78, 80, 82, 88
Mortosh 17

Mother 10, 12–15, 25, 157
Mother Earth 14–15
Motherland 13, 25
Motherliness 157
Mount of Lud 148
Mountain of Tears 148
Muredin 10
Muspel 11

N

Name 67
Nana 9–10, 16
Nana the Mighty Mother 10
Nanara 9
Naniku 8
Nantladiwen 156
Nara 146
Nasarines 137
Nathaniel 155
nation 18, 26–28, 35, 37–39, 41, 43–44, 46, 48, 50, 52, 54, 58, 65, 70, 72–73, 75, 78–82, 84–85, 87–88, 90, 99, 101, 104, 113, 115–116, 119–120, 122, 125–126, 137, 139–140, 142–143, 146, 150–152, 158
Nature 66, 68, 70, 75, 77, 80, 100, 111, 120, 123, 139, 146
Nature of the Place 139
Nature Spirits 146
Nematon 143
Nemids 146
Neptoran 8–9
Nero 136
Nertha 8
Netherfolk 10–11
Nethermen 13
Netherogre 10
New God 29
New One 29
Newcomer 71
Newlyn 8–9, 16
Newlyn of Warnwilt 16
Newlyn the Fairmaid 8
Newlyn the Ravenfaced 9
Niad 8
Nick-o-the-nights 146
Nobility 140, 158
Nodinos 7–8
Nonima 10
North 5, 7–9, 12–13, 16

North Saxondom 5
Northern Beauty 8
North-spawned 13
Nud 7–8, 10
Nudlanders 10
Nuvrie 146

O

Oben 9–10, 12
Ogmosian 162
Ognana 9
Okther 5
Old Faith 8, 17, 23
Old Keltica 25
Old Yearteller 9
Olva 19
Olwin Keesabeg 25
One 5–8, 11–12, 17, 23, 25, 28–29, 35–36, 38, 56, 65–66, 70, 74, 82–85, 89–90, 95, 97, 99, 102–103, 114, 121, 133–134, 137, 139–140, 142–146, 150–151, 155–156, 158
One Creation 156
One Flame 143
One God 25, 156
One Pure Essence 66
One So Great 6
One Sole Consciousness 74
One Supreme Being 146
One Supreme Truth 114
One True God 134
Orma 18
Owainbartha 25
Owin Wiseheart 8

P

Pafamba 10
Pain 24, 48, 69, 161
Painted People 24
Pair Keridwen 161
Palader 151
Parables 151
Parsis 14
Partain 18
Path 45, 58, 66, 98–99
Paul the Martyred in God 136
Paynim 155
Peace 11, 18, 27, 47, 152
Pemantris 66

Pencluith the Dalradan 5
Pendora 8
Pentercil 22
People of the Bear 16
Perfection 89
Perfume of the flowers 145
Peter 141
Pharisee 141
Pilgrim 45, 47, 49, 56–57
Pilgrims on the Path 45
Pilgrims on the Way 47, 49
Place of Brandigan 148
Place of Decision 116
Place of Rest 10
Place of Terror 38
Poise 57
Pokatha 16
Poverty 151
Power 39, 52, 54, 119, 136, 148, 156
Powers 39, 52, 54, 136, 148
Powers Above 39, 52, 54
Powers of Darkness 148
Pray 53, 114
Prayer 114
Pretankely 10
Prince of Darkness 137
Pritan 23
Prize of Seduction 7
Progress 35, 150
Prophet 52, 121
Protecting Spirit 25, 42
Protecting Spirits 42
Protectiveness 157
Prudence 156
Pudens 136, 147
Pudentia 147
Punishment 77

Q

Queen 161
Queen Helena 161

R

Rada 12
Rafinia 133, 148
Raith 25
Rathkelder 22
Real Man 157, 159

Reality 73, 82, 158
Reality and Truth 82
Realm of Darkness 160
Red Eagle and Snake 24
Ree 16
Religion 101–104, 106, 110–113, 117, 120, 122–127, 151
Resounding Halls 147
Respect 107–108, 157
Reverence for the sacred 157
Rights 107
Rimvady 23
River of Sweet Waters 145
Robeth 8
Roman 135–136, 142, 145–147
Roman Nierotes 136
Rome 134–136
Rowland Gasson 142
Rule 66
Ruler 66

S

Sabrin 134
Sacred Books 100, 102–104, 107, 109, 111, 113–115, 118, 120–121, 126, 135
Sacred Circle 148
Sacred island 142
Sacred Scriptures 58
Safety 156
Salog 146
Salt 137
Samaritans 141
Samhain 9
Sankel 135
Sap of the Trees 145
Sayings of Jesus 142
Scots 5
Sea of Heavy Salt 137
Sea of the Setting Sun 135
Self-control 56
Self-mastery 86
Senmag 14
Sensuality 157
September 5
Service 106
Setnaspor 18
Shadow 29, 116
Shadowland 116
Shaker 37

Shieldmakers 5
Shindekra 17
Shindy 11
Shrine of the Heart 95
Sibel 8
Sibel the Strange Priestess 8
Siluria 134, 147
Simon 137
Skill 98
Skymother 7
Slayer of Niktoran 16
Society of Saints 137
Solmanth 17
Solomon 140
Son 6–7, 12, 16–17, 23–25, 40, 135, 138, 144–145, 148, 152
Son of Dewi 145
Son of Kaswalen 25
Son of Man 135, 138
Song of Life 6–7
Sons 12, 16–17, 23–24, 40, 144, 148, 152
Sons of Brittania 152
Sons of Fire 17, 148
Sons of God 144
Sons of May 16, 23–24
Sons of Men 144
Sons of the Nightcrow 12
Sons of the Plough 144
Sophists 155
Sorrow 44, 99–100
Soul 28, 30, 98, 145
Soul Form 30
Soul spirit 28
soulspirit 37–40, 48–50, 53–57, 59, 66–74, 77–90
Source 37, 146, 149, 156
South 7, 9–10, 24
Southward 9
Sowithy 8–9
Sowithy of the Fair Isle 9
Sphere 65–80, 82–84, 88–89
Sphere Above 75, 80, 82–84
Sphere of Beauty and Glory 67
Sphere of Matter and Mortality 65–66, 68, 70, 75–78, 80, 82, 88
Sphere of Mortal Man 66
Spheres of Existence 65–66
Spirit 25, 29, 35, 37–44, 46, 48–50, 52–54, 57, 65–80, 82–84, 86–90, 95, 98, 111, 114–116, 124, 142–143, 146, 149, 152, 157, 161

Spirit Above 57, 149
Spirit Above All Spirits 149
Spirit cankerers 29
Spirit Force 75
Spirit Form 29
Spirit in the Outer Circle 157
Spirit of Divinity 114
Spirit of God 152, 161
Spirit of Life 146
Spirit of the Shadow self 29
Spiritual Realm 95, 111, 115–116, 124
Spring 145
Spring of Truth 145
Stability 156
Stone Chambers 37–38, 43, 47
Stranger 142
Strathard 5
Study 53, 79, 85, 120
Subspheres 66
Success 77
Suffering Just One 137
Summer 17, 134, 138, 148, 151
Summerhouse of the King 134
Summerland 17, 134
Sun 5, 14, 19, 135, 143
Sun of my life 143
Sunderstow 5
Sunfaced 19
Superstition 114
Supreme 27, 37–44, 46, 48–50, 52–54, 57, 65–70, 72–79, 82–84, 86–87, 89–90, 114, 146, 158
Supreme Being 146, 158
Supreme Commander 27
Supreme Ruler 66
Supreme Spirit 37–44, 46, 48–50, 52–54, 57, 65–70, 72–79, 82–84, 86–87, 89–90
Supreme Spirit and His Great Plan 76
Supreme Spirit Himself 41
Supreme Vision 72
Sweetness of the Fruits and Perfume of the flowers 145

T

Taishan 143
Talesman who writes 5
Tanagekil 5
Taning 14
Tanis the Moonmaid 8

Taran 17, 133
Tarant 133
Tarsis 133, 135
Teacher 8, 137, 149
Teacher of Righteousness 137
Tendency Towards Evil 119
Terror 38
Thames 147
Thaneros 8
Thanis 8
The Frightener 53
The One 74, 134, 155
The Source 146, 156
Thespendu 25
Thom 140
Thomas 140
Thunderwolf 11
Thunor 15
Tiberius 135
Tirfola 15
Tishana 8
Tiz 16
Tomb Chamber 38
Tothnaelethan 5
Tothsolars 10
Townfounder and Metalmaster 7
Traith the Whitehaired 8
Trebethew 148
Trees 6, 145
Tribulation 100
Troubadours 161–162
Trowtis 143
True God 134
True Way 58, 73, 79, 81, 98–99
Truth and Justice 52
Tuwait 7
Tuwait the Eastern Father 7
Twice Born 35
Tydain 146

U

Uksening 13
Underearthman 7
Unhappiness 74
Universal 7
Universal Hub 7
Universe 65
Universes of Matter 65
Upstanding Ones 12

V

Vala 8
Vale of Tadwylch 148
Vale of the Dead 148
Victory Winner 7
Vision 66, 72, 81

W

Wains 133
Waiths 146
Wanderers 133
Watcher 8
Water Spouter 7
Way 40–41, 47, 49, 58, 73, 79, 81, 98–99, 150
Way of Truth 40–41
Weak 36, 51
Weal 49, 151
Wealth 49, 151
Weary Wanderer 12
Welcomer 8
Welsh 25, 146
Wenda 18–19
Wenda the Wise 19
West 5, 7, 9, 14–16, 23–25, 135
West Saxondom 5
Western 9, 14–15, 135
Western Sea of the Jews 135
Wickedness 52
Wicta 9, 133
Wictarin 9
Wildland Cultivators 13–14
Wildwave Wanderer 16
Will Smith 155
Wind Fighter 7
Winter 17, 138
Wisdom 30, 37, 48, 105, 115, 140, 149, 151, 153, 156, 161
Wisdom and Truth 105
Wise 8, 10, 19, 134, 142
Wise One 134
Wise Ones 134
Wise Strangers 142
Wives 46
Woadica 147
Woe 10, 13, 19
Wokelyn 9
Wolfbane 163
Women 105, 107, 142, 145
Word 103, 121, 151, 155
Worker of Strange Metals 16
World 6, 49
Wothin 8

Y

Yasus 16
Yelpa 16
York 73
Yoshan 13
Your Presence 142
Your Spirit 142

www.ingramcontent.com/pod-product-compliance
Lightning Source LLC
Chambersburg PA
CBHW080245170426
43192CB00014BA/2578